EDWARD PECHTER

OTHELLO

and Interpretive Traditions

UNIVERSITY OF IOWA PRESS

Iowa City

University of Iowa Press, Iowa City 52242

Copyright © 1999 by the University of Iowa Press

Printed in the United States of America

Design by Richard Hendel

http://www.uiowa.edu/~uipress

Printed on acid-free paper

Library of Congress Cataloging-in-Publication Data

Pechter, Edward, 1941–

Othello and interpretive traditions / by Edward Pechter.

p.   cm. — (Studies in theatre history and culture)

Includes bibliographical references (p.   ) and index.

ISBN 0-87745-685-2

1. Shakespeare, William, 1564–1616. Othello.   2. Shakespeare, William, 1564–1616—Criticism and interpretation—History.   3. Shakespeare, William, 1564–1616—Stage history.   4. Muslims in literature.   5. Blacks in literature.   6. Tragedy.   I. Title.   II. Series.

PR2829.P43   1999

822.3'3—dc21   99-20943

99   00   01   02   03   C   5   4   3   2   1

FOR STANLEY FISH

CONTENTS

This book tries to describe *Othello*'s design and effects in a way that can account for the play's extraordinary power to engage the interests of audiences and readers, both at present (it has become, arguably, the Shakespearean tragedy of our time) and earlier, as recorded in the rich traditions of interpretive response going back nearly to the play's original production. As I see *Othello*, its effects develop out of the peculiar way it shares out the central space of its action — and fractures its attractive power — equally between the protagonist and the antagonist. This design has made harsh and perhaps impossible demands on theatrical production; the stage history of the play may be plotted as a continuous refusal or inability to allow for Othello's and Iago's equivalent attractive power. The critical tradition, too, has piled up a consistent record of appalled frustration, frequently in response to the play's problematic structure and affective economy, the burden of which may be summed up in Dr. Johnson's comment about the play's catastrophe: "I am glad that I have ended my revisal of this dreadful scene. It is not to be endured."

Putting it this way suggests that *Othello* stands in a generating position prior to its critical and theatrical interpretation: the interpretation is produced by and responds to the play. This commonsense view has, like so many others, been subjected to a withering skeptical analysis in our time. Its apparently objectivist assumptions seem to be unsustainable: what and where is the "*Othello*" to which I just insouciantly gestured? and how do we get to it without substantial mediation? It can be argued that we engage with the play only by joining an ongoing conversation (or, indeed, fierce argument), whose terms have been established by, say, Edwin Booth, Helena Faucit, Thomas Rymer, Laurence Fishburne, Stephen Greenblatt, Henry Jackson, and Karen Newman, a list that could be extended almost indefinitely and supplemented with yet another list, itself almost infinitely extensible, including people like Kwame Anthony Appiah, Steve Biko, Ben Okri, and Nicole Brown

Simpson, some of whose texts and voices we may not have read or heard or perhaps even heard of. For this reason, it is equally plausible to reverse the order of priority I suggested earlier, claiming now that it is the interpretive tradition that stands in an anterior position, producing whatever it is we can see as the play.

The chicken/egg question here cannot be resolved on its own terms. As a theoretical matter, *Othello* and its interpretive traditions are not distinguishable. They are mutually dependent, reciprocally constitutive ways of talking about the same thing, and the distinction is merely a matter of analytic convenience. But that's a major qualification. In practical terms, we cannot say anything about *Othello* without deciding (consciously or otherwise) this matter of priority. This decision will have a substantially determining influence on both the object and the subject of analysis — on the shape and nature of "*Othello*," on the discourse produced about it, and on the question of whether this discourse is most at home under the roof of textual analysis, performance history, or cultural studies.

In the following pages, I travel around among these different disciplinary sites, but textual analysis is my home. Reflecting on the changing theatrical and cultural situations within which the play is produced, I am nonetheless inclined to keep my eye (or perhaps interpretive imagination) on an original *Othello*, whose energies continue even now to determine — that is, to *re*produce — the cultural and theatrical forms within which we know the play. For reasons suggested just earlier, such a text-centered position is problematic in the current critical climate. Although I touch on this matter occasionally in the following pages, the argument of "*Othello*" *and Interpretive Traditions* is shaped primarily by practical concerns and proceeds along interpretive rather than theoretical or metacritical lines: after an opening survey of *Othello*'s stage and critical reception, five chapters follow the action of the play in a way that tries to account for its tremendous power over the centuries to engage theatrical and literary interest.

In one important respect, though, the theoretical collapse of differences continues to provide a fundamentally strong motivation driving this book, trained precisely on the distinction between traditions and our time. Current *Othellos*, critical and theatrical, frequently claim power for themselves to interrogate and displace an impoverished history. But if the lines separating our *Othello* from interpretive traditions blur and disappear, how can anyone sustain the detachment necessary for such enlightened critique? Faced with this play's relentless crushing of hopes for escape from a benighted past, we may be driven to feel that the transformative claims driving so much contemporary interpretive practice are illusory — an experience truly "not to be endured."

This book is inextricably involved with Concordia University, where I feel lucky to have worked for thirty years. I owe a lot to many students who listened to my ideas about *Othello* as they developed and who were not bashful about advancing their own. Let one stand for all, the young woman who interrupted my earnest plea about the need to historicize in order to appreciate the power of Desdemona's public avowal of sexual interest in Othello by saying, "What do you mean — my father would have slapped me across the face." I owe a lot also to colleagues who gave me useful tips about what to read and even sometimes what and how to write: Peter Feder, Marcie Frank, Judith Herz, Robert Martin, Kevin Pask, Eyvind Ronquist, David Sheps, Neil ten Kortenaar, and Andras Ungar. I am grateful to the Faculty of Arts and Science for granting me a study leave in the winter 1998 term during which the book was completed.

Much of my work was facilitated by a grant from the Social Sciences and Humanities Research Council of Canada. It was facilitated in different ways by McGill colleagues in the Shakespeare in the Theatre Research Group, especially Mike Bristol, Leanore Lieblein, John Ripley, and Kate Shaw, and by people at the University of Victoria, where I spent the sabbatical during which I completed the book, including Ed Berry, Michael Best, Kim Blank, Evelyn Cobley, Arnie Keller, Joe Kess, and Terry Sherwood.

Unless otherwise indicated, *Othello* citations are taken from E. A. J. Honigmann's Arden 3 edition, and other Shakespearean citations from the second edition of the Riverside Shakespeare. Unreferenced quotations from Honigmann can be found in his commentary about the lines under discussion. Parts of chapter 4 and the appendix, chapter 5, and the afterword appeared in earlier versions as "'Have you not read of some such thing?': Sex and Sexual Stories in *Othello*," *Shakespeare Survey* 49 (Cambridge: Cambridge University Press, 1996), 201–216; "Why Should We Call Her Whore? Bianca in *Othello*," in *Shakespeare in the Twentieth Century: The Selected Proceedings of the International Shakespeare Association World Congress, Los Angeles, 1996*, ed. Jonathan Bate, Jill Levenson, and Dieter Mehl (Newark and London: University of Delaware Press and Associated University Presses, 1998, 364–377); and "*Othello*, the Infamous Ripley and SHAKSPER," in *Shakespearean Con-*

tinuities: Essays in Honour of E. A. J. Honigmann, ed. J. B. Batchelor, T. G. S. Cain, and Claire Lamont (London: Macmillan, 1997), 138–149.

I owe thanks to the anonymous reader for the University of Iowa Press for many useful suggestions and to Holly Carver of the press, who was always there for me with prompt and smart and funny answers to my questions. I am very grateful to Thomas Postlewait, who took a lot of time from his own work in order to locate this book closer to theatrical history and further away from narrowmindedness than it would have been otherwise. In addition to my incalculable obligations to his work, I am personally indebted to Ernst Honigmann, who encouraged me when I made a midcareer shift to Shakespeare studies. My greatest professional debt is acknowledged in the dedication to Stanley Fish, who has been generously supplying me with useful ideas, and with letters of recommendation, for more years than either of us would care to acknowledge.

OTHELLO

and Interpretive Traditions

Othello and Interpretive Traditions

Sunday, June 19, 1994, the day after the white Bronco chase on the L.A. freeways, the blood still tacky at the Rockingham crime scene, when it began. "Has anyone yet noted the similarities between Othello and O. J. Simpson: black male and white woman, history of spousal abuse, murder of wife and friend, claims to have loved his wife 'too much,' etc.?" The author of these words, a Shakespearean who teaches at a university in the western United States, was addressing himself to an electronic discussion group called SHAKSPER, many of whose subscribers had probably made the connection to which he was referring, all of whom were now obliged to consider its implications.[1] A discussion began immediately under the rubric of "Similarities," fine-tuning the analogy ("where's the 'history of spousal abuse' in *Othello*?" "forgot the 'suicide' theme in his list of similarities") and questioning its appropriateness and taste. This discussion was often overheated. The originator was accused of racism, the accuser of "political correctness." The language was unusually strong ("the son of a bitch," "what the hell?"), to the discomfort of SHAKSPER's goodhearted and latitudinarian moderator, Hardy Cook of Bowie State University in Maryland ("I too share many . . . misgivings"), who tried to nudge the discussion back to safer and more familiar ground: "I do not consider Othello's death a suicide . . . I also view Cleopatra's death as a noble act." Cook was not immediately successful. The discussion continued, meandering into long and frequently enraged arguments about wife-battering, the biases of the media, the need to assume innocence until guilt is proven, among other controversial topics.

Many people, on and off SHAKSPER, in and outside of academia, were intrigued by the resonance they thought they heard between *Othello* and the "crime of the century" (James McPherson, Hodgdon). It was another — rather belated and melodramatic — piece of evidence to suggest the play's unusual power to generate interest in our time. *Othello* has become the Shakespearean tragedy of choice for the present generation. During the last twenty years or so, it has replaced *King Lear* in the way *Lear* had earlier replaced *Hamlet* as the tragedy that speaks most directly and powerfully to current interests. Robert Scholes, for instance, helping to design a new capstone English course for grade 12, selects *Othello* as the one obligatory Shakespeare play because "the issues of cultural conflict are in the foreground" (136). Writing without direct pedagogical interests and for a different audience, Mitchell Greenberg sees much the same thing: *Othello* has a peculiar power "to haunt us as an uncanny projection, from the past, of our conflicted present" (1).

Conflict, though, is not unique to *Othello*; we need to be more specific. During the period of *Othello*'s growing ascendancy, criticism has been transformed by feminist, African American, and postcolonialist studies, to whose central concerns the play seems directly to appeal. *Othello* focuses on marriage as a domestic relationship, where the most intimately private experience is nonetheless shaped by the pressures of society and political power. The play is preoccupied with questions of gender difference, the expectations of men and women for themselves and about each other, including those that underwrite and undermine marriage. It is preoccupied with racial difference as well. Its protagonist is an alien to white Christian Europe, what we would now call an immigrant, whose visible racial difference seems to be the defining aspect of his identity, the source of his charismatic power to excite interest and to generate horror. As Mythili Kaul puts it, introducing a collection of new essays by black writers on the play, "All the contributors" see *Othello* as "of utmost relevance today in terms of" a variety of "pressing contemporary issues," including "politics, colonial exploitation, cultural relativism, and, above all, race" (preface, xii). The play begins with a graphically violent image of sexual and racial difference, "Even now, now, very now, an old black ram / Is tupping your white ewe!" (1.1.87–88); and it ends with the tableau of Othello and Desdemona locked in a perverse embrace on the marriage bed revealed finally as the place of murder.

"Traditions" in this book's title introduces a different set of concerns, one that looks to be (and in some respects truly is) at cross-purposes with what I have just said about the play's immediate appeal to present interests. For *Othello* remains in many ways a strange play, lodged in a past whose beliefs and assumptions are not easily accommodated to our own. The SHAKSPER discussion suggests as much. Most of it was motivated by the belief that the presumed fit between the play and the murders was rather a misfit; either it placed the tawdry facts behind the bloodbath at Rockingham in an artificially dignified setting, or it diminished the play's power to generate the response appropriate to heroic tragedy, or both. "Let's stop talking about this!" SHAKSPERians kept saying, in the angry and inevitably self-defeating denials that have characterized so much *Othello* commentary going back to its origins in Rymer. Eventually, in this case anyway, the message got through. The discussion petered out in about three weeks. It may be that we simply lost interest. These striking coincidences tend to be short-lived.[2] As we'll see in the afterword, when in March 1995 discussion on SHAKSPER returned to *Othello*, no one mentioned the Simpson case. Either we were being careful, or it never entered our minds.

The relation, then, between our *Othello* and the *Othello* constructed out of and inherited from interpretive traditions is a complicated one. As a way of getting into the complications, let me describe a lecture I attended a few years ago, in which a visiting intellectual historian cast a critical eye on nineteenth-century European views of Africans. He read from a Victorian ethnographic description of tribal sexual practices. "Listen to that," he said, "he's getting turned on." Later he showed us some slides of the "Hottentot Venus," a fertility icon that fascinated the Victorians, especially because of its enlarged and prominently displayed vagina, to which the lecturer repeatedly gestured with his pointer. This went on for some time. Eventually my companion, himself an intellectual historian of the European nineteenth century, gripped my arm. "If someone came into this room by accident," he said, "what would they think was going on?"

European attitudes to Africans and to women's sexuality are central questions for anyone studying *Othello*, but I tell this story for different reasons. My colleague's question emphasized the importance of contextualization for interpretation. If you don't understand the context of academic lectures you might miss the point, taking the critical analysis of prurient interest for an expression of the interest it is analyzing. Something like this could be said about, and in the midst of, any academic lecture, but it usually isn't. My colleague was violating the conventional norm, which calls for audiences at academic lectures to be attentively silent. In this respect, he was performing the transgressive action recounted in endlessly repeated anecdotes from the performance history of *Othello*, some of which I shall discuss in chapter 1, of audiences so moved by the play that they found it necessary to assert their presence and even intervene in the dramatic action.

Underlying my colleague's outburst, I believe, was an intuition that anyone inside that lecture room, even *knowing* the context, might find it hard to be sure that some prurient form of interest wasn't involved. The same uncomfortable sense had emerged earlier in the lecture. How could the lecturer detect that the ethnographer's relation to his material had migrated from scientific observation to erotic arousal unless he too was aroused? How could we in the audience be convinced of his claim unless (however diverse in age, gender, sexual orientation, etc.) we experienced a similarly increased sense of sexual interest? Perhaps most troubling of all, what if the lecturer's claim *was producing* a corresponding interest in us, which would then count as evidence to justify the claim in the first place? Of course, we might always disagree with the lecturer's contaminating interpretation. "No," we would say, "that's wrong. This description of tribal sexual practices does not evoke my sexual interest." But denial, especially in connection with a subject like sexual interest (or racial prejudice: "Some of my best friends are people of color") is almost invariably the reverse of convincing. Anyone listening to such a denial ("'Tis not to make me jealous / To say my wife . . ." [3.3.186–187]) is likely to have suspicions heightened rather than dispelled. Hearing yourself speak ("By heaven, thou echo'st me / As if there were some monster in thy thought" [3.3.109–110]), you might even begin to wonder about yourself.

Even without my parenthetical quotations and my reference to the play's performance history, I would hope that by now *Othello* seems virtually to force itself upon us, for it focuses directly and centrally on the questions I have been raising here about the nature of belief, the fraught and problematic process by which convictions are settled in the mind. In A. C. Bradley's *Shakespearean Tragedy*, which may be taken as representative of nineteenth-century interpretive practice, the matter led to the question "Is Othello easily jealous?" This question is still generally current for actors, theatrical audiences, and students (constituencies we may ignore at some risk), but many academic critics have tended to back away from it. By isolating the protagonist from the dramatic action

Othello and Interpretive Traditions

and seeking to understand his behavior in terms of an independently motivating inner nature, the question seems to be driven by the hero-worshiping and psychological assumptions of nineteenth-century commentary — assumptions whose relevance to our own and to Renaissance concerns we have some reason to doubt. But a version of it still drives our efforts to make sense of the play, though now fixed to the antagonist rather than the protagonist, and to systems rather than to individual instances of belief. How can we explain Iago's spectacular success in shaping not just Othello's understanding but almost everyone else's as well? Brabantio, Iago's first victim, feels defenseless against Iago's suggestions: "This accident is not unlike my dream, / Belief of it oppresses me already" (1.1.140–141). Cassio and Othello seem to be defenseless as well. Auden remarked that he couldn't "think of another play in which the villain is so completely triumphant" ("The Joker in the Pack," 246). What accounts for Iago's apparently irresistible power?

This is where the lecture comes back into the picture. Like the "Hottentot Venus," that image of Iago — "Even now, now, very now, an old black ram / Is tupping your white ewe!" — seems too powerful to control, uncontainable within any appropriately reasonable frame. For the characters inside the play, Iago's speech functions like free indirect discourse: a tissue of clichés and proverbs belonging to nobody in particular and everybody in general, it becomes absorbed into an amorphous "honesty" — "a whispering," as Kenneth Burke says ("Othello," 169), floating independently of any designatable source. Identifying the speaker, the contextualizing gesture that inaugurates all interpretive action, is effectively impossible for Othello and Cassio and Brabantio, who are doomed rather to reproduce Iago's fearful anxieties. Audiences are better off; the play identifies Iago for us in no uncertain terms as "a villain" whose pronouncements shouldn't be trusted, but this doesn't really help. By the end of the first act, we know enough to say that "it is wrong to think that *blacks are the devil* or that *women are whores*"; but the italicized propositions seem to have a life of their own, *blacks are the devil, women are whores*, unimpeded by "wrong" in the same way that erroneous convictions ("'Tis not to make me jealous") are reinforced rather than eliminated by "not." Iago's hatred breaks through the constraints of syntax and of all logical structures, immune to the skeptical analysis that might be provided by our considered beliefs and values. Whatever our intentions or advantages in knowledge, we wind up like his victims inside the play, trapped inside the reproduction of his contaminated and contaminating malice. There seems to be no effective critical purchase on Iago, no judicious higher knowledge by means of which we can eliminate his prejudiced opinions. As Iago himself puts it in his final speech, "What you know, you know" (5.2.300).

One consequence of this argument is to blur if not totally erase the distinction between *Othello* and its interpretive traditions. If critical reflection on the play winds up reproducing the malignancy it seeks to repudiate, then we can say that the play is so deeply embedded in its interpretive traditions that effectively it is those traditions. Critical reflection on critical reflection doesn't help either. You can, as I have tried to do, describe the mechanism by which *Othello* traps us, saying that "it doesn't help to say that 'it is wrong to think that *blacks are the devil*,'" but as you see, the description does not free us from the machinery, just enriches our sense of its complexity, thereby perhaps trapping us even more securely.[3]

A further consequence is to highlight the contradictory purposes I mentioned earlier between the play's special appeal to current audiences and our relation to inherited interpretive traditions. Feminist, African American, and postcolonialist critics have jettisoned some of their original emancipatory claims, but not the absolutely foundational one of standing in some critical relation to the past. It is, however, precisely this claim that the play, as I see it, works to undermine, and the result is a peculiarly painful double bind. Focusing on race and gender (and on class, ethnicity, sexuality, and nationality too, as we shall see), the play talks about exactly what we want it to talk about, but then tells us exactly what we do not want to hear ("'Sblood," as Iago says in his first words, "but you'll not hear me" [1.1.4]) and shows us what we cannot bear to see ("The object poisons sight," Lodovico tells us in the play's final speech. "Let it be hid" [5.2.362–363]).

Starting from this position, where do we go? If the play may be collapsed into its interpretive traditions, then we might want to look at these traditions on their own terms; and if interpretation is defined theatrically, we will find ourselves doing performance history. The performance history of *Othello* is extraordinarily rich. The play was evidently successful when new, to judge from the recorded performances and allusions. It was "probably the second revival" in the Restoration (Spencer, 12) when its popularity "was second, perhaps, only to that of *Hamlet*, among Shakespeare's plays, and the tragedy has never been long from the stage in later times" (Sprague, *Shakespeare and the Actors*, 185). But although the play has held the stage, exciting great theatrical interest,

Othello and Interpretive Traditions

without a significant hiatus from its own time to ours, any sense we might have of continuity in *Othello*'s performance history needs to be skeptically examined. The play's stage history is constituted out of many different elements: variously edited scripts, played by different, and different kinds, of actors in assorted theatrical settings, transformed over time by a variety of technical innovations in lighting, costuming, and scene design, and sometimes by technical regressions or restorations (Poel, the new Globe) as well, all of these phenomena realized in a kinesthetic experience that alters not only over the long sweep of time but from one performance to the next of what we uncritically call "the same production." Performance history, then, might (and often does) dissolve into a miscellany of greatly memorable realizations, momentous but also momentary as a sound.

Anyone with only a rudimentary knowledge of theater history (I include myself in this category) is bound to be struck with the self-enclosed and self-referential nature of theatrical meaning, in which various histrionic gestures or production decisions are defined against previous practice ("Fishburne's action there replicates a move of Olivier's which ultimately derives from Macklin . . ."). But theatrical culture is, after all, only "relatively autonomous"; it is, willy-nilly, part of culture more comprehensively defined. Hence we might find ourselves doing cultural history. In the manner that James Shapiro has used *The Merchant* to trace different ideas of Jewishness in English self- and national identification, we could examine the ways in which *Othello* has been made to signify at various times and on various stages in the complex and overdetermined process of establishing (or destabilizing) racial ideas. Joyce Green MacDonald has done just this, taking off from a confluence of theatrical and sociopolitical events clustered in the early 1830s, including the exchange of roles between Kean and Macready, the former playing Othello as the "tawny Moor" he had introduced in 1814, the latter in blackface; Ira Aldridge, the "African Roscius," offering the first black performance of the role on the English stage; the opening of Maurice Dowling's *Othello Travestie, An Operatic Burlesque Burletta*, which imported American minstrel-show style to England where it achieved a popularity comparable to its American prominence; recent slave revolts and the parliamentary debates that led to a bill emancipating British-owned slaves in the West Indies. The focus here is not on particular theatrical performances of *Othello* or even on performances of other tenuously related theatrical pieces, but on the conflicted meanings of race in English society during the fourth decade of the nineteenth century when, as MacDonald shows, "playing race became a deadly serious kind of cultural work aimed at appropriating discourses of racial difference . . . often . . . inadequate to the problem of incorporating black or African things into the dual western consciousness of white self and alien other" (234).

There is a third possibility apart from theatrical and cultural history, derived from a reversal of the procedures that generate these two practices. Instead of emphasizing the distinct and momentary impressions of theatrical performances or the discontinuous constructions appropriate to particular cultural situations — instead of these, we might rather emphasize the *consistency* of the response record. The sense of painful double bind I described earlier in contemporary response to *Othello* is not unique to our time. Trying to account for "the peculiarity of *Othello*" as "the most painfully exciting and the most terrible" of Shakespeare's tragedies, Bradley pointed to the way our "heart and mind are held in a vice, experiencing the extremes of pity and fear, sympathy and repulsion, sickening hope and dreadful expectation" (*Shakespearean Tragedy*, 143). Bradley's terms may seem vague and abstract, even clichéd (or perhaps just different from our own). But Bradley is talking about the Temptation Scene (3.3), acknowledging the unique structure and emotional economy that draws audiences equally to the attractive powers of Othello and Iago, and thus describing a play recognizably like the one we know in our time. As we'll see in chapter 1, the reception history of the play, whatever its local detail and particular inflections, is remarkably consistent, registering the impossible demands of responding at once to Othello's and Iago's voices and constituting a record of grief, rage, and resistance that testifies to the felt presence of a fundamentally intolerable experience. From this perspective, our *Othello* and the various *Othello*s of the past, recent and remote, are not at cross-purposes after all. Each of them shares with all the others the excruciating anxiety of being at cross-purposes with itself.

In conjunction with the lines I quoted from the play's opening and close ("but you'll not hear me"; "The object poisons sight"), this coherence in the play's reception history, critical as well as theatrical, might lead us to think that the interpretive traditions of *Othello* are not autonomous or generative: they do not produce but are rather produced by the play. In this case, we would now find ourselves asking how the play produces the interpretations, and perhaps even why. What are the dramatic strategies by which *Othello* has managed to achieve its extraordinarily intense effects on audiences and readers over such a long span of time, and why should we continue to value the play (as we apparently do by returning to it so often) for its achievement? These questions introduce a different set of concerns, formalist and esthetic, to the ones motivating theatrical and cultural history, thereby constituting a different interpretive procedure which might be (and has been) called practical criticism.

The umbrella term "interpretive" in the title of this book is designed precisely to allow access to the different domains of theatrical and cultural history as well as textual criticism. Nonetheless, there are distinct priorities at work here. This book is more practical criticism than cultural studies. *Othello* and racial questions are inseparable, I think (though not everyone thinks so, and until around 1800 it seems almost nobody thought so), but I'm less interested in *Othello* as a document in the history of racial relations than in the literary and theatrical energies which have driven so many readers and audiences over such a long period of time to acknowledge (or indeed refuse) racial (and related sorts of) anxieties. And again: this book is more practical criticism than theater history. Despite the equivalence just earlier ("literary and theatrical energies"), the theater history here is conceptually secondary to a text-centered sense of the play's possibilities. Performance does get roughly equal attention in chapter 1's synopsis of the play's theatrical and critical history, and again in chapters 3 through 6, discussing the last four acts of the play (as we have become accustomed since at least Rowe to designating them). But in chapter 2, about the play's opening and (I believe) foundational actions, the discussion is grounded almost wholly in a text-centered interpretation; and even as subsequent chapters focus increasingly on the ways *Othello* has been performed, my prior commitment remains to describing the kinds of performances I believe to be encouraged — even authorized — by the words in the script.

To treat *Othello* as primarily a literary text, however accommodated to the particular conditions of various theatrical performances and cultural situations, means occupying a position that may seem oblivious to much of the strongest work in current critical analysis. Indeed, to invest in the artistic design of a Shakespearean play as though it embodied the presumably fixed status of an author's printed text has been described, by one of the most authoritative voices on the current scene, as "historically inaccurate, and blind . . . to the true nature of phenomena we are dealing with" (Orgel, "The Authentic Shakespeare," 10). Whenever truth and historical accuracy are invoked, there is always an argument to be made; and as a battle-scarred veteran of disciplinary turf wars,

I am almost always eager to return to the fray. But not here, not now. Except for an appendix about the concept of "character," this book simply proceeds from the conviction that, given our current situation, it is a good and useful function of criticism at the present time to sustain a focus on the formal and affective qualities of a play like *Othello*. "To vouch this is no proof," of course, as the Duke tells Brabantio (1.3.107). "Good" and "useful" are empty and evasive terms, and to fill them with meaning would require developing substantial arguments about the current scene of Shakespearean interpretation and about the value and historical depth of poetics as a basis for interpretive practice. But I doubt that even a systematically sustained argument would constitute "proof" in the sense of demonstration: the analysis that claims to justify a disciplinary preference is likely to be supported with evidence produced by the same disciplinary preference it purports to be justifying — and therefore circular. I have in any case written on the basis of my convictions rather than as an attempt at their justification. *"Othello" and Interpretive Traditions* is a description of the play's extraordinary capacity to generate literary and theatrical interest as recorded in its long and rich critical and theatrical histories, not a theoretical prolegomenon to such a description. What it does, it does.

Othello
in Theatrical
and
Critical History

The earliest recorded performance of *Othello* dates from November 1, 1604, when the play was staged at the Whitehall Banqueting House. The response record begins six years later with a performance at Oxford in 1610, as described by Henry Jackson:

> They also had tragedies, which they acted with propriety and fitness. In which (tragedies), not only through speaking but also through acting certain things, they moved (the audience) to tears. But truly the celebrated Desdemona, slain in our presence by her husband, although she pleaded her case very effectively throughout, yet moved (us) more after she was dead, when, lying on her bed, she entreated the pity of the spectators by her very countenance. (Quoted Evans, 1978)

In emphasizing the play's strongly direct appeal to an audience's emotions, Jackson sets the tone for a tradition of response that continues more or less unbroken to our own day. The stage history of *Othello* is full of stories about audiences so disturbed that they could not contain themselves within the bounds of conventional response. Jean-François Ducis's French adaptation (1792) "had to provide a happy ending because Desdemona's unmerited death resulted in mass fainting" (Rosenberg, 93). Sixteen years earlier, Ludwig Schröder's version was said to have

> exceeded by far what the nerves of the men of Hamburg, and even more those of the women . . . could bear. The closer the performance approached the catastrophe, the more uneasy the audience grew.

"Swoons followed upon swoons," reports an eyewitness. "The doors of the boxes opened and closed. People left or, when necessary, were carried out; and, according to trustworthy reports, the miscarriages suffered by various prominent ladies were the result of seeing and hearing the overly tragic play." (Quoted Habicht, 5)

Less extreme though similarly transgressive behavior is reported in Samuel Pepys's *Diary* of a Restoration performance where "a very pretty lady . . . called out to see Desdemona smothered," and by the biographer of Edwin Forrest, one of the memorable American Othellos in the nineteenth century, whose performance provoked "a refined and lovely young lady" to declare that " 'if that is the way Moors look and talk and love, give me a Moor for a husband.' " [1]

Such testimony resonates interestingly with Jackson's reaction. Audiences are so moved by the play that they seem to lose their concentration on the "propriety and fitness" of the actor's performance and become absorbed instead in the roles being performed ("the celebrated Desdemona," "a [noble] Moor"). Perhaps the most striking instance of such bizarre overinvolvement comes in an anecdote transcribed in Stendhal of an 1822 performance in Baltimore, during which a soldier on guard duty, "seeing Othello . . . about to kill Desdemona, shouted: 'It will never be said that in my presence a confounded Negro has killed a white woman!'" whereupon "he fired his gun and broke an arm of the actor who was playing Othello" (quoted Bate, 222). Here again, the intensity of engagement seems to have erased the line separating the performer and the part, "Othello" and "the actor who was playing Othello." It is as though this "overly tragic" play does not allow for the distance we normally associate with dramatic representation.

There are many anecdotes to suggest that the actors themselves have been similarly affected: we hear of Edmund Kean, probably the premier Othello in the early nineteenth century, spitting up blood after one performance, collapsing into the arms of Iago (played by his son Charles) in the midst of another, never to recover; [2] of Junius Brutus Booth, who on one occasion "would have smothered Desdemona in earnest if the other actors had not rushed in from the wings and pulled him off his victim" (Shattuck, 46); or of Forrest again, who, known as a betrayed (though also betraying) husband, played the role continually against the background of a divorce case which dragged on for eighteen years, prompting a contemporary witness to declare that "in place of interpreting Othello, he interpreted himself, enacting Forrest under a bor-

Othello in Theatrical and Critical History

rowed name" (quoted Rosenberg, 98). This identification may help to explain the stories of recent Othellos such as Robeson and Welles falling in love with their Desdemonas. The idea underlies *A Double Life*, the film in which Ronald Colman, playing a modern actor performing Othello to his wife's Desdemona, becomes obsessively jealous with predictably murderous consequences in "real life."

We should treat these anecdotes with caution. The elder Booth went over the top in roles other than Othello, and off the stage as well as on. For Forrest "certain of his principle roles," not just Othello, "became briefs for the defense" in his divorce, and again as part of a pattern of jealous ambivalence (as in his relationship with Macready) independent of performing the Noble Moor (Shattuck, 85). Theatrical performers become passionately involved with one another quite apart from performances of *Othello*, just as chartered accountants do, as a consequence of proximity and shared experience. And theatrical anecdotes are nothing if not theatrical. They tend to exaggerate (all the stories about disastrous productions of "the Scottish play" simply ignore the many *Macbeth*s that went off without a hitch), and some of them may not even be true to begin with. They feed off each other. Would the refined and lovely lady's comment about Forrest have been recorded if not for the familiarity of the very pretty lady in Pepys?

But *Othello* does seem to be a special case. Consider Kenneth Tynan's questions about Olivier's Othello: "Will the public and critics realise that this is an egocentric Othello, not an egocentric performance? . . . It is Othello, not Olivier, who is indulging himself emotionally . . . but will the audience know the difference?" (7–8, 10–11). Since these questions might be asked of any performance, the real question is why Tynan feels constrained to ask them; something to do with a great actor in a particularly intense production, but something to do with the play, surely, as well. Even with all allowances made for skepticism, the sheer proliferation of such stories about performers and audiences going over the top is remarkable ("a year does not go by without the newspapers' reporting similar stories," as Stendhal adds after reporting the Baltimore soldier's murderous assault). So is their consistency. Sprague tells one of a Macready performance in Liverpool: during the "collaring" episode of the Temptation Scene, when Othello takes Iago by the throat on "Villain, be sure thou prove my love a whore" (3.3.362), "'a gentleman in the upper boxes' is said to have 'started up and exclaimed, loud enough for all around to hear, "Choke the devil! choke him!"'"; stories "of this sort," Sprague adds, "are particularly numerous in the case of *Othello*, and furnish a curious tribute to its tragic intensity" (*Shakespeare and the Actors*, 199). Julia Genster, who seems to be remembering a version of the Macready story, referring to "those outraged theatergoers who have stood, shaking their fists, shouting to Othello that Iago is lying," draws the same conclusion as Sprague: "The ideational matrix of this play puts its audience under a particular kind of pressure, one to which the anecdotal history bears witness" (805). *Othello* is in some sense simply too painful to tolerate.[3]

In this respect theatrical history is reinforced by critical history, beginning as early as Dr. Johnson's declaration about the ending that "I am glad that I have ended my revisal of this dreadful scene. It is not to be endured" (Vickers, 5.165). Johnson said much the same thing about the ending of *King Lear*, the chief competitor to *Othello* in its capacity to afflict audiences, and the connection was clearly on A. C. Bradley's mind in the remark I quoted in the introduction, seeking to explain "the peculiarity" of the play: "Of all Shakespeare's tragedies," he wrote, "not even excepting *King Lear*, *Othello* is the most painfully exciting and the most terrible" (*Shakespearean Tragedy*, 143).

At least as important are those critical responses where the play's disturbing power is revealed but remains unacknowledged. The earliest sustained commentary on *Othello* is in Thomas Rymer's *Short View of Tragedy* (1693), which includes an often wittily detailed invective against what he contemptuously calls the "Tragedy of the Handkerchief" (160). As Joel B. Altman points out, Rymer's catalog of improbabilities in *Othello* is the determining origin of the ensuing traditions of *Othello* commentary. Although most critics have disagreed with his conclusions, "Rymer turns out to have been the most influential of Shakespeare's readers after all, by setting the crucial question" (131). For my present purposes, the most striking thing about Rymer's attack is the tone. Restoration polemics takes no prisoners, but the extraordinary intensity of irritation and anger in Rymer's assault on the play, and on the perverse stupidity of his contemporaries for liking it so much ("From all the Tragedies acted on our English Stage," he says in his opening words, "*Othello* is said to bear the Bell away" [131][4]), suggests an emotional investment of his own he can neither control nor understand. In this respect, Rymer established not only the agenda for *Othello* criticism but its aggressive and embattled atmosphere as well.

During the nineteenth century, when Shakespearean commentary began to coalesce into something like a systematic discipline, the play's capacity to generate intense anxiety tends to center on the issue of race.

Othello in Theatrical and Critical History

Through the end of the eighteenth century, playing Othello in blackface wasn't a matter of concern; but "the question of Othello's color, so confidently assumed by Garrick, soon became a stumbling block for actors" (Carlisle, 189). In the second decade of the nineteenth century, Kean abandoned blackface for a light brown makeup. The decision may have been "motivated primarily by theatrical considerations" (Carlisle, 190); Kean depended greatly on facial expressions (too greatly, Hazlitt thought; Sprague, *Shakespearian Players*, 73), and he thought the lighter color helped audiences to see what he was doing, especially difficult in the huge buildings where he performed. Kean's innovation profoundly changed subsequent performance; the fact — or better, question — of Othello's color became a basis for nervous theatrical excitement throughout the nineteenth century. Hence the report of a woman who "hysterically fainted" is now attached to a "'thrilling' effect" Macready devised for his performance of Othello: "He thrust out 'his dark despairing face, through the curtains' forming in its 'contrast with the drapery a marvellous piece of colour.'"[5] Though Macready was not particularly successful in the part, this bit of stage business "was later repeated by Forrest, Phelps, Booth and Irving as late as 1881" (Sprague, *Shakespeare and the Actors*, 216).

These theatrical matters obviously have a broader cultural context; a similarly nervous kind of excitement seems to have generated or been generated by critical response in the increased racial self-consciousness of nineteenth-century thought. Kean's new makeup corresponds to a critical innovation, usually said to originate with Lamb and Coleridge, claiming that Othello must be a tawny Moor rather than a black African (of these matters, much more in the next chapter and the afterword). Nineteenth-century commentators typically acknowledge a deeply affectionate admiration for Othello on the one hand and on the other an abhorrence of his blackness and repulsion at the prospect of interracial marriage. As a consequence of these contradictory desires, they are frequently driven to desperate expedients of disguise or denial. In one notorious instance, Mary Preston, writing in Maryland four years after the end of the American Civil War, acknowledged that "I have always *imagined* its hero as a white man," and then simply changed the facts to correspond with her desire. "Othello," she peremptorily declared, "*was* a *white* man!" (quoted Furness, 395).

Race is still a problematic concern for theatrical production, as Jonathan Miller found out when he produced the play in 1981 for the BBC. Deliberately downplaying the issue and casting Anthony Hopkins as though Othello were "a Hashemite warrior, drilled in British army manners," Miller found himself in "terrible trouble." The "issue of race," he concluded, "has now become as inescapable in the theatre as in real life" (159). Race is still profoundly important in criticism as well, of course, but the peculiarly nineteenth-century kind of denial and shameful anxiety about racial matters has not occupied a central position since Bradley's *Shakespearean Tragedy*. We have, though, our own embarrassments and anxieties, our own sources of shame in the face of this play, which seem to have been passed down to us from the origins of modern critical response. There are two key figures here, Bradley and T. S. Eliot. *Shakespearean Tragedy* sums up and caps off the great Romantic and Victorian traditions of commentary, predicated on a sympathetic imaginative engagement with a heroic protagonist. Against this background, Eliot casually remarks that Othello's final speech always struck him as an attempt at *"cheering himself up."* Designating this attitude as *"bovarysme,* the human will to see things as they are not," Eliot deftly reduces the Noble Moor of received opinion to a feminized and bourgeois banality ("Shakespeare and the Stoicism of Seneca," 111, Eliot's emphasis).

Here as elsewhere, Eliot was enormously influential. His casual impression precipitated a fundamental shift in twentieth-century criticism away from an admirable to a deeply flawed protagonist. It was F. R. Leavis who systematically developed Eliot's point about Othello's final speech, projecting this view backward to reveal a protagonist who "has from the beginning responded" with a self-dramatizing egotism: as early as the opening scenes of the play, according to Leavis, "the essential traitor is within the gates" (139). And this is where Bradley comes back into the picture. Like many of Eliot's memorable Shakespearean remarks — that *Hamlet* is "most certainly an artistic failure" because it lacks an "objective correlative," or that along with *Antony and Cleopatra, Coriolanus* is "Shakespeare's most assured artistic success" ("Hamlet," 123, 124) — the *bovarysme* comment seems to be directed against particular opinions of Bradley or the general consensus of belief represented in Bradley's work. In Leavis, this anti-Bradleyan focus is made explicit. His essay is from first to last a ferocious *ad hominem* attack on Bradley for the "sentimental perversity" of his affectionate admiration for the Noble Moor (141).

As several commentators have pointed out, the intensity of Leavis's assault on Bradley's version of *Othello* seems excessive (as does the early twentieth-century reaction against Bradley in general). Christopher Norris observes that the

difference of views between Bradley and Leavis becomes oddly intertwined with the drama played out between Othello and Iago.
Leavis conceives himself as speaking up for a tough-minded realist
assessment of the play inherently at odds with Bradley's "idealizing"
approach. . . . It is not uncommon for critics to become thus involved in curious patterns of compulsive repetition. . . . Interpretation can only repeat, in compulsive fashion, the acts of misreading
exemplified by various, more or less deluded characters *within the
tale.* (59–61, Norris's emphasis)

Norris is right to characterize Leavis as a "typically combative" writer
and plausible in his claim that this obsessive kind of involvement is itself
"not uncommon," typical of critical response in general. Nonetheless,
propelled like Rymer at the end of the seventeenth century by a manic
rage against the play's and the protagonist's appeal to current taste,
Leavis surpasses his own controversial norms and norms of critical involvement in general. This excess suggests something about *Othello* in
the extraordinary intensity with which it engages our vulnerably angry
identification.

If such overreaction does not start with Leavis, neither does it end
there. In his influential study of the tragedies, *The Story of the Night*,
John Holloway includes a ten-page appendix responding to Leavis's
essay. Commenting on Othello's refusal to confront Desdemona, "I'll
not expostulate with her, lest her body and beauty unprovide my mind
again" (4.1.201–203), or rather on Leavis's claim that the speech reveals
Othello's "voluptuous sensuality," Holloway sharply disagrees:

These words do no such thing. What Dr Leavis takes as the decisive
proof of how Othello's love is at bottom voluptuous sensuality is no
proof at all. This is because — I take it that I am now about to repeat
a commonplace — it is simply false that women's bodies and beauty
unprovide men's minds through exciting "voluptuous sensuality." . . .
The words are grotesquely irrelevant. What is in question is what
makes part of everyone's familiar knowledge about love, marriage
and attraction between men and women. And . . . it would be out of
the question to suppose that any of these simple facts are unknown
to Dr Leavis — indeed, it is difficult to believe that they are unknown
to anyone in normal health. (164–165)

The assault on Leavis here is as violent as Leavis's own on Bradley.
Where Leavis's Bradley was "perverse," Holloway's Leavis is perverted,

pathologically disconnected from reality. Private quarrels and the nasty politics of British literary studies in midcentury are no doubt relevant to all this, but so is the play, whose "whole tendency," as John Bayley remarks, "is to make us partisan" (148).

Commenting on the "surprising . . . *personal* acrimony" in *Othello* criticism," Peter Davison speculates that "the peculiar viciousness that animates some critics . . . may stem from what in *Othello* subconsciously disturbs them" (10 and 53, Davison's emphasis). For Holloway, this disturbing "what" in *Othello* is clearly sexual in nature. In disagreeing with Leavis, he evokes the authority of "everyone's familiar knowledge about love, marriage and attraction between men and women." It is not uncommon for *Othello* critics to claim that their interpretations are not just valid but true, yet another piece of evidence for the special pressures the play puts on us.[6] In Holloway's case, however, this claim is especially problematic. Given the difficulty of talking about one's own sexual experience, who can claim to speak authoritatively of anyone else's, let alone *everyone* else's? This appeal beyond Othello's speech to a presumed consensus allows Holloway to play fast and loose with the speech itself. It is hard to see what Othello can be acknowledging in refusing to speak to Desdemona if not precisely his experience of her attractiveness as undermining self-command, especially when a similar sentiment is expressed elsewhere in the play and generally in a wide variety of texts, theatrical and otherwise, written during the play's period.[7] Yet this sentiment Holloway summarily dismisses as "grotesquely irrelevant" and "simply false."

The denial is as fully astounding as Mary Preston's of the protagonist's color, but as with Preston we are better off emphasizing exemplarity than idiosyncrasy. If "repression pervades the entire world" of *Othello* (Snow, "Sexual Anxiety," 384), then critical denial, the refusal of an intolerably painful reality, serving (as in Norris's description) to reproduce the compulsive behavior of characters inside the dramatic action, may seem understandable, even appropriate, as a response. Moreover, just as Preston's refusal of Othello's blackness is only an extreme instance of a typical (and therefore in a sense normal) response, so obsessive denial on the sexual register is not unique to Holloway; it is relatively common in modern *Othello* criticism, which includes a still-active cottage industry producing claims that Othello and Desdemona never consummate their marriage, and arguing for them with the same peculiar rage and personal edge as in Holloway's appendix.[8] In this context, Holloway's quarrel with Leavis may be joined to Leavis's with Bradley at the foun-

Othello in Theatrical and Critical History

dation of twentieth-century critical response to the play. In their over-heated anger, they exhibit the early signs of a process by which sex has displaced race as the topic about which modern anxieties in the face of this play most densely cluster.

Current interpretation, theatrical and critical, has been notably will-ing to acknowledge the play's uncanny ability to evoke thoughts, feel-ings, and images of a disturbingly intimate nature. For some years, crit-ics have been focusing on the way *Othello* makes us think "not merely generally of marriage but specifically of the wedding night" (Cavell, 131). By now (as we shall see in some detail in chapter 4) there is a thriving enterprise at the center of *Othello* commentary claiming that the play works by evoking "a hidden scene of desire [as the] focus of compulsive fascination for audience and characters alike" (Neill, "Hidden Malady," 98). A similar focus characterizes theatrical performance. Almost every-one agrees, even those who didn't like it, that the John Dexter–Olivier *Othello* at the National Theatre in 1964 is the most powerfully memo-rable performance of modern times, and almost everyone agrees about the "strong physical aura of this performance" (Bamber Gascoigne, quoted in Tynan, 107). To take a lesser-known example, consider the dumb show by which Harold Scott introduced his 1990 production at the Shakespeare Theatre in Washington:

> Othello and Desdemona entered from behind a large bed, placed centerstage and covered with crimson draperies. They walked slowly around it from opposite sides, while an African talking drum played in the background. Othello and Desdemona approached the bed and knelt on it. Each let fall the robe s/he wore and, nude, they con-tinued to kneel and embraced and lay down across the bed, which was then drawn back into the shadows and off-stage, not to reappear until the final scene. (Johnson-Haddad, "Shakespeare Theatre at the Folger," 477)

In our willingness, even eagerness, to engage with the play's disturb-ing sexuality, we have moved a healthy distance away from Holloway's obsessive denials. It is not clear, however, what claims we are entitled to make about our increased frankness, or about its benefits in coming to terms with this play. Davison's "subconsciously disturbing" suggests the reassuring idea that consciousness is therapeutic, that knowledge pro-duces self-possession and interpretive power. But Holloway's problem was not primarily ignorance or repression; on the contrary, he was fully aware of the factors motivating his outrageous claims:

The spectacle of literary critics and university lecturers engaging in disputes where to say anything worth saying, they must draw upon their intimate comprehension of the many ways in which sexuality may prove a good force or an evil one in men's lives, is a spectacle which is not remote enough for comfort from the ridiculous. (37)

The beautifully sustained control of this sentence conveys the suggestion of a commanding self-knowledge, but the style is contradicted by the subject, the substance of his knowledge, which is his own embarrassed folly: by exposing his own most deeply personal convictions and feelings about intimate sexual experience, he will make a ridiculous spectacle of himself — like the play's protagonist, becoming "the fixed figure for the time of scorn / To point his slow and moving finger at!" (4.2.55–56). In playing Othello to Leavis's Iago, Holloway is much more fully cognizant than his adversary of the risks involved; but the understanding produces no practical benefits. Able to analyze *Othello*'s "whole tendency . . . to make us partisan," he still has no effective protection against the play's power to generate a compulsive advocacy.

Here again he resembles Othello, who proclaims the utter foolishness of believing Iago —

> Exchange me for a goat
> When I shall turn the business of my soul
> To such exsufflicate and blown surmises,
> Matching thy inference. (3.3 183–186)

— and then promptly performs the utter foolishness he proclaims. Holloway just doesn't seem to be able to help himself. His predicament, moreover, derives not from personal inadequacy but from the general condition of literary and theatrical response. As he rightly understood his situation, he had no choice but to engage with the inherited traditions of *Othello* commentary. The only way he had "to say anything" that might be recognized "as worth saying" was "to engage in dispute" with Leavis (or agree with him). Once entered into that angry argument, he has become vulnerable to the sense of painful exposure which seems to have generated the argument to begin with.

As a cautionary tale about the limits of knowledge, Holloway might make us skeptical about our own potential mastery of *Othello*, for whatever advantages we might claim in literary or sexual sophistication, we operate under the same constraint. Our abilities to see what we see in *Othello* (let alone say something worth saying about it) are determined in fundamental ways. We can connect with the play only by joining a conversation (or argument) whose agenda and tonality have already been established — and in many cases by voices we have never directly heard and writers we have never even heard of. Holloway himself now functions as one of our determinants, along with much subsequent writing and performance, absorbing into themselves the claims made earlier — by Leavis, Eliot, Bradley, Preston, Coleridge, and the other intensely engaged and frequently enraged readers and audiences of this play going back to Thomas Rymer and Henry Jackson. Whatever their peculiarities, these witnesses all offer consistent and corroborating testimony about the power of the play. They suggest that no acknowledgment of the disturbing element in *Othello* will succeed in managing the disturbance, and that nothing we can do will defend ourselves adequately against the threat represented by *Othello* to our "unprovided" mind.

How has *Othello* sustained its extraordinary power to affect audiences over four centuries? What is it about the play that accounts for this remarkable continuity of response? Its themes and subject matter must be relevant here. Love and jealousy, sexual desire and creaturely difference (racial or otherwise) — these seem to be subjects of deep and ambivalent fascination throughout human history, mattering greatly to all societies that have left us records of their interests. It might be claimed that *Othello* is resonating on a universal register, transcending the partialities of particular audiences and appealing to an essential humanity shared across cultural differences. In fact, of course, it has been so claimed: this idea — not just about *Othello* but about Shakespeare's plays generally — goes back to Ben Jonson at the beginning of the First Folio ("He was not of an age, but for all time!"), and similar claims were often — even routinely — made through the end of the nineteenth century. They have been subjected to a skeptical scrutiny in the twentieth century and a downright hostile one in our own time, but the idea of Shakespeare's transcendent appeal remains generally familiar, and substantial vestiges of it survive, however qualified, even among those current critics who are most skeptical about the existence of an essential humanity and most committed to a materialist explanation for the transmission of cultural values.[9]

Too many smart people have committed themselves to one version or another of Shakespeare's universality for us to dismiss it out of hand. But it doesn't seem to get us very far; once we declare it, what next? Moreover, contemporary suspicion about universals is justified; they can be vague and amorphous abstractions, obscuring important differences. Whatever race means now, for instance (and it's hardly an identical meaning for all of us), it seems implausible to assume that it meant the same thing for audiences four hundred years ago (who presumably had to endure internal contradictions of their own). Neither could the concept of gender difference as the constituting feature of male and female identity or of sexual desire. There is good evidence to believe that Shakespeare's audience did not identify human nature in terms of a core racial or sexual self. In fact, the very concept of an inner core of being, however identified, is probably something Shakespeare's audience would not have recognized, at least not in our sense as the self-evident motivating factor by which to understand human action.

From this angle, the reception history of *Othello* is apt to look very different from the narrative earlier in this chapter. There I represented the nineteenth-century concern with race as simply a particular inflection of the play's generally anxiety-producing effect, a specific version of the same phenomenon, but we can turn this material the other way around to emphasize not continuity but discontinuity. Now we might say that interpreters in the early nineteenth century — in Britain and America, at least — *invented* color as a central topic in the play, as part of a major shift in basic cultural values with far-reaching ramifications for *Othello* and beyond. For it was at about the same time that (*a*) sexual identity became a normative concept along with the concept of the inner self as the natural locus for explaining and analyzing what we do; (*b*) a pathological indecisiveness was discovered as Hamlet's defining feature; and (*c*) Shakespearean commentary and literary criticism in general first took recognizable shape as a practice with which our own is continuous.[10] In the face of such fundamental and apparently interconnected transformations, it is hard to claim real kinship with pre-Romantic response to Shakespeare. On the contrary, earlier audiences of *Othello* (or *Hamlet*) should seem very strange to us in not being preoccupied with the protagonist's race (or tendency to delay). It does not seem too much to say that they were looking at a different play.

The strangeness of the original *Othello* is something we ought to respect; we need to do more than acknowledge the readiness with which the play speaks to our own interests. We should keep in mind the historical distance of the audiences for which it was written. Although *Othello* has become our play, we need to see it as their play too. But these look like contradictory or mutually exclusive endeavors. If we want to retrieve *Othello*'s historical particularity, we seem bound to detach ourselves from its present power; but removing ourselves to a position above the action, we seem to abandon the very qualities of *Othello* that generated its historical interest for us in the first place. We then risk losing not just our play but theirs as well.

One way out of this impasse is to get a clearer sense of what we mean by their play. By returning to the original *Othello*, we go with the flow of contemporary critical work. "Always historicize" has become our rallying cry. But what does it mean to be historical? Common sense suggests that it means, first of all, interpreting texts in their original contexts, but what are they? Historical studies tend frequently to conceptualize the original context as an amorphous thematic whole — the patriarchy, social struggle, power, the cultural text; but there is nothing resembling consensus on this matter, and in more usefully suggestive and influential current versions, the problem is treated with such subtlety that the very idea of an original context begins to disintegrate.[11] If we are interested in *Othello* as a play, moreover, the problem becomes even more complicated. "No preposition," Wai Chee Dimock remarks, "is more important to a synchronic historicism than the reassuring *in*" (1061); but even if we could determine what they were in, the phenomena we designate as literary or theatrical texts can be claimed to exist precisely by virtue of their resistance to such enclosure.

Hence Kathleen E. McLuskie, writing about the "*reproducibility* of the early modern playtext" (her emphasis), claims that because it

> dealt with recurring tropes and images, it was the more easily separable from particular theatrical and social contexts, more open for its meanings to be reconstructed with the cultural toolkit of a different audience. It allowed the plays to be "not of an age" and, if not for all time, for the times when their varied and contradictory representations . . . could be reanimated by contemporary preoccupations, to generate theatrical if not political excitement. (100)

McLuskie is interested in the economic and social materialities within which the institution of Renaissance theater developed, but her point is that a play is not a political tract or a medical textbook or a legal commentary; it is a play. Although a play can be a window onto a different culture and strange past, it serves as a cultural artifact only in very peculiar and specific ways. It is designed to "generate theatrical . . . excitement," producing in its audience a powerful affective engagement with the dramatic action and characters. A theatrical audience is made up of different individuals, and in the Renaissance public theater for which

Othello was written, the audience was much more socially and ideologically diverse than what we are used to.[12] Playing to such a big room, Renaissance plays were especially reliant on "recurring tropes and images," because such stylized conventions made them available for various kinds of interpretation or appropriation. One consequence of this flexibility is that audiences in later theaters and even readers, separated not just historically but phenomenologically from the plays' original reception conditions, could nonetheless feel that Shakespeare was talking directly to them. Hence McLuskie's claim for the *"reproducibility"* of Shakespeare's plays, what John Ripley calls their "mechanism for self-renewal" (121), may be understood as entirely consistent with their original conditions of production and reception.

If we're interested in the play's capacity to "generate theatrical excitement," then themes won't matter so much. Love and jealousy — the asymmetrical power relations defined with reference to race and gender — are highly interesting topics. But sex and race do not by themselves explain the extraordinary power of *Othello* as a theatrical or literary vehicle. If they did, *Oroonoco*, Aphra Behn's prose romance about a royal African slave who has lots of sexual charisma, would matter to us as much as *Othello* and in the same way. *Oroonoco*, to be sure, had a rich afterlife in a variety of prose and theatrical spinoffs, powerfully feeding off of and feeding into the slavery debates throughout the eighteenth century. The book's hesitancies, changes of direction, and downright confusion must have made it wonderfully useful as a vicarious expressive access to the confused racial and sexual feelings of Restoration and eighteenth-century England. Along with the female author, this probably helps to explain its extraordinary appeal to us after centuries of almost total neglect: it engages historical interest in direct relation to its esthetic indifference. Yet even in its moment of textual power, no one felt faint or angry reading *Oroonoco*, or found the protagonist's murder of his wife and his own torture and suicide at the end so dreadful as "not to be endured."[13]

Instead of themes, we might focus on the dramatic action as it unfolds before us, and we might ask which of the characters speak most directly to us and for us, drawing us most deeply into their own positions inside the action of the play. The obvious answer here is the protagonist. According to G. Wilson Knight, "*Othello* is dominated by its protagonist" (97); this, however, is not true, or certainly less true than of Shakespeare's other tragedies. *Othello* is the only tragedy in which the protagonist does not have the most lines to speak. This distinction belongs to Iago, who speaks almost one-third more lines than Othello.[14] On top of his quantitative dominance, Iago enjoys a position of qualitative power. In his frequent soliloquies, spoken directly to us, he makes us party to his own thoughts, feelings, and purposes, which themselves generate and determine the plot. Iago's extraordinary prominence as a surrogate dramatist within the action of *Othello* has frequently been acknowledged:

> Because of his privileged placing in the play's development, which allows him to confide in the audience directly, he involves us, draws us into a kind of complicity in his designs. . . . The key to the play is not the extent to which Othello is infected by Iago, but the extent to which we in the audience are seduced by him. (Foakes, "The Descent of Iago," 26, 28)

> Iago enjoys a privileged relation with the audience. He possesses what can be termed the discourse of knowledge in *Othello* and annexes not only the other characters, but the resisting spectator as well, into his world and its perspective. By virtue of his manipulative power and his superior knowledge and control over the action, which we share, we are implicated in his machinations and the cultural values they imply. (Newman "'And Wash the Ethiop,'" 151)

The remarkable thing about these two recent descriptions of Iago is not only how much each sounds like the other but how applicable they both are to both Richard III and Hamlet, who happen to be the only two characters in the entire Shakespeare canon with a higher line count than Iago (only Hamlet has a higher percentage of his own play). But Richard III and Hamlet *are* the protagonists of their plays — in fact, particularly dominating examples of the dominant part (hence the phrase "*Hamlet* without the Prince of Denmark" to indicate the absence of the defining center — no one says "*Macbeth* without the Thane of Cawdor" or even "*Lear* without the old kind king"). Iago is not.

Othello is unique in its dramatic structure and emotional economy. Nowhere else does Shakespeare divide the central space of a tragedy between two inhabitants with different but equally strong claims on our interest.[15] This shared top billing was apparently acknowledged by the early audiences: for Leonard Digges, "Honest *Iago*, or the jealous Moore" are equivalent examples of Shakespeare's "ravishing" power.[16] "Jago for a rogue, and Othello for a jealous husband," Abraham Wright wrote in his commonplace book around 1637, "two parts well penned"

(John Munro, 411). The play's peculiarity is reflected in the complications of its subsequent performance history. "Here," as Irving's biographer says, "the lover and the violator of order are almost equally prominent, and Irving tried his hands at both parts" (Alan Hughes, 142). So did Kean, Macready, and Edwin Booth, among others, at a time when the star system made sure that leading actors concentrated their efforts on leading parts. The role-swapping arrangements get at the same point (Macready and Charles Mayne Young in 1816, Irving and Booth in 1881, for examples). These arrangements transferred the approximately equal competition between the characters in the dramatic action to a contest at the performative level between evenly matched actors. Such a double competitive potential seems to have been part of *Othello*'s stage history for as far back as we can see. Carol Carlisle quotes the actor Samuel Foote's remark about Othello in 1747 "that he could recall no other character which 'so absolutely depends on . . . the Returning of the Ball,' for 'the greatest Othello that ever was born, unless he be well provided with an Ancient, [cannot] properly . . . express either the Hero or the jealous Lover.'" This view, she adds, survives into the present as in Olivier's "view of the play as a duelling ground for actors" (184).

Two stories about Kean illustrate these at once dramatic and histrionic possibilities. In 1817, when the sudden popularity of Junius Brutus Booth "seemed briefly to challenge" his own, "Kean flatteringly invited [Booth] to enter into a contract with his own management at Drury Lane and to play, among other parts, Iago" (Hankey, 60). Booth played Iago opposite Kean's Othello on February 20, to "a house 'crammed to the very Ceiling,'" including "several of the Nobility" and "'the most eminent among literary men and critics.' When Booth as Iago mentioned that he knew his price, the pit attached significance to the words and applauded them wildly.'" But Booth was thoroughly upstaged: "Kean's *Othello* smothered *Desdemona* and my *Iago* too," he said, and declined to repeat the experience, as billed, five days later (Sprague, *Shakespearian Players*, 77). At the end of his career, in 1833, by then old and gouty and a drunk, Kean nonetheless scored another triumph as Othello, this time over Macready's Iago. As George Henry Lewes remembered it, "How puny he appeared beside Macready . . . until the third act when he seemed to swell into a stature which made Macready appear small. . . . I would again risk broken ribs for the chance of a good place in the pit to see anything like it" (Hankey, 60).

These were Kean's triumphs, but they were also Othello's. The 1833 performance opposite Macready was part of a swapping arrangement in which Kean refused to take on Iago, even though Macready was a better Iago than an Othello and Kean himself excelled at both.[17] But Kean believed "that however engagingly he played Iago, he could never win the sympathies of his audience . . . and he is reported to have warned a young actor 'not to peril the sympathies of the audiences as Iago, while he can assuredly possess them wholly by only a moderate picture of Othello'" (Hankey, 54). He "insisted that he had acted [Iago] merely to show that he had carefully studied both characters but that he could not imagine anyone's seriously entertaining the notion of their equality. . . . 'Othello holds all the interest'" (Carlisle, 218). In this respect, Kean reflected contemporary taste in general; Othello's role dominated during the first half of the century. But by the time Irving and Booth traded roles in 1881, in performances that "revealed two masterly Iagos and two unsatisfactory Othellos" (Odell, 376),[18] things had changed. It was now "quite clear that Iago had emerged as the most interesting role" (Hankey, 91).

Not that either preeminence was ever absolute. Kean's warning to the anonymous young actor would have made no sense about Claudius, say, or any other tragic nonprotagonist, none of which might have tempted a young actor "to peril the sympathies of the audience" in the way Kean warned against. Kean's resistance to Iago's role testifies to its availability as a theatrical possibility, an acknowledgment of its suitability for an actor of Kean's preeminent stature — an intuited awareness, even at a time when Othello's role is self-evidently dominant, that maybe it is Iago who is really the play's star turn. But it works the other way around as well. With Iago's eventual supremacy comes also a sense of regret for the diminished power of Othello's part. There is a long tradition going back from Fechter to Garrick of celebrated actors regretting that their performances of Othello failed or failed to achieve the powerful success of their Iagos. Othello was "a negligibility in Irving's career" (Odell, 310), but as "the greatest actor-manager of his day" and "an accepted standard for Hamlet, Macbeth and Lear," he kept trying until, after the 1881 performances with Booth, he finally gave up: "He rolled up his clothes that he had worn as the Moor, one by one, carefully laying one garment on top of the other, and then, half humorously and very deliberately, said: 'Never again'" (Rosenberg, 79). Such disappointment may say something about the unlimited nature of histrionic ego (like Bottom, who wants to play all the parts himself in A Midsummer Night's Dream);[19] but it also reflects the intuition, even when Iago's dominance has become the norm, that Othello without the Moor of Venice at the center is a diminished thing. Carried over into our century, the failure of modern

Othellos to hold their own against their Iagos represents the norm. According to Martin Wine, commenting on five midcentury productions, "most reviewers felt that, with the exception of the National's [Dexter-Olivier], these belonged aesthetically more to Iago than to Othello" (43);[20] the Othellos "were no match for the vividly realised Iagos who . . . developed their parts with such high spirits that they threw the emotional balance of [their] productions out of kilter" (62). By now, to judge from response to the Branagh-Fishburne film, this lament has become something of a routine.[21]

As with theatrical history, so with critical history; a similar transformation has occurred, with similarly ambivalent results — though later. The shift away from Othello as the affective center occurs, as we have seen, with the anti-Bradleyan insurgence of Eliot and Leavis; but Bradley himself was already forced to some desperate expedients in order to sustain his focus on the Noble Moor, isolating the character of Iago more or less consciously to guarantee that his fascination for us does not interfere with our admiration for Othello.[22] As in later critics working out of Bradley's basic feeling, this strategy had the reverse effect, highlighting Iago even more.[23] Indeed, Leavis's attack was predicated on the claim that Bradley made too much of Iago, as if he and not Othello were the play's central concern. But as Norris says, Leavis himself was carrying on further in the same direction: his contemptuous dismissal of idealized nobility is delivered in Iago's voice and testifies to his own unconscious absorption. We have been echoing him ever since. Well before Norris called attention to the way Leavis's commentary "becomes oddly intertwined with . . . Iago," critics were remarking on the fact that the unillusioned and antiheroic readings that have dominated twentieth-century critical response to *Othello* all wind up in one way or another sounding like Iago.[24]

The ascendancy of Iago is a major triumph of modern *Othello* criticism. Our ability to acknowledge the extent to which Iago speaks for us and to reproduce his voice have added immeasurably to the energy of interpretive response to the play. By Bradley's time, celebrating the Noble Moor's heroic simplicity had become something of an empty routine. This is true as well about the huge theatrical spectacles that framed the heroic *Othellos* of the nineteenth century. They had become unsustainable esthetically as well as economically, either disappearing or removing themselves into the more capacious accommodations of grand opera. But by now this may seem too much of a good thing — even, like the modern theatrical *Othello*, a diminished thing. An absorption into

Iago's point of view has allowed us to see through Othello as bombastic from the beginning, or at least deeply flawed and vulnerable; but if Othello's collapse seems merely predictable and even in a sense justified, then all the testimonials we have witnessed to an unendurably painful play must be dismissed as mistaken. The privileges of membership in Iago's sophisticated club are not gratis; we have purchased power over the play at the cost of the play's power over us. Modern criticism of *Othello* is turning out to be a mixed blessing, maybe even a poisoned gift.

According to Michael D. Bristol, "the best commentators on this play have recognized the degree to which it prompts a desire to prevent the impending débâcle and the sense in which it is itself a kind of theatrical punishment for the observers" (200). In this remark, Bristol claims for *Othello* a special power to generate contradictory desires — the one, suffering with the play's protagonist, the other acting with its antagonist (and then suffering punishment as a result). In suggesting the need to acknowledge roughly equal and certainly opposite kinds of involvement, Bristol may be aligned with John Bayley who, after his claim that "the whole tendency of *Othello* is to make us partisan," immediately adds that it works "to underline the incommensurability of opposed emotional states." In effect Bristol and Bayley ask us to see the play from a position shared with and fractured by Othello and Iago. Along with others among "the best commentators" on this play, they invite us to play Leavis and Holloway at once, or Leavis and Bradley, or (more generally) to inhabit not just our own disillusioned versions of the play but earlier heroic versions as well.

This is a difficult course to follow in many respects: methodologically (criticism is supposed to be coherent); epistemologically (you can't stand in two different places at the same time); and above all emotionally (the consequences of such a course are bound to be deeply painful). As a result, it is bound to be resisted. Indeed, the play itself, as Jane Adamson describes it, may be said to generate our resistance to its own fierce energies, revealing "the impossible difficulty of sustaining . . . a life open to doubt and uncertainty" not just for its characters but for its audience as well, making "us acutely aware of our *own* needs for emotional and moral certainty, simplicity and finality [as a] way of sheltering ourselves from the full reality of its ending" (300–301; Adamson's emphasis). Our resistance to *Othello*, then, may be appropriate and even inevitable. As we have seen in this brief tour of the play's theatrical and critical history, however, resistance seems to be futile as well.

Disconfirmation

If we try to imagine ourselves back into an early seventeenth-century Globe audience, what do see at the beginning of *Othello*? Two men enter, arguing. We know they are angry — "abhor," "hate," and "despise" are spat out in the first few seconds — but not why. Presumably the black cloth hung at the rear of the stage signals a tragedy, but what's the matter — what's the subject of the play? Sometimes Shakespeare provides this information directly and immediately (*Troilus*, *Lear*, and *Antony*), but *Othello* is much less obliging. What is the "this" to which the first speaker refers? Who is the "him" that Iago has claimed to hate? The answers become available only gradually. "Him" turns out to refer to a military commander whom Iago resents for some perceived slight, but what is "this"? Sixty lines into the play, Roderigo refers to a triumph, "What a full fortune does the thicklips owe / If he can carry't thus!" where the "it" carried thus may seem to refer to Cassio's promotion, as though *that* is the "this" and now the "it" we have been looking for since the beginning; but with "her father" in Iago's next speech, we discover that "it" must refer to something else again: the promotion only explains why Iago hates "the thicklips" and therefore was not party to whatever "full fortune" he now possesses — the nature of which, however, we still do not know. Iago's speech here helps to shed some light on this matter, but also to obscure it:

> Call up her father,
> Rouse him, make after him, poison his delight,
> Proclaim him in the streets, incense her kinsmen,
> And, though he in a fertile climate dwell,
> Plague him with flies! Though that his joy be joy
> Yet throw such changes of vexation on't
> As it may lose some colour. (1.1.66–72)

The pronouns are unstable, offering contradictory suggestions. Honigmann thinks that "him," "him," and "his" in line 67 all refer to "her father" and is skeptical about the view of "some editors" who think "the 'him' throughout is Othello." But even coming back to this speech after reading or seeing the play many times, we can't be sure whether in "his delight" and "his joy" Iago is thinking of "her father" or "the thicklips"; and the joyful and delightful "it" on which Iago proposes to throw changes of vexation remains still to be defined.

In no other play of Shakespeare's except maybe *Hamlet* do we have to work so hard and over such a sustained period in order to determine what the play is about. "What is the matter there?" Brabantio's entering question a moment later echoes Iago at the very beginning, "If ever I did dream / Of such a matter, abhor me" (4–5) and is in turn echoed by Othello in the next scene, "What's the matter, think you?" (38). As John Shaw demonstrates, versions of this question recur like a litany throughout the action of the play. They represent the often anguished perplexity of the characters in the face of an often threatening action whose contours need to be defined. The play works hard to make it our question as well.

And to make Iago the source of our answers. The play names him right away (for Roderigo's name we are made to wait until line 55) and thus immediately gives him a special accessibility beyond physical presence ("the shorter one in the brown," or whatever). He clearly knows more than Roderigo, providing the background information to us as well as to him inside the action. Iago is the commanding figure, leading them to the position Roderigo announces they have reached ("Here is her father's house"), from which to proceed with the plan Iago has devised ("I'll call aloud"). Thanks to Iago, we have been propelled beyond discussion to the more decisive and revelatory mode of action where we might hope finally to find the clarification we seek.

In the event, we are not disappointed.

> Zounds, sir, you're robbed, for shame put on your gown!
> Your heart is burst, you have lost half your soul,
> Even now, now, very now, an old black ram
> Is tupping your white ewe! (85–88)

Here at last is the "this" we have been looking for. After so much gray indefinition, Iago gives us a sudden sharpness of focus. Passing references to "the Moor" and "the thicklips" and maybe even Iago's threat to make "his joy . . . lose some colour" emerge precipitously into a new and stunningly definite light. Roderigo's motivation is illuminated as well. Though we have to wait for a bit before he is identified as a disappointed suitor, Iago's description of interracial copulation is so appalling in its graphic specificity that it can absorb all the feelings of angry resistance and resentment we have sensed till now. The image is intensified temporally as well as pictorially. "Even now, now, very now" repeatedly thrusts the action home into the present moment of our hearing it. "Tupping" is a nasty word used of animals, a variant of "topping." The word probably sounds like "fucking" to modern audiences but must have violated the ears of Renaissance audiences as well. Iago's speech enacts the monstrous violation it describes, indecently assaulting not just Brabantio (can we avoid hearing "ewe" as "you?") but us.[1] We have been longing for knowledge, and now Iago thrusts it on us with a vengeance.

At the minimal level of being able to specify "the matter," then, we are required to enter this play under the rough guidance of Iago who, moreover, seems designed to determine not just the subject but our attitude toward it as well. Subsequent audiences come to the play knowing that Iago is not to be trusted, information picked up either from the general cultural data bank or from the dramatis personae in printed texts. Shakespeare's audience might have had some pretextual clue in the costuming equivalent to "the black wig and heavy eyebrows used by the conventional Iago" of the nineteenth-century stage (Carlisle, 222), but they saw the play before it had been assimilated into received tradition and without the advance information furnished by a playbill. Lacking such prejudicial knowledge, what would they have understood?

Obviously Iago is self-serving in claiming he deserved Cassio's promotion, but he expresses his complaint more generally in terms of a lament for a world where old ties of loyalty have disintegrated:

> 'Tis the curse of service:
> Preferment goes by letter and affection
> And not by old gradation, where each second
> Stood heir to th'first. (34–37)

Renaissance plays are full of speeches yearning for a simpler past; their audiences seem to have been peculiarly susceptible to nostalgia, a sentimental predisposition for which there are plausible social and economic explanations.[2] In any case, by the time of *Othello*'s first performances the tone and values of Iago's speech had become part of the standard theatrical repertoire, one of McLuskie's "recurring tropes and images," a recognizable dramatic type (sometimes designated the *laudator temporis acti*, the "praiser of times past"). It can be played for laughs, as by Falstaff, but in the tragic mode it has a more or less autonomous authority, expressing the truth for the purposes of theatrical engagement. We can trust dramatic characters who talk like this, at least provisionally.

Iago's frank resentment and willful misrepresentation are unlovely qualities, but in terms again of theatrical values, even they tend to command respect, the consequence of Iago's enacting another dramatic type that achieved great prominence in the early seventeenth century. "The Malcontent," as we have come to designate this type, serves to pass harsh judgment on a thoroughly contaminated social order. At the same time, he sees no alternative but to accept his situation as a participant in this corrupt world ("Nay, there's no remedy") and protect his own interests ("In following him I follow but myself"). Like Hamlet, who may be seen as among other things an early and probably formative version of the same dramatic type, Iago believes that "something is rotten in the state," but for strategic reasons he cannot reveal his true feelings ("I am not what I am"; compare Hamlet's "I have that within that passes show"). Like the *laudator temporis acti*, the Malcontent may be explained with relation to social and political context, but by the time of *Othello* it too had, like Iago's nostalgia for the "old gradation," assumed a more or less autonomous authority.[3] Iago is resentful, alienated, and hypocritical, but the Malcontent's position he seems to occupy is the best one available from which both to judge and to take part in the peculiarly stressful world he inhabits. Since this combination of judgment and participation is a good working description of a theatrical audience's position, small wonder that we tend to trust him.

For modern audiences the most serious obstacle to trusting Iago is his blatant racism, yet all the available evidence suggests that the original audiences would have assented easily, even automatically, to Iago's slurs about the as-yet-unnamed old ram's color. Shakespeare evidently assumes such assent in his representation of Aaron in *Titus* and Portia, the pretty much unambiguously sympathetic heroine of *The Merchant*, who insouciantly dismisses Morocco with "May all of his complexion choose me so" (2.6.79). G. K. Hunter demonstrates that "a traditional view of what Moors are like, i.e., gross, disgusting, inferior, carrying the symbol of their damnation on their skin," was normal and overt in Shakespeare's time (45). As he labors to terrify Brabantio, Iago makes systematic use of conventional ideas about black origins in acts of sexual transgression and diabolically inspired violation of the father's authority and property rights ("thieves, thieves, thieves!"; "the devil will make a grandsire of you"), resulting in the debased deformity — in Iago's inflection, the bestiality — of a sinfully contaminated progeny ("coursers for cousins and jennets for germans").[4] Such insults may have seemed exceptional to Shakespeare's audience only in their wit and verbal cleverness, the alliteration here and the slyly sarcastic pun at the very beginning ("his Moorship" for "his worship"), commanding assent reinforced by delighted if anxious laughter.

Globe audiences not only felt differently about dark skin, they must have seen something different. The play lumps together black and Moorish attributes in a way that can perplex modern audiences, who have assimilated (and in many cases more recently come to reject) the understanding of distinct racial identities from the ideas systematically deployed by scientists during the nineteenth century (the same period when, as a parallel development, the debate raged whether to play Othello as "a black African" or "a tawny Moor"). The Elizabethans were clearly able to think in terms of distinct and biologically determined identities, but such a "racialist" consciousness was a long way from full development or general dispersion. Rather, it was contained within and typically driven by "pre-racialist" assumptions of a religious nature. Skin color was not so much a thing in itself as the marker of a theological category; black is the color of the devil, evil, sin. Its significance was "moral and religious," as Julie Hankey says, "rather than racial and geographical" (11). According to Hunter, the new knowledge derived from exploration had no effect in displacing the dominant theological mode that fundamentally structured the Elizabethans' understanding: "The vocabulary at their disposal frustrated any attempt at scientific discrimination. The world was still seen largely, in terms of vocabulary, as a network of religious names. The word 'Moor' had no clear racial status" (40); it was used indiscriminately to describe any people "in that outer circuit of non-Christian lands where the saving grace of Jerusalem is weakest in its whitening power" (41). In fact, the standard term in the Renaissance to describe a character like Othello is "Blackamoor," as in Best's "all these black Moores which are in Africa," which conflates North African and sub-Saharan racial types in just the way we don't. Richard Burbage, the original Othello, probably performed the part in blackface and Moorish costume — as a "Blackamoor"; but Renaissance audiences probably wouldn't have registered the suggestions as scientifically contradictory, perhaps partly as a result of contemporary histrionic conventions, but chiefly because they weren't used to thinking in terms of the scientific (or pseudoscientific) categories of race and geography that were being contradicted.[5]

Relatively unencumbered with a racial consciousness, the original audiences may have been more rather than less vulnerable to the play's peculiarly anxiety-producing effects. The indiscriminate mixing of black and Moorish impressions serves to endow Othello with an unstable quality that adds to and may indeed be at the heart of his terrifying strangeness. In Brabantio's incredulous question whether Desdemona would have "run from her guardage to the sooty bosom / Of such a thing as thou? to fear, not to delight" (1.2.70–71), "thing" is a functionally imprecise word. Caliban in *The Tempest*, a "salvage and deformed slave" according to the character list in the Folio, a monstrously amorphous creature in the action, is described as a "thing of darkness" (5.1.275). "What, has this thing appear'd again to-night?" Horatio asks at the beginning of *Hamlet* (1.1.29). We do not yet know he is referring to the ghost of Hamlet Sr., and the question inspires fear precisely through the totally unconstrained suggestiveness of "thing." In the same way, Brabantio's speech associates the indefinite with the effect of fear, both here and later in the next scene: "what she feared to look on" (99). These usages imply that the various suggestions about Othello's color might have seemed not so much contradictory to Elizabethans as emphatic, reinforcing the anxious sense of a volatile and moving target, like the ghost in *Hamlet* who cannot be fixed in a local habitation even after it is given a tentative name: "'Tis here, 'tis here, 'tis gone." As Roderigo describes him, the "lascivious Moor" is "an extravagant and wheeling stranger / Of here and everywhere" (1.1.135).

A tawny Moor, a black African, Othello is also the "turbanned Turk" of his own description at the end (5.2.351). In the opening scene, Iago refers to "the Cyprus wars, / Which *even now* stands in act" (148–149), and the emphasized words help to establish a structural analogy: as Othello invades the space of Brabantio's authority, so the Turks threaten Venice's political and economic interests. The Turkish peril seems to be playing on primal fears as well; according to the Duke, it is experienced "in fearful sense" (1.3.12), a word that echoes Brabantio's response to "such a thing" as Othello a moment earlier at the end of the preceding scene. The Turkish invasion raises the age-old specter of barbarian hordes assaulting Europe from the margins. Brabantio evokes the idea in order to dismiss it. "What tell'st thou me of robbing? This is Venice: /

My house is not a grange" (that is, not a "country house or outlying farmhouse," as Honigmann glosses "grange" in 1.1.105). By the next scene, however, Brabantio's confidence has been eroded:

> the duke himself,
> Or any of my brothers of the state,
> Cannot but feel this wrong as 'twere their own.
> For if such actions may have passage free
> Bond-slaves and pagans shall our statesmen be. (1.2.99)

Othello's action in eloping with Desdemona has in effect transformed Venice from the protected and protecting center to a vulnerable outpost overrun by infidels.

If the Turks are terrifying phantoms, they are also actual personages. The threat of invasion evokes recent history; the "Turks took Cyprus from the Venetians in 1570–3 and, though heavily defeated by a Christian navy at the Battle of Lepanto (1571), henceforth dominated the eastern Mediterranean" (Honigmann, 8). These events would have been part of living memory for at least some of Shakespeare's audience, and they would have been revitalized by the presence, much commented on, of a Moorish retinue representing the King of Barbary at Elizabeth's court during 1600–1601 and by the republication on his accession in 1603 of King James's 1595 poem celebrating Lepanto.[6] Moreover, the Turkish domination in the Mediterranean was still consequential; it furnished an effective obstacle to the eastward expansion of European economic interests, providing a material reason why the English invested in the roundabout project of a western passage to the riches of the East.

But if economics helps to reinforce the fear of a demonic other, it can also account for friendlier and more familiarized images. For the Turks were themselves partners with the English in the highly profitable enterprise of the "Levant trade"; in fact the English were displacing the Venetians as the chief beneficiaries of this trade.[7] To complicate matters further, the Moors were partners for the English as well, at least potentially, in a political sense. Jack D'Amico details negotiations undertaken throughout Elizabeth's reign (the embassy of 1600–1601 was part of this) and sustained into James's, seeking to enlist Moorish support against the threats represented by continental European powers, especially France and Spain. "Relations between England and Morocco were extremely complex," D'Amico tells us, "and the opinions generated by those relations [varied] from the dangerously inscrutable alien to the exotically attractive ally" (39).

The context of religious feeling lets us most fully appreciate the intensity of contradictions during the period and their possible resonances for the play's first audiences. The threat of European invasion, which antedated the Spanish Armada of 1588 and lasted well into the seventeenth century, was consistently perceived in the context of religious disputes: a Catholic assault against Protestant England. The intensity of anti-Catholic feeling in Elizabethan and early Jacobean England is difficult to exaggerate. The specter of a Catholic invasion combined with convictions about a secret Catholic conspiracy operating inside England must have contributed to what one Tudor historian has characterized as a prevalent paranoia.[8] Since the Catholics were routinely represented as anti-Christ, the Elizabethans may well have sensed themselves positioned between two forces of invading infidels, uneasily playing off one against the other — like the Venetians in the play, using Othello to protect themselves against a danger that Othello himself symbolically represents.

This sense of ambivalent anxiety is yet further intensified by the Venetian setting. Venice serves as the center of civilized stability, as in Brabantio's speech, but the confidence of this claim may well have seemed tenuous to an English audience, from whose perspective Venice occupied an exposed position at the edge of Christian Europe. At the same time, since England occupied a comparable position at the other edge, Shakespeare's audience probably felt inclined to identify its own position with that of Venetian authority — father Brabantio and the "brothers of the state" — "feeling this wrong as 'twere their own." Like the historical realities of material commerce, the geographical facts seem to be operating inside a symbolic economy structured by deeply felt contradictions.[9] Venice worked powerfully on English imaginations during the Renaissance (and later) as an object of desire, evoking wealth, art, and Italian sophistication, but also as an object of repulsion, evoking Italianate greed and decadent sexuality.[10] This mythic Venice, something Shakespeare could count on his audiences' including with the baggage they carried into the theater, is at once where you dream of being and where you fear you already are, a "dangerously alien" and an "exotically attractive" image at the same time: D'Amico's words to describe Elizabethan feelings toward the Moors seem to fit Venice as well, and the results are "extremely complex" indeed. The conflict between Venetian and Turk defines the play's foundation, but since each of the terms reproduces the conflict in itself, the foundation tends to disintegrate. Where is the center? Where is the margin?

It is not that we cannot answer these questions (really one question with two parts), but as we are propelled by Iago through the violently shifting emotional landscape at the beginning of the play's action, each answer lasts only long enough for suggestions to emerge requiring us to change places: *here* becomes a strange and unfamiliar place, *there* turns into the position from which we find ourselves engaging with the action.[11] The negotiation of such an action need not be a fearful thing. In Montaigne's *Essays*, for instance, such volatile instability is contained within the cosmopolitan amusement of the author's controlling point of view. Like the "wise man" in the humanist adage "All the world's his soil," secure in his own self, Montaigne is at home "here and everywhere."[12] In *Othello*, though, our guide is Iago, and from his anxiety-driven and anxiety-producing perspective, the erosion of the distinction between here and everywhere else transports us violently into nowhere, an amorphously engulfing space where the constituting differences of individual identity, as between black and white, self and other, seem to be collapsing — even now, now, very now — into a monstrous undifferentiation.[13]

To judge from the immediately following scenes, *Othello* labors so consistently hard in its earliest action to absorb us into the threatened aggression of Iago's point of view only in order to disconfirm the impressions it has carefully produced. For when we meet Othello in 1.2, he is totally unlike what we have been led to expect. Iago's description of "bombast circumstance / Horribly stuffed with epithets of war" conjures up *miles gloriosus*, a ranting buffoon spun off from the Prince of Morocco in *The Merchant*. But all the aggressive self-justification at the beginning of 1.2 belongs to Iago himself; as Empson remarked, he sounds "like a ruffian in Marlowe" ("Honest in *Othello*," 234). His big talk about loyalty may be a show of passion designed to work Othello up, but even so the contrast is striking and surprising. Othello is poised and dignified. In the midst of Iago's sixteen jittery lines, complete with exaggerated physical gestures acting out his own proclaimed bravado ("Nine or ten times / I had thought t'have yerked him here"), Othello's "'Tis better as it is" stands as a stable bulwark.

We had been threatened with a disruptive "thing . . . to fear," but it is Iago and then Brabantio who propel the action toward a brawl, while Othello maintains order: "Keep up your bright swords, for the dew will rust them" (59). When Kean delivered this line, according to Keats, "it was as if 'his throat had commanded where swords were as thick as reeds. From the eternal risk, he speaks as though his body were un-assailable'" (Sprague, *Shakespearian Players*, 79). Irving, by contrast, "stood with his back to the audience, 'throwing up his arms in an excited manner and speaking petulantly'" (Alan Hughes, 143), but Irving's was an anomalous (and unsuccessful) rendition of the role. Readers are also impressed. "Othello's scorn is that of the professional fighter towards civilian brawlers" (Sanders, 66), but something more powerful is also at work. Along with "I must be found" a moment earlier, the "bright swords" might evoke Jesus in the Garden of Gethsemane (Honigmann provides biblical references). These resonances shouldn't be exaggerated, but they serve to provide another specific instance of the way in which Iago's suggestions ("The *devil* will make a grandsire of you") are directly contradicted by what we see and hear.

One of these suggestions turns out to be confirmed, though in a sur-prising and fundamentally disconfirming way. Othello's supremely un-ruffled self-confidence in the face of Brabantio's expected challenge is consistent with Iago's accusatory description of "loving his own pride and purposes":

> Let him do his spite;
> My services, which I have done the signiory,
> Shall out-tongue his complaints. 'Tis yet to know —
> Which, when I know that boasting is an honour,
> I shall promulgate — I fetch my life and being
> From men of royal siege, and my demerits
> May speak unbonneted to as proud a fortune
> As this that I have reached. For know, Iago,
> But that I love the gentle Desdemona
> I would not my unhoused free condition
> Put into circumscription and confine
> For the sea's worth. (17–28)

But this speech might be characterized as *amour-propre* only in a sense emptied of any pejorative connotations. Othello manages to assert his own worth in a nonboastful way. More important than his explicit con-tempt for self-advertisement (for as much could be said about Corio-lanus) are the apparently unintended and unconscious suggestions of an authentic modesty. "Demerits" acknowledges fallibility as it claims jus-tification; "unbonneted" evokes a gesture of deference, removing his hat to his superiors even as he asserts his own rights. Above all, Othello is disarming in his feelings about Desdemona. He hasn't fallen in love in the usual sense of that metaphor; Othello is not Romeo, driven by an overwhelming need, still less the desperately needy suitors or petitionary courtiers of the sonnet sequences, begging for mercy. He experiences the freedom of his soldierly celibacy as a self-sufficient condition, which he trades in quite clearheadedly for something better. If this were all, Othello might indeed resemble Iago's description, loving his own pride like a self-satisfied pragmatist — a sort of high-style Pertinax Surly proposing to the Spanish Lady in *The Alchemist*, say. But the last lines of the speech defeat any such impression. Playing off a simple and direct expression of affection, "I love the gentle Desdemona," against the reiterative Latinate polysyllables and syntactic inversion by which he represents his single state, and then climaxing with the image of infinite and transcendent value (how much is the sea worth? how much more is Desdemona worth?), these beautiful lines make it clear that, whatever it means to say so, Othello is in love.

Othello's deference invites us to reconceptualize the categorical distinction between self-love and the social order, or the individual ego and the corporate order. Othello's claims for his own merit are equally claims for the fairness of "the signiory" in acknowledging his services and rewarding them appropriately. His self-confidence seems to be coterminous with a confidence in the legitimacy of Venetian political authority. And with religious authority as well:

> as truly as to heaven
> I do confess the vices of my blood
> So justly to your grave ears I'll present
> How I did thrive in this fair lady's love
> And she in mine. (1.3.124–128)

In these remarkable lines introducing his long autobiographical narrative to the Senate, Othello associates the love between him and Desdemona with guilt and sin — demerits indeed! The linkage is arresting but in the present context it works to augment the protagonist's image. By acknowledging the vices of his blood, Othello affirms an orthodox Christian and emphatically Protestant belief in original sin. *Not* to acknowledge this would constitute an arrogant claim of self-sufficiency, like Caesar's bragging just before the assassination. The words, therefore, convey an appropriate modesty, but at the same time an absolute confidence: even as he confesses to a sinful nature, he rests secure in the redemptive power of divine authority. As the "grave ears" of the Senate will perceive the merits of his demerits, so a listening heaven has already restored the defects of his spiritual nature. The Q variant of "faithful" for "truly" in the first line reinforces the theological context, as does the way in which Othello, like a good Protestant, imagines a direct relationship to heaven, unmediated by any ecclesiastical apparatus administering the sacraments. The speech clarifies Othello's statement of conviction earlier about "my perfect soul" (1.2.30) and helps to account for the fact that the statement doesn't sound as though he is in love with his own pride — quite the reverse.

Self-worth and public recognition reciprocate and mutually sustain each other for Othello, as though interchangeable and identical phenomena. A large part of his charismatic power at the beginning derives from the apparently effortless way in which his sensibility unifies categories we normally think of as distinct and even contradictory.[14] Where Iago says, "I am not what I am," Othello is what he is. This extraordinary integrity comes across most powerfully in the Senate narrative. Like all life stories, Othello's has displacement as its subject: growing up, leaving home, enslavement, liberation, religious conversion; but these potential traumas are represented (if at all) not as rupture but as continuity, the accumulation of undifferentiated experience. Hence the sense of ongoing action, things happening "oft" and "still" (meaning "always," as usual in Shakespeare), an unbroken succession of marvelous events, encountering a sequence of wonderful creatures in one romantic landscape after another. The effect has been described as "unchanging in its monotony" (Sypher, 122), but Renaissance audiences, greedily devouring reports about the exotic new worlds opening to exploration, may well have found all the "novelties" in Othello's speech the opposite of boring.

The most striking effect of continuity derives from the oddly recursive narrative. Recounting his life becomes part of the life he is recounting. His journey goes from "boyish days / To th' very moment" of the telling (1.3.133–134), and now, even now, to the very moment of his telling it again. The "antres vast and deserts idle, / Rough quarries, rocks and hills whose heads touch heaven" seem at first to belong to his life, but with "it was my hint to speak," they migrate ("here and everywhere") to the story of his life as he recounts it to Brabantio and Desdemona, and once again to the Senate and to us (141–143). "Such was my process," he says (143), referring at once to his experience and his relation of that experience, his life and his life story. At the very beginning of the "personal history" that bears his name, David Copperfield acknowledges uncertainty as to whether he will "turn out to be the hero of my own life," deferring to a text behind his own control: "These pages must show."[15] This problematic split between narrator and narrative subject, the self telling the story and the self whose story is being told, seems to be inevitable in autobiography. But Othello has somehow eluded it. He and his narrative are perfectly identical. How can we know the storyteller from the story?

The speech is a great set piece, an aria in the "*Othello* music." It is set up with the Duke's "Say it, Othello," an "unusual turn of phrase," as Honigmann points out, whose formality tends therefore to set the speech apart as well. As he introduced the speech, so the Duke has the first response to it: "I think this tale would win my daughter too." Whether speaking to Brabantio or himself, the Duke ignores Desdemona's entry: Othello's mesmerizing speech has allowed no room for other impressions.[16] At the end of the scene, the Duke is given a pithy couplet that helps to clarify the nature of his response. "If virtue no delighted beauty lack / Your son-in-law is far more fair than black" (290–291). Inevitably patronizing to modern ears, the remark must have sounded on a fundamentally different register if heard inside the theological context, powerfully present to Renaissance imaginations, that (in Hunter's description) although "all nations are Ethiopians, black in their natural sinfulness," nonetheless, "they may become white in the knowledge of the Lord" (48).

Othello, in Hunter's view, "manipulates our sympathies" in its opening movements, "supposing that we will have brought to the theatre a set of careless assumptions about 'Moors,'" on to which it then, by evoking different traditions of belief, "complicating factors which had begun to affect thought in this day," "is able to superimpose . . . new valuations" of Othello, diametrically opposed to the fear and loathing first generated by Iago (49).[17] The Duke's response here, testifying to the overwhelming power of Othello to generate affectionate admiration in those who see and hear him, squares with the declaration of the "refined and lovely young lady" at a Forrest performance: "If that is the way Moors look and talk and love, give me a Moor for a husband." Othello is not a thing to fear, but a man to love.

Desdemona provides the major confirmation — or, more precisely, disconfirmation of the beliefs originally impressed on us by the play. She enters at a crucial point in the action. Whatever the climactic quality of Othello's speech for the Duke and maybe the audience, it functions only as an interim measure, filling up the time "till she come" to provide her own evidence. Brabantio insists on Desdemona's version as the final determinant: "I pray you, hear her speak" (1.3.175).

In "The Design of Desdemona: Doubt Raised and Resolved," Ann Jennalie Cook argues that in the context "of Elizabethan courtship customs" (189), Desdemona's apparent willingness to let her own marriage be arranged behind Brabantio's back and in flat contradiction to his wishes would have seemed like a serious transgression against appropriate daughterly obedience. The social norms are perhaps less consistent than we might think, but Cook's claim is convincing, partly owing to generic signals,[18] and in larger part because it is supported by critical traditions. The sentiment attributed to Coleridge that "it would be something monstrous to conceive this beautiful Venetian girl falling in love with a veritable negro" underlies a lot of uncertainty in nineteenth-century and later response to Desdemona (Raysor, 1.42). Bradley hotly contested this view, claiming that it represented Desdemona's "love, in effect, as Brabantio regarded it, and not as Shakespeare conceived it"; but the only way Bradley could manage "to see what Shakespeare imagined" was to argue that the "later impression of Desdemona" as sweetly virtuous and self-sacrificing "must be carried back and united with the earlier," more problematic one (164–168). As we shall see in chapter 5, this is pretty much the effect of nineteenth-century theatrical performances of the part, but since this procedure of reading backward from the end inverts the process by which Shakespeare's audience processed the play's material, such critical and theatrical denial may tend only to confirm the evidence for an anxious sense of Desdemona's transgressive nature.

Cook speculates that the "unlikely alliance with a Moor might have been far less troubling than the elopement itself," but the anxieties Iago produces about Desdemona go beyond the violation of social norms (188). She is involved only passively in the image of "an old black ram . . . tupping your white ewe," but with "Your daughter and the Moor are now making the beast with two backs" (1.1.114–115), Iago represents Desdemona as equally and actively cooperating in the expression of bestial passion. Roderigo's description a moment later evokes similar suggestions:

> your fair daughter
> At this odd-even and dull watch o'th'night,
> Transported with no worse nor better guard

> But with a knave of common hire, a gondolier,
> To the gross clasps of a lascivious Moor . . . (120–124)

Before we fill in the gaps,[19] this elliptical speech seems to be describing Desdemona's multiple sexual transports with (that is, attractions to) first an unspecified common knave who then emerges into more particularized view as a gondolier and is finally defined as the lascivious Moor.[20] The superimposition of images metastasizes beyond the violation of social norms to suggest a perversely promiscuous sexual appetite. These suggestions are further reinforced by Roderigo's claim that Desdemona

> hath made a gross revolt,
> Tying her duty, beauty, wit and fortunes
> In an extravagant and wheeling stranger
> Of here and everywhere. (132–135)

"Gross revolt" echoes the Moor's "gross clasps" just earlier; it provides a metaphorical linkage between Othello and Desdemona beyond the literal alliance in the dramatic action. In effect, they connect with one another in a free space of erotic wandering, outside the constraints of stabilizing order, to perform even now and again by the end of the next scene the specific but unspecified deeds (for what exactly is Brabantio referring to in "such actions?") whose monstrous consequences will invert the hierarchical structure of patriarchal Christianity ("Bond-slaves and pagans shall our statesmen be").

Desdemona, thus, is absorbed under Iago's general direction into the prospect of anxiety and terror embodied in Othello. Like his racism, Iago's blatant misogyny may sound bizarre now but probably represented an entirely unexceptional story to the play's first audience.[21] And as with Othello, the images Iago evokes about Desdemona turn out to be either surprisingly wrong or right only in a way that fundamentally disconfirms the expectations Iago has set up. In response to Brabantio's request to describe "where most you owe obedience," Desdemona responds:

> My noble father,
> I do perceive here a divided duty.
> To you I am bound for life and education:
> My life and education both do learn me
> How to respect you; you are the lord of duty,
> I am hitherto your daughter. But here's my husband:
> And so much duty as my mother showed

To you, preferring you before her father,
So much I challenge that I may profess
Due to the Moor my lord. (1.3.180–189)

In this entry speech, Desdemona confirms Brabantio's fears. She was not
bewitched, was indeed "half the wooer" (176), and despite Brabantio's
description of "a maiden never bold," she forcefully declares, with unequivocal emphasis in "hitherto" and "here's my husband," a transfer of
affectionate loyalty from Brabantio to Othello. The transfer, however, is
represented not as a violation or betrayal but an affirmation of traditional order. In moving from father to husband, Desdemona claims to
be reenacting the movement of her own mother from her father to Brabantio himself. In this exchange of loyalty and duty, she nowhere affirms
her own rights against the prerogatives of male authority and therefore
does not seem to challenge but reinforce the structure of order on which
Brabantio's own authority is based.[22]

When the focus shifts from social to sexual transgression, Desdemona's boldness is even more pronounced. In the following exchange,
the Duke is responding to Othello's request for "fit disposition for my
wife" while he is in Cyprus:

Duke. Why, at her father's.
Bra.   I'll not have it so.
Oth. Nor I.
Des. Nor I, I would not there reside
      To put my father in impatient thoughts
      By being in his eye. Most gracious duke,
      To my unfolding lend your prosperous ear
      And let me find a charter in your voice
      T'assist my simpleness.
Duke. What would you, Desdemona?
Des. That I did love the Moor to live with him
      My downright violence and scorn of fortunes
      May trumpet to the world. My heart's subdued
      Even to the very quality of my lord:
      I saw Othello's visage in his mind,
      And to his honours and his valiant parts
      Did I my soul and fortunes consecrate,
      So that, dear lords, if I be left behind,
      A moth of peace, and he go to the war,
      The rites for which I love him are bereft me,

> And I a heavy interim shall support
> By his dear absence. Let me go with him. (1.3.241–260)

The context gives a full sense of Desdemona's purposiveness, especially the speech rhythms at the beginnings. "Nor *I*," as the third voice in the sequence, is emphatically decisive.[23] Although she defers to the Duke's authority to charter her voice, she nonetheless claims the right to choose her own fit disposition — to dispose of herself. She makes the claim on her own initiative (no one has asked for her opinion, as Brabantio did earlier, when his "Come hither, gentle mistress," suggested a reluctance on her part to enter, let alone speak to the Senate). In asserting her rights to the pleasures of Othello's company, she clearly means sexual enjoyment. The suggestions of "his valiant parts" and "the rites for which I love him," and even the metaphor by which Desdemona describes deprivation, "I a heavy interim shall support" — all these represent how consistently she imagines experience in bodily terms. Her words express a powerful sexual desire for Othello, openly declared in the public forum.

Why then does her speech tend to diminish rather than to reinforce the fears Iago has evoked? Hunter's terms to account for the disconfirmation of Iago's racism can account for his misogyny as well: the play superimposes one system of belief and feeling on another — in this instance, different ideas available in the sixteenth century about sexuality and marriage. Desdemona's speech resonates powerfully within the emergent context of "companionate marriage."[24] Her love for Othello is predicated on the desire "to live with him," to share his life in all aspects. Sex is unequivocally part of this, but so is exotic travel and the heroic romance of military affairs. So is his inner beauty: "I saw Othello's visage in his mind." Like the Duke's couplet about Othello's fairness, this line creates awkwardness for us, but adjusted to the appropriate context, it strongly confirms our conviction about Othello's "perfect soul" — and about her own, which she "did . . . consecrate" to him.

In *Table-Talk* for 27 September 1830, Coleridge indulged in some reflection about Desdemona's appeal:

> "Most women have no character at all", said Pope, and meant it for satire. Shakespeare, who knew man and woman much better, saw that it, in fact, was the perfection of woman to be characterless. Everyone wishes a Desdemona or Ophelia for a wife — creatures who, though they may not always understand you, do always feel you, and feel with you. (Foakes, *Coleridge's Criticism*, 185)

Despite the idealized sentimentality, there is something useful in emphasizing Desdemona's capacity to "feel" and "feel with." As Stanley Cavell remarks about "I saw Othello's visage in his mind," although "it is commonly felt that she means she overlooked his blackness in favor of his inner brilliance," nonetheless "what the line more naturally says is that she saw his visage as he sees it" — that is, so fully enters into Othello's existence that she experiences the world from inside his own sensibility (129). Othello himself had acknowledged this capacity in describing Desdemona's response to his story: "She wished / That heaven had made her such a man" (1.3.163–164) bespeaks a desire not just to find a man like Othello with whom to connect but to become the being that is Othello. In "my heart's subdued / Even to the very quality of my lord," Desdemona's declaration to the Senate suggests that she already has.

In the Quarto, Desdemona's heart is subdued in a more explicitly sexual phrase to Othello's "utmost pleasure," but for Edward Snow the Folio is preferable as

> a more radical expression of the ontology of sexual exchange; it stresses the active investment in Othello's masculinity that Desdemona's acquiescence to it entails. (When Juliet similarly anticipates the "manning" of her blood by Romeo, she is thinking not only of being dominated by him but of feeling her own phallic stirrings achieve mastery.) . . . Q's "utmost pleasure" loses F's rich fusion of submission and self assertion. ("Sexual Anxiety," 407–408)

This description beautifully acknowledges Desdemona's powerful presence in an actively desiring selfhood where desire is explicitly though not exclusively sexual. Since Desdemona's "subdued" condition might be characterized as a literal self-abnegation or even selflessness, we can understand Coleridge's description of emptiness and lack, as though she had no self to begin with. For Coleridge, Desdemona's abundant capacity to feel and feel with is predicated on an apparently compensatory absence of intellectual character, an inability to "understand." Snow detaches us from this image of mindless affection and brings us closer to Othello's own response just after Desdemona's declaration, supporting her wish to accompany him in order "to be free and generous to her mind."

Coleridge claims to know "in fact" what all men want. The traditions of *Othello* interpretation and indeed the action itself of the play suggest that such generalizations (about men, women, blacks, Florentines, whatever) are a risky business, "dangerous conceits," as Iago says (3.3.329). Who knows what men want? [25] Snow, who implies an answer to the question very different from that of Coleridge, nonetheless winds up in basically the same position: both of them manifest a profoundly affectionate regard for Desdemona. I think this is the place the play wants us to be, or wants us to feel we ought to be (a distinction I shall turn to in a moment). However diversely edited and performed in a variety of theatrical settings to audiences interpreting according to the historically specific cultural determinants shaping response (race, class, gender, ethnicity, sexuality, nationality, etc.), the performance cues in the text as I understood it are too numerous and consistent to resist our finding ourselves by this point, despite the powerfully convincing quality of Iago's initial suggestions, in love with the gentle Desdemona.

To sum up: in its opening movements, the play aligns us with Iago's views and then, by revealing Othello's and Desdemona's stunning attractions, requires us to dissociate ourselves from him. As Hunter suggests, this process of disconfirmation is preeminently rational, assuming an open-minded audience who, in the face of negative evidence, "will find it easy to abandon" Iago's prejudiced hypotheses for more plausible ones (47). It is therefore particularly appropriate that the doubts are resolved in a meeting of the Venetian Senate, an elaborate scene where formal process endows the action with an aura of political and judicial authority. The Senate scene not only enacts disconfirmation; it focuses our attention on the process as a subject for reflection. Hence the Duke at the very beginning: "There is no composition in these news / That gives them credit." Before we know what incoherences he is talking about, we may hear in these words an echo of our own experience of contradiction in the juxtaposition of the old black ram and the noble Moor during the two preceding scenes. Then, for the next almost-fifty lines (far more than we need, as Joel Altman points out, to cover Othello's travel time [136]), we are required to watch the Senators scrupulously sifting through the conflicting reports and contradictory evidence in order eventually to reach the right conclusion ("'Tis certain then for Cyprus"). The play is going out of its way to make us conscious of the way in which belief is appropriately constituted — "to anatomize composition," in Altman's words, "specifically the way the mind composes an acceptable simulacrum of reality" (136). The passage serves to legitimate at once the Senate's interpretive procedures and our own; by the end of act 1, we should apparently be in a state of secure resolution about the noble Moor, the gentle Desdemona, and their marriage.

It hasn't quite worked out this way. This position is basically consistent with performance traditions, especially in the nineteenth century, and even the diminished Othellos of the more recent stage and film versions are generally sympathetic figures, but critical commentary, especially in our century, constitutes another story. As Arthur Kirsch demonstrates, "most of it is driven by the impulse to convict Othello of moral or psychic failure," with a similar "quest for pathology" characterizing commentary about Desdemona as well (11).[26] Kirsch thinks this is wrongheaded; he too understands the opening scenes of the play as an enactment of disconfirmation. One consequence of this situation is that Kirsch is caught in the trap Holloway recognized. The only way he has "to say anything" that might be recognized "as worth saying" is "to engage in dispute" with an inherited tradition of *Othello* commentary that is "driven by the impulse" to make negative judgments about Othello and Desdemona.

> Desdemona is not Helen or Cressida, . . . she is true, and . . . there is no service greater than she deserves. One would suppose these to be self-evident propositions, but there are notable critics who dispute them. [Othello's big speech] should alone suggest that Desdemona is hardly an overaggressive schoolgirl. [Her] feeling for Othello is . . . a sign not that she is silly or guileful, but that she has a capacity to sympathize. . . . We may be disposed to regard tears and the capacity for pity as cheap commodities, but Shakespeare did not. . . . It is nonsense to imagine that Shakespeare created [Desdemona's opening] speech for a character who was to be an unpleasant homiletic example [and] even greater nonsense to imagine that such a speech would introduce a girl incapable of "mature affection." (11–15)

All this (and more) in four pages devoted to Desdemona; still much more follows when Kirsch comes to the protagonist ("Othello's marked worship of her is an expression, not as so many critics would have it, of . . . intrinsic weakness," etc. [21]). Kirsch finds himself in the unenviable position — discomforting to watch and presumably painful to occupy — of harping with increasingly irritated emphasis ("nonsense . . . even greater nonsense") on denials that cannot help but repeat and therefore potentially reinforce the interpretive errors he is seeking to eliminate.

What accounts for the perversity of the interpretive tradition that has put Kirsch into this position? Kirsch holds Rymer responsible for originating the nonsensical view that Desdemona is an "unpleasant homiletic example," and this squares with Altman's point that Rymer is in general responsible for "setting the crucial question" for all subsequent *Othello* criticism. Altman's phrase suggests an analytically self-conscious process, but there are times when going back to Rymer is just something *Othello* critics do. Like the mountain for the mountain climber, Rymer is monumentally there. Furness, for instance, reproduces a substantial passage from Rymer complaining about Desdemona's pleas for Cassio (I quote the passage in chapter 4) and then says, "It is to be hoped that the reader comprehends the motive which prompts the occasional insertion of these criticisms by Rymer. He has read his Shakespeare to little purpose who does not appreciate the relief, amid tragic scenes, afforded by a dash of buffoonery" (167). Comic relief in this sense is a form of motiveless benignity, but motivelessness is not meaninglessness, and Kirsch, commenting on the same passage, gets at the meaning — namely Iago: "To stage or read those scenes in which [Desdemona] pleads for Cassio as the exercises of a wilful woman or a domineering wife is to misconstrue her motives and to become as subject to Iago's inversions as Othello does" (17). If Rymer is just "a kind of critical Iago" (Newman, "And Wash," 152), then behind Rymer, the original impulse still driving a perverse critical tradition, is Iago himself.

But then how do we explain Iago's power to shape belief? Kirsch himself acknowledges that the play itself is responsible for Iago's initial power ("Shakespeare has deliberately implicated us in . . . primordial prejudice"). He claims this is only to engage us actively in the process of reevaluation ("We ourselves thus experience, we do not merely witness, the process of perception Desdemona describes"); but if "that process is kept constantly in our consciousness by Othello's literal appearance, by the pervasive imagery of blackness and fairness and of true and false vision, and by Iago's increasingly ominous and explicitly diabolic threats" (21), why is the effect not to reinforce rather than to disconfirm the original impression?

It is precisely this process — first in, last out; not disconfirmation, but reconfirmation — that Michael Neill claims to be operating in our perception of *Othello*'s opening movements:

> The play thinks abomination into being and then taunts the audience with the knowledge that it can never be *un*thought. . . . Since

the audience is exposed to [Iago's] obscenities before it is allowed to encounter either Othello or Desdemona in person, they serve to plant the suggestion, which perseveres like an itch throughout the action. . . . The scenes that follow contrive to keep alive the ugly curiosity that Iago has aroused.[27]

Disconfirmation assumes a mind free and open to new evidence, but the model Neill describes here, "a technique that works close to the unstable ground of consciousness itself" (395), accounts for the generation of belief as a fundamentally irrational process.

This model too is not only enacted but thematized in the play, in Brabantio's initial response to Iago's appalling first image: "This accident is not unlike my dream, / Belief of it oppresses me already" (1.1.140–141). Brabantio is persuaded, even before he acts on Roderigo's advice to see if Desdemona is at home, by the subconscious fear of an apparently recurring nightmare. His conviction of female betrayal is not the product of conscious assent; he seems to have no choice but to yield to its oppressive anxiety. Once convinced, he looks for and of course finds confirmation in the idea of witchcraft to explain what has happened:

> Is there not charms
> By which the property of youth and maidhood
> May be abused? Have you not read, Roderigo,
> Of some such thing? (1.1.169–172)

At first just another straw at which Brabantio grasps, witchcraft is quickly transformed to a plausible hypothesis ("I'll have't disputed on, / 'Tis probable and palpable to thinking" [1.2.75–76]) and then elevated to the absolute certainty of a self-evident fact: "For nature so preposterously to err / Being not deficient, blind, or lame of sense, / Sans witchcraft could not" (1.3.63–65).

If we are meant to see through Brabantio's "superstition," then the Duke's skepticism —

> To vouch this is no proof
> Without more certain and more overt test
> Than these thin habits and poor likelihoods
> Of modern seeming do prefer against him. (107–110)

— and senatorial due process should act out the triumph of rationality.[28] But the resolution represented at the end of act 1 produces profoundly equivocal effects. The legal resolution somehow misses the point, a legal fiction.[29] It cannot altogether eliminate the intense fear and anxiety Iago has generated at the beginning, or totally erase the memory of Iago's suggestion that senatorial impartiality is a hypocritical facade ("the state . . . Cannot with safety cast him" [1.1.145, 147]).[30] The Duke's comforting maxims at the end of the scene do not satisfy Brabantio, whose sarcastic echoes seem designed to emphasize their banality. The elaborate suspense raised about Desdemona's "fit disposition" is left unresolved. The Duke simply avoids a decision, pleading time constraints.

Even more troubling are the suggestions that senatorial due process is significantly similar to the irrational epistemological model developed in Brabantio. Despite the sober reflection and the careful examination of contradictory hypotheses at the beginning of the scene, the Duke becomes convinced of Turkish intentions before confirming evidence comes in the form of the messenger. As with so many of the "preposterous" acts of judgment Altman and Parker describe in the play, the Duke seems to have leaped to a "foregone conclusion." He is apparently "driven by impulse" (to recall Kirsch's phrase for the perversity of *Othello* commentary), a preconception which (like Brabantio's dream) may itself be inaccessible to rational scrutiny. He believes the messenger, who is himself no closer to events or personally more authoritative than the sailor, presumably because the messenger's version conforms to what he already believes — that the Turks are a violently threatening force: "the main article I do approve / In *fearful* sense" (1.3.11–12). Senatorial judgment seems to be determined by a variant of the same frightful nightmare oppressing Brabantio.[31]

The element of time is crucial here, as always in dramatic experience. We of course know there's a lot more play to come, and the signals of an ultimately tragic denouement by themselves make suspect the stability of the generically comic resolution we have apparently negotiated here. The rapidity and volatility of the action in the first act of *Othello* are bound to leave remnants of disquietude. That Iago has residual authority even through the Senate's resolution is entirely reasonable. "Primordial prejudices" are not so "easy to abandon"; anyone who has experienced "the grip of a guilt" knows better than to expect immediate release. We need some time to get more distance from Iago's contaminating malice. But that's not what the play gives us. Instead of time and distance, the play restores Iago to a commanding presence at the end of act 1. Then it awards him almost sole proprietorship of the second act.

Disconfirmation

Iago

The Duke and the senators have resolved the questions of Othello and Desdemona and of the Cyprus wars, so they depart the scene. Othello and Desdemona exchange a few words of business and follow the others offstage, leaving us with Iago and Roderigo again, back where we started:

> *Rod.* Iago!
> *Iago.* What sayst thou, noble heart?
> *Rod.* What will I do, think'st thou? (1.3.302–304)

Roderigo's single-word utterance is punctuated with a period in the early texts. Honigmann's exclamation point follows one editorial tradition (Ridley, Walker and Wilson); the other is a dash ("Iago — "), going back to Dr. Johnson (Bevington, Evans). These emendations acknowledge that Roderigo's speech seems to make sense only as a way of breaking a silence; he is seeking attention from Iago, whose mind must be engaged elsewhere. This pause was much expanded and elaborated in nineteenth-century productions, where new techniques of *mise-en-scène* (box sets replacing movable scenes in grooves, large property pieces, platforms, stairs, extensive furniture, etc.) required time to clear the stage. These productions invented elaborately ceremonious dumb shows of formal departure, sometimes supplemented with stage business predicated on character psychology, to accommodate their needs.[1] Such inventions, though inconsistent with production practices and histrionic conventions at the Globe, nonetheless work to produce a similar effect: the early texts too seem to be going out of the way to write a pause into their theatrical action at this point.

The pause serves to focus our attention on Iago: perhaps he is ruminating, as we probably are, on his failed attempt to poison Othello's delight; perhaps, as Stanislavski advises, he is now "deep in thought" how to try again.[2] An interval here makes much more sense than between the first and second acts. The act division, largely a fiction of printed texts and divorced from the experience of the play's early audiences, is positively misleading. In terms of the action, Montano has probably already entered on the large platform stage, calling out his question to the remote first gentleman, "What from the cape can you discern at sea?" even before Iago has disappeared. Moreover, since Iago's incantatory soliloquy at the end of act 1 seems to "engender" the storm, "any interval between Acts I and II destroys the effect of Iago's 'monstrous birth'" (Wine, 21).[3] Hence the continuity here reinforces the sense derived from discontinuity — the pause — earlier on. In both cases, we are made to focus on Iago, specifically on his power to shape the action of the play.

R. A. Foakes notes that Iago's dominant position in the play is concentrated at the beginning: he has "43 per cent of the lines" in the first two acts compared to "32.58 per cent of the words in the play" as a whole ("The Descent of Iago," 29). The concentration is most intense in this second movement of the play. From 1.3.302 ("Iago!") to the end of 2.3, Iago is on stage for 700 of 805 lines, during which time he is conspicuously shown to be controlling the action, for the other characters onstage as well as for the audience.[4] How do we explain this extraordinary domination? What are the strategies by which the play endows Iago with power, and to what ends?

We are by now so habituated to Iago's power that we think the role is "actor-proof," but it wasn't always so. Kean's remarks about the part's limits are worth remembering, especially because they grow out of eighteenth-century interpretive traditions, within which Iago had relatively little interest. The sheer length of the role was not a sign of dramatic power but a source of dramatic discomfort. In Bell's acting editions (first published in 1773 and often reprinted through the nineteenth century), the role was heavily cut; "This part," the annotator remarks, "though much curtailed in the acting, is still so long, and had so many soliloquies, that, without capital abilities and strict attention, it must pall an audience" (quoted Odell, 35). According to Carol Carlisle, "there was no hint of admiration for his intellectual ability" in the eighteenth century; "the character was too 'underhand,' too 'mean' and 'base' to inspire any such feeling." As late as 1817, William Oxberry could describe Iago as "not a part for applause" as though it were a self-evident fact (quoted Winter, *Shakespeare on the Stage*, 259). But it was around this time when "a new Iago emerged — an Iago with a light touch, a light step, a sprightly wit, who reveled in his own ingenuity and some-times charmed the audience into reveling with him" (Carlisle, 224–225).

The new Iago, then, is an invention of Romanticism, part of the cul-tural transformation which produced Othello's color, Hamlet's delay, and inner identity as topics for critical and theatrical interest. The inner self is crucial here. One reason why "motiveless malignity" became and still is an irresistible phrase in talking about Iago is its power to concen-trate the mind on the mystery of Iago's character. (This wasn't really Coleridge's main interest, as we'll see, but the misappropriation only reinforces the point.) Lamb's argument about the superiority of the read text to the performed play gets at the same thing: the latter is superficial appearance and declamatory rhetoric, "low tricks upon the eye and ear," when what we want is to "know the internal workings of a great mind" (98) — even a greatly criminal mind like Iago's or (in the following passage) Richard III's. "Nothing but his crimes, his actions, is visible," Lamb complains about theatrical performance, whereas in reading, a "horror at his crimes blends with the effect which we feel, but how is it qualified, how is it carried off, by the rich intellect which he displays, his resources, his wit, his buoyant spirits, his vast knowledge and insight into characters, the poetry of his part" (105–106). Lamb's argument purports to distinguish between general phenomena, reading texts ver-sus watching plays. His objections, though, are perhaps less to theater as such than to the residual histrionic conventions of the eighteenth-century stage; and even as he wrote, actors were developing techniques to accommodate the new psychological interest.

The power of the role developed gradually. Even with its ascendancy securely established by Irving's and Edwin Booth's memorable perfor-mances in the late middle of the nineteenth century, Iago's conventional costume and makeup sometimes persisted. By this time, however, they were subject to objection as "tasteless attempts to proclaim his villainy on sight" (Carlisle, 222). Both Irving and Booth "reiterated the need for preserving Iago's apparent guilelessness" (Carlisle, 220). Irving's perfor-mance in particular depended on exploiting "a sharp distinction be-tween Iago's outward geniality and his real villainy" (Carlisle, 221), and the result was a stunning histrionic display. In a public reading of 1877, his "'great ambition as a destroyer' was hidden beneath an 'alternating surface personality' which offered each victim a deceiver fashioned to exploit his individual weaknesses" (Alan Hughes, 144). Four years later he developed these energies opposite Booth's Othello: "Deceiving every-one 'in right of his superior intelligence', he changed his masks with dazzling virtuosity: 'to Roderigo, a fantastic trifler, to Cassio, the best of good fellows; to Othello, a complex composition made up of cynical philosophy and bitter truth'. Instant transitions underlined his duplicity" (Hughes, 145).

Irving had no investment in historical authenticity (we're a long way from Poel), but his busy performance — full of "small, fidgety business" and "never for an instant still" (Hughes, 146) — may evoke images of the "bustling," chameleon-like villains of the Renaissance stage: the Alchemist and Face, Volpone and Mosca, Shakespeare's Richard, and Marlowe's Barabas, going back through Lorenzo in *The Spanish Tragedy* to the Vice. Irving was particularly effective in directly engaging his audience:

> His humour was as brilliant as his clothes, and spectators frequently found themselves caught in a laugh, unwillingly and at times insidiously, because they seemed to be sharing a joke with the devil: "the flavour of grim comedy . . . is effectively exhibited, and the audience is moved in the most tragic scenes to a kind of merriment. The asides are delivered in a gibing, acrimonious, yet self-contented spirit, the effect of which is indescribable." (Hughes, 145)

In this respect Irving seems to anticipate modern tastes as much as echo those of the Renaissance. The "privileged" position Iago occupies in current criticism (see Foakes and Newman, quoted in chapter 1) derives from his soliloquies and asides. They make us joint venturers with him, invested in the project of moving the action along. "And what's he then that says I play the villain?" (2.3.331) "picks up where he left off at 2.1.308," as Honigmann remarks, "but now *knavery* sees clearly how to proceed." The direct address at once invites us to engage with him and requires us to acknowledge a continuing engagement. In a way at best tenuously connected to morality, we share an identity with Iago that is rooted in theatrical pleasure. Irving's Iago seemed to understand this; he not only talked to us, he talked for us. Push this further and you can get to a deliberately outrageous postmodern production like Peter Zadek's for the Deutsches Schauspielhaus, Hamburg, in 1976, where the audience is provoked into talking (indeed, shouting) back.[5]

Booth's Iago went in a diametrically opposed direction. Compared to the kaleidoscopic variety of Irving's busy performance, Booth was subdued, stable, and restrained in playing to the audience's insider knowledge. According to Winter, the gay, light-hearted, good-humored soldier whom he thus presented would have deceived anybody. . . . Nothing could be more absolutely specious and convincingly sympathetic than Booth's voice, manner, and whole personality were when he said, "There's matter in't *indeed*, if *he* be *angry!*" The duplicity of the character, when visible in association with others, was made evident to the audience by the subtle use of gesture and facial play, by perfect employment of the indefinable but instantly perceptible expedient of *transparency*, — and it was only when alone that his *Iago* revealed his frightful wickedness and his fiendish joy in it, and there was, in that revealment, an icy malignity of exultation that caused a strange effect of mingled admiration and fear. (*Shakespeare*, 271, Winter's emphases)

Booth himself is even more austere in the description he furnished Furness. Commenting on his insouciant dismissal of reputation:

With a significant glance at Cassio. Do not smile, or sneer, or glower, — try to impress even *the audience* with your sincerity. 'Tis better, however, always to ignore the audience; if you can forget that you are a "shew" you will be natural. The more sincere your manner, the more devilish your deceit. I think the "light comedian" should play the villain's part, not the "heavy man"; I mean the Shakespearian villains. Iago should appear to be what all but the audience believe he is. Even when alone, there is little need to remove the mask entirely. Shakespeare spares you that trouble. (Furness, 146, Booth's emphasis)

Where Irving played to the audience's pleased awareness in a multiplicity of deceptions, Booth sustained a single distinction, between his public persona and private self, and then tried to reduce or eliminate even that one. Where Irving in effect amplified the performative possibilities of the part, Booth diminished and played against them, sensing that the play text guarantees their felt presence independent of his own histrionic effort. Or better, the requisite effort was to conceal effort. "Shakespeare spares you that trouble" is the remark of a very smart actor.

There is no easy way or good reason to choose between Irving's and Booth's Iagos. Individual spectators had their preferences, of course. Many commentators key on Irving's business when, commenting on Cassio and Desdemona in 2.1, he nonchalantly munches on grapes and spits out the pits (Alan Hughes, 145; Winter, *Shakespeare*, 275; Sprague, *Shakespeare and the Actors*, 189); it is clearly a brilliant realization of "the wine she drinks is made of grapes" (2.1.249–250). Yet Mowbray Morris thought that Irving's business was "much less really natural to the character than Mr. Booth's still, respectful attitude, leaning against the sundial, alert to execute any command, seeming careless what goes on so long as he is ready when wanted, yet ever watching his prey with sly, sleepless, vigilance" (quoted Sprague, *Shakespearian Players*, 129). Winter believed that Booth's Iago was "incomparably the best . . . that has been on our stage within the last fifty years" (*Shakespeare*, 271). Winter was a Booth booster but may have had a point. Booth's was virtually the only nineteenth-century Iago who stayed onstage during Othello's last speeches and suicide, trumping the Moor's death with his own exultant power (more of this in chapter 6), and the dark terror of his triumph suggests a power deeper than what was realized in Irving's delighted and delightful bustling.

Theatrical values cannot alone account for Iago's power. Something in his way of seeing and dealing with the world must be convincing and appealing. Here Coleridge's remark about motiveless malignity is helpfully suggestive:

> The last speech [1.3.381–403], the motive-hunting of motiveless malignity — how awful! In itself fiendish — while yet he was allowed to bear the divine image, too fiendish for his own steady view. A being next to devil, only *not* quite devil — and this Shakespeare has attempted — executed — without disgust, without scandal! (Foakes, *Coleridge's Criticism*, 113)

Coleridge is frankly amazed at Shakespeare's ability to represent such evil "without disgust." His admiration for the authorial achievement implies a confession about readerly responsibility: Coleridge himself is undisgusted contemplating Iago in a way that might seem (and is therefore vigorously denied to be) a "scandal." The question of motivation speaks to emergent psychological concerns, but Coleridge is working chiefly within a residual theological framework, where the ethical questions — was Shakespeare right to create Iago this way? are we right to feel this way about Iago? — have a particular intensity. If we are interested in the original reception of the play, this theological framework needs to be taken seriously.

One way to get at this point is to contrast Iago with the "modern cynics" Peter Sloterdijk describes as proliferating on the current scene:

> They do not see their clear, evil gaze as a personal defect or an amoral quirk that needs to be privately justified. Instinctively, they no longer

understand their way of existing as something that has to do with being evil, but as participation in a collective, realistically attuned way of seeing things. It is the universally widespread way in which enlightened people see to it that they are not taken for suckers. . . . It is the stance of people who realize that the times of naïveté are gone.

These "asocial characters" of Sloterdijk sound a lot like Iago, in his consistent and overt contempt for (as he sees it) hypocritical or self-deluded idealization. But there are significant differences as well. In Sloterdijk's description, cynicism has become "universally widespread," normalized to the point where it no longer seems to need any justification. Modern cynics "are no longer outsiders"; they "lose their individual sting" and "have long ceased to expose themselves as eccentrics."[6] Iago, to be sure, is unapologetic, even self-congratulatory about the canniness of his views, but he is aware of the official and normative status of an idealizing view which makes him look eccentric. Evil, moreover, is very much part of his vocabulary. He acknowledges "double knavery" and aligns himself with "hell," "night," and the "monstrous" in the first soliloquy and consistently thereafter. This is mockery, of course. Iago invites his audience to take religious virtue as part of the deluded official version of human nature. Renaissance audiences must have been open to such materialist arguments and even atheistic opinions;[7] these were, however, truly risky and blasphemous and, most important, contained within a culture still profoundly dominated by religious feeling. However widespread the skepticism about orthodoxy in Shakespeare's time, any doubt would have been entertained from inside a structure of religious belief and understanding, the vocabulary of faith within which the audience saw the world and without which there would have been no world to see.[8]

If hell and the devil are not just metaphors, let alone naive fictions, Iago's self-designations must have been more than a joke among enlightened insiders; but the substantial constraints these concepts might be expected to establish on his attractive power don't seem to work. Iago is apparently irresistible — certainly for the characters inside the play and apparently for audiences as well who, if Iago is the devil, come nonetheless to sympathize (in the root sense) with him to the extent of forgetting any obligations to the theological values that allowed for the designation in the first place. No wonder Coleridge was amazed.

Modern interpreters have been inclined to follow out the psychological rather than the theological implications of Coleridge's response. "Let's think about Iago for a moment," Jonathan Miller says. "He is the personification of evil — but what does that mean? I cannot make any sense of the notion of evil in the abstract, or as a general principle that might be personified in a particular character. Instead I ask myself: what does this character do or mean?" Miller's inclination leads him to stress the social context for Iago's envy. "Iago is an unpromoted officer who could never aspire to promotion because his class rules him out. . . . In casting Bob Hoskins as Iago" in his 1981 BBC production, Miller made him "into a working-class sergeant" in order "to stress the idea of social frustration" (146–149). In this respect, Miller is working in a strong tradition of modern Iagos, which goes back to Frank Finlay's "solid, honest-to-God N.C.O." opposite Olivier (Tynan, 2) and further to Olivier's own Iago in 1938 opposite Ralph Richardson. This line carries on to Ian McKellen, opposite Willard White in Trevor Nunn's 1989 RSC production: "McKellen's northern accent sets him apart from the rest of the cast, particularly Othello and Cassio," who "speak in traditional BBC tones. . . . Iago is excluded from the inner circle" (Vaughan, 222).

The *locus classicus* for this Iago in critical commentary is Empson's "Honest in *Othello*," which anticipates many of Miller's points (and which the Cambridge-educated Miller may have known). Empson, too, is skeptical about theological abstractions. The only way "to justify calling Iago" the devil is to psychologize and socialize the concept: "What is really in view is the spectator or reader . . . recognising, in a manner secretly, the complementary truths projected into the figure of Iago" (249). "The Victorians," Empson believed, "were not ready enough to approve" honest Iago; they "took him as an abstract term 'Evil,'" and by lifting him out of the social dimension of the action effectively limited an audience's ability to recognize themselves in the sentiments Iago expresses (234, 230). (Empson's "Victorians" are critics, not theatrical performers and audiences, but as we'll see in chapter 6, the nineteenth-century stage itself imposed substantial constraints on Iago's power, so Empson's general argument is not without relevance to traditions of theatrical interpretation as well.) Empson keys on Iago's remark about Cassio near the end, "He hath a daily beauty in his life / That makes me ugly" (5.1.19–20). For Miller this was Iago's "most revealing line" because it "seems to summarize . . . the nature of envy" (147); Empson uses it to disagree with Bradley's belief that the speech was about moral beauty. "Iago only means that Cassio has smart clothes and more upper-class manners, which give him an unfair advantage over Iago" (234). Perhaps most important, Empson emphasizes military society as a site of rank, privilege, and resentment. "Many of the audience were old soldiers disbanded without pension; they would dislike Cassio as the new type of officer, the boy who can displace men of experience because he knows enough mathematics to work the new guns" (229).

The interest here is chiefly historical; Empson is trying to reconstruct a Renaissance audience's experience. He may well be exaggerating the size of the old-soldier constituency, but his argument doesn't depend on the point. The "honesty" of Empson's Iago involves "the good qualities of being 'ready to blow the gaff' and 'frank to yourself about your own desires'" — an unillusioned pragmatism about human behavior as motivated by appetite and power (235). The general sense of resentment inherent in such a view must have had a particularly strong appeal: the disenchanted drama of the Renaissance frequently represents social privilege as residual, unearned, and arbitrary.[9] Iago's status and age may have reinforced the effect. The play gives us contradictory signals about Iago's social position, leaving him somewhere in an indeterminate middle and thus easily accessible to a broad range of the spectators in the public theater who felt themselves in a variety of ways similarly displaced.[10] On the other hand, the play goes out of its way to specify his age as twenty-eight (1.3.311), but twenty-eight must have seemed older in 1601–1604 than it does to us, perhaps a chronologically middling position corresponding to his flexible social status, so this detail may produce a similar effect.

Most important, the play consistently grounds Iago's galling sense of exclusion in the dramatic action — as in the way, just after his attempts at witty entertainment in the "praise of women" at the beginning of act 2, Desdemona turns away from him and enters into conversation with her natural ally. "How say you, Cassio, is he not a most profane and liberal counsellor?" She speaks about Iago as if he were not there, as if he did not exist. Cassio responds in kind: "He speaks home, madam, you may relish him more in the soldier than in the scholar" (2.1.163–166). This is an especially "unfortunate remark," Honigmann observes, "as Cassio's bookishness particularly irritates Iago"; a social marker, Cassio's learning signals cultural capital, the right stuff. His remark immediately precipitates Iago's ominous and vindictive aside. Like the comparable dramatization of Shylock's exclusion (*Merchant*, 1.3.70–105), this little fillip of action confirms and (theatrically speaking) justifies the villain's motivation.

But this brings us back to the same problem: trying to relate theatrical values to nontheatrical values — to real life, as we conventionally call it, authentic or sincere belief. The psychological framework leaves us in a perplexing situation fundamentally similar to the theological — this is really Coleridge's point. Consider Iago's desire to ruin Roderigo:

> Thus do I ever make my fool my purse:
> For I mine own gained knowledge should profane
> If I would time expend with such a snipe
> But for my sport and profit. (1.3.382–385)

The profit motive seems inconsequential, and why is it pleasurable to destroy somebody, as part of a regular and continual practice ("ever"), simply because the somebody is irritatingly there?[11] Iago's hatred for Othello, expressed just after, at least purports to be explicable: "I hate the Moor / And it is thought abroad that 'twixt my sheets / He's done my office" (385–387); but as Heilman says about the "and" in line 386, "rarely is a conjunction used so effectively: the hate is prior, and a motive is then discovered."[12] Iago's motivations are fabricated after the fact out of little or nothing; even the real ones seem inadequate to explain the intensity of his malice. They are legion, but despite or rather because of their capacity for apparently unconstrained proliferation, they seem unconnected to a constant and free-floating malice, the sadistic pleasure in poisoning people's delight for the sheer unmotivated joy of doing so.

The more we see of Iago, the less sense he makes. Despite his self-congratulatory rationality, he is full of contradictions.[13] He has contempt for what he takes to be others' self-delusions, but he is nothing if not delusional himself. His canny self-protectiveness disappears into an obsessive plotting whose purposes are obscure, even to himself, and whose consequences, it becomes increasingly clear, are bound to be suicidal: "his goals," as Auden said, seem to "include his self-destruction" ("The Joker in the Pack," 246). In short, Iago is a paranoid psychopath, the equivalent in psychological jargon to a diabolical villain; yet — amazingly again — this seems to make no difference, or at least it doesn't effectively curtail his extraordinary power to engage us with his point of view. Despite the evident signs of his pathological perversity, he manages, as a vast array of very differently positioned critics agree, to occupy the position of a felt norm.[14] The threats he imagines everywhere are obviously hallucinations, yet somehow we become convinced that they are true, if not literally real, that his conviction of being besieged by an assaultive hostility is the bedrock fact of human existence. How does the play manage to produce this conviction?

Maybe the question shouldn't be asked. Carol Carlisle quotes Margaret Webster: we "do not stop to fuss for reasons." The "pure venom" of Iago's hatred "chills the blood; it also compels us to belief." Carlisle thinks this may be "*too* simple, since, in concentrating upon audience effect, it takes no account of the actor's own understanding" (239). More to my purposes, it takes no account of interpreters, who have an irritable tendency to reach after explanation. One way to accommodate this tendency is to take with some seriousness the idea of a "bedrock fact of human existence." Iago appeals to us because he plays to aspects of identity and self-understanding that, however modified through the contingencies of history, seem essential to the way we experience ourselves in the world.

In his earliest self-explanatory speech, Iago builds from the premise that "we cannot all be masters, nor all masters / Cannot be truly followed" (1.1.42–43). Well, yes; who could disagree? There are masters and servants, because gradation inheres inevitably in any social order; that some servants are loyal and others not corresponds to the obvious facts of human nature. Iago is a canny and unillusioned realist; he "knows all qualities, with a learned spirit, / Of human dealings" (3.3.262–263), as Othello says, explaining why he is willing to credit Iago's claims. But it's more than just an ability to describe the way things are that makes Iago seem right; his words call attention to the way we know things to be what they are. "We cannot all be masters" because without servants to define their different position, the masters themselves would disappear: the concepts of master and servant would simply not exist. In the same way, if there were no disloyal servants, there would be no loyal servants either, because loyalty exists by virtue of contrast to disloyalty. In this sense Iago's speech may be understood as doing epistemology rather than ontology. It works not by describing already-existing categories of existence but by pointing to the concept of difference required to summon the categories into being.

This may seem to be overreading a simple and casual turn of phrase, but the differential basis of identity keeps returning throughout Iago's speech. Hence, a moment later: "It is as sure as you are Roderigo, / Were I the Moor, I would not be Iago" (55–56). "The simplicity," as Greenblatt says after quoting the second line of this statement, "is far more apparent than real." He then proceeds to unpack the assumptions about the nature of identity attached to "the 'I' in both halves of the line": does the "ego underlie . . . all institutional structures" or is it "constituted by institutional structures" (*Renaissance Self-Fashioning*, 236)? But to hear

Iago's words as problematizing the concept of identity depends on ignoring the in-every-sense-prior line, "It is as sure as you are Roderigo." [15] This seems indisputable: Roderigo *is* surely Roderigo. On to this axiomatic concept of self-identity the speech superimposes an apparently equally axiomatic concept of differential identity. Iago surely is Iago . . . because he is not Othello. Iago is not in the business of fleshing out the equivocal meanings of human identity but rather of asserting its unequivocal existence. Whatever the perplexities attached to the "I," it self-evidently exists on the basis of the differentiation that is its enabling condition. Hence the speech's outrageous conclusion: "I am not what I am" (64). By parodying Jehovah's "I am that I am," these last words constitute the first signal in the play of Iago's diabolical identity. But timing is everything. At this point Iago seems generally reliable (perforce, since he is our usher into the action of the play) and the parody nothing more than a risqué piece of wit, a joke wicked only in the idiomatic and strictly nontheological sense of the word. The main significance, "I am not what I appear to be," reinforces the commonsense truth about differential identity that has underwritten the speech as a whole.

In a funny exchange later in the scene, the same idea seems to be in play: "*Brabantio*: Thou art a villain. *Iago*: You are a senator" (116). Editors almost always feel the need to clarify this exchange with some sort of stage business, often drawing on theatrical traditions that go back to the eighteenth century (Sprague, *Shakespeare and the Actors*, 186): Iago pauses before "a senator," "senator" is spoken in a contemptuous way to suggest less respectful designations, exclamation points are substituted for the periods after each statement (as by Honigmann, whose text I have restored to the original periods). But leave the words alone, for an uninflected or even blandly insouciant delivery, and you get, once again, identity realized in difference. A senator is . . . not a villain, and vice versa. This is too simple; sometimes senators are villains. The moral and the sociopolitical can overlap as well as differ, and their relationship will vary in individual cases. Nonetheless, we need a simple map or basic grid in order to start the interpretive business of definition and evaluation — something like a dramatis personae, the list of characters modern readers depend on as they try to follow the action. Such lists were rarely included in the original printed texts, and the first audiences made do without playbills. Still, they would have needed something comparable in their minds in order to place the characters, if only in some provisional and tentative way, and the placement would have been of necessity differential: the short one — that is, not the tall one; the senator, not the villain. Iago's response makes this exchange into a kind of mini–dramatis personae, identifying the roles by differentiation.

Othello happens to be one of the few plays in the Folio (seven in all) which include such a list and, perhaps influenced by this exchange, it designates Iago as "a villain." (In the same list Brabantio is designated "father to Desdemona," but most modern lists, again perhaps influenced by this exchange, indicate that he is a senator as well.) The designation in this exchange adds some retrospective weight to the diabolical implications of "I am not what I am" and looks ahead to "who calls me villain?" But timing is still everything, and at this point Iago's surprising comeback is still likely to sound more like a joke than a real fact. The real fact, at least in terms of the sophisticated understanding Iago invites us to share with him, is that there are no real facts, or none that we can know without differentiation.

Iago is on to something fundamental about the way we make sense of the world. In "The Antithetical Meaning of Primal Words," Freud puzzles over the anomaly that the language of ancient Egypt includes "a fair number of words with two meanings, one of which is the exact opposite of the other": the "word 'strong' meant both 'strong' and 'weak'" and "'light' was used to mean both 'light' and 'darkness.'" In addition, the Egyptian lexicon possesses many "words in which two vocables of antithetical meanings are united so as to form a compound which bears the meaning of only one of its two constituents." Hence for words such as "old-young," "far-near," "bind-sever," "outside-inside," the meaning, "in spite of combining the extremes of difference," is limited to "young," "near," "bind" and "inside," respectively. This "riddle," Freud tells us,

is easier to solve than it appears to be. Our concepts owe their existence to comparisons. If it were always light we should not be able to distinguish light from dark, and consequently we should not be able to have either the concept of light or the word for it. It is clear that everything on this planet is relative and has an independent existence only in so far as it is differentiated in respect of its relations to other things [and that] the essential relativity of all knowledge, thought or consciousness cannot but show itself in language. (Strachey, 11.156–157) [16]

Freud's system is heavily invested in origins, and he characteristically emphasizes the antiquity of this phenomenon. Ancient Egypt, he says in a significant metaphor, "was one of the cradles of the development of human reason" (156). Differentiation as the basis of identity does indeed seem to go back to the creation in Genesis ("and God divided the light from the darkness") and then to the origin of human history, when "the knowledge of good and evil, as two twins cleaving together, leaped forth into the world. And perhaps this is that doom which Adam fell into of knowing good and evil, that is to say, of knowing good by evil" (Merritt Hughes, 728).[17]

By defining himself differentially, then, Iago is right: in contrast to Sir Thomas Browne's God, who "onely is," all other entities "have an existence with dependency and are something by a distinction" (34). But how then does Iago construct such a lunatic existence on this evidently stable foundation? Consider Werner Sollors, introducing the concept of ethnicity:

> It makes little sense to define "ethnicity-as-such," since it refers not to a thing-in-itself but to a relationship: ethnicity is typically based on a *contrast*. If all human beings belonged to one and the same ethnic group we would not need such terms as "ethnicity," though we might then stress other ways of differentiating ourselves such as age, sex, class, place of birth, or sign of the zodiac. Ethnic, racial, or national identifications rest on antitheses, on negativity, or on what the ethnopsychoanalyst Georges Devereux has termed their "dissociative" character. Ethnic identity, seen this way, "is logically and historically the product of the assertion that 'A is an X because he is not a Y'" — a proposition which makes it remarkably easy to identify Xness. By the same token, the definition of Xs as non-Ys threatens to exaggerate their differences in such a way that if the Xs think of themselves as human, they may therefore consider the Ys as somehow nonhuman. Unless the equation is offset by the positive acceptance of its opposite, "B is a Y by being a non-X," contrastive identification may overrule the shared humanity of different groups and erect symbolic boundaries that may resemble those between human beings and animals or being living beings and dead things. (288)

Sollors allows us to see both Iago's normality and his deranged excess: he "threatens to exaggerate . . . differences." He says not just that he is different from Othello, but that he hates him. He is convinced that Othello is out to diminish and ultimately destroy him. As with the Moor, so with women. Iago's sense of himself as a man is based on differentia-tion from women. But Iago *hates* women. The point of his witty banter at the beginning of act 2 is that women are by nature manipulative crea-tures who use men for their own distinct purposes. When Desdemona says that this is slander, Iago's disagreement, "Nay, it is true, or else I am a Turk" (114), slips from gender to religion in a way that calls attention to the general mechanism. Difference experienced as hostility ("otherness") metastasizes into an all-encompassing phenomenon. Blacks, women, Turks, aristocrats, Florentines ("One Michael Cassio, a Florentine" — this is presumably spat out: *you know those bastards from Florence, let them in and they steal your job!* [1.1.19]): everybody is out to get him.

In fact, their assaults are what create him; they constitute the varying conditions for his existence. Iago does more than disagree with Desde-mona's charge of slander; he stakes his identity wholly on the existence of a hostile (in this case female) otherness. Take that away, and you've taken him away. "I am nothing," he says just after, in a statement we need to understand literally rather than idiomatically, "if not critical" (117). He is pure negativity, difference without positive terms. He wants whatever they (blacks, women, etc.) are denying him; he is only what-ever they are seeking to destroy. His agenda is a parody of the golden rule: destroy them before they destroy you. The destruction of others is the origin of the self. Iago is identity politics reduced to its absurdity, a bundle or rather a series of besieged special interests, each of them sum-moned into being by the presumedly hostile special interests of whoever is his immediate company. Around Desdemona, Emilia, and Bianca, he is a man; around Othello, white; around Cassio, professionally and so-cially déclassé. He can do it all — race, class, and gender — whatever fills his emptiness with a sense of injured merit.

The play gives us ample basis to see Iago's lunacy for what it is. Some-times it does so by verbal suggestion, as in the perverse apartheid by which Iago imagines the proper managing of our bodily gardens: "We will plant nettles or sow lettuce, set hyssop and weed up thyme, supply it with one gender of herbs or distract it with many" (1.3.322–324).[18] Chiefly, though, it's in some of the other characters that we are made to see Iago's position as pathological, and of these chiefly Desdemona:

> She swore in faith 'twas strange, 'twas passing strange,
> 'Twas pitiful, 'twas wondrous pitiful;
> She wished she had not heard it, yet she wished
> That heaven had made her such a man. (1.3.161–164)

Desdemona experiences Othello's difference as foreign, the usual sense of "strange" (as in Roderigo's "extravagant and wheeling stranger / Of here and everywhere"), even potentially threatening (wishing "she had not heard it"). Her response, though, is not selfishly protective but socially welcoming; she does not seek to try to destroy difference but to identify affectionately with it as an expression of desire for her own enrichment.

Desdemona's generosity in the play is unique in degree, but not in kind. Montano, hearing of Othello's imminent arrival "in full commission here for Cyprus," declares "I am glad on't, 'tis a worthy governor" (1.2.30). This is "ungrudging praise from the man replaced as governor," as Honigmann astutely observes. It bespeaks a generous affection for Othello and a feeling of community with Venice transcending his own individual interests. How different from Iago's resentment about Cassio's promotion. And how different Cassio is himself in appreciating (misguidedly, to be sure) Iago's intercession on his behalf: "I never knew / A Florentine more kind and honest" (3.1.40–41). Cassio is aware of national (or civic) differences, but finds what Sollors calls a "shared humanity," or at least a shared interest, that seems more important.

Cassio is very good at this, especially in the early part of the play. Entering the scene in 2.1 and overhearing expressions of solicitous care for Othello's safety, he speaks with gratitude. "Thanks, you the valiant of this warlike isle / That so approve the Moor" (43–44). His love identifies with Othello's interests; their kindness to the Moor is experienced as kindness to himself. This identification is nowhere stronger than in his imagining of Othello and Desdemona's lovemaking a moment later:

> Great Jove, Othello guard,
> And swell his sail with thine own powerful breath
> That he may bless this bay with his tall ship,
> Make love's quick pants in Desdemona's arms,
> Give renewed fire to our extinct spirits
> And bring all Cyprus comfort! (2.1.77–82)

Cassio loves Desdemona as well as he loves Othello, but not in the way Iago supposes. Instead of possessive jealousy, "his, not mine," Cassio imagines participating in their lovemaking; it gives renewed fire to his own spirits, to all of them. Unlike Iago, who experiences other people's joy as poison, Cassio so identifies with Othello and Desdemona that he shares their "comfort." It's a wonderfully surprising word, but Othello and Desdemona will use it themselves in their ecstatic reunion just after (192, 206), as if to confirm the self-fulfilling prophecy of Cassio's generously affectionate response.[19]

Cassio has a beauty that makes Iago ugly, and absorbed in his or Desdemona's loveliness, who would be distracted by Iago? The trouble is, the play doesn't allow us to be absorbed very often or for very long in Cassio and Desdemona. When Iago enters the scene in 2.1, he immediately upstages them and takes control of our interest. If hate upstages love, does this mean that hate is stronger than love? When Milton's Satan speaks of "*immortal* hate" or when Emilia speculates about "some *eternal* villain" poisoning Othello's mind, the words imply a claim for diabolical hatred as at least equivalent in power to divine love.[20] Theologically speaking, the claim is heretical nonsense. God was there first, at the beginning; the devil is antimatter, the adversary; hatred, like all sin, is a perversion of ontologically prior love. But in terms of theatrical experience rather than orthodox Christian values, *Othello* makes us feel Iago's power as virtually irresistible during the first two acts.

According to Samuel Huntington in *The Clash of Civilizations and the Remaking of World Order*, the fact that "people define their identity by what they are not" leads to the conclusion that "it is human to hate. For self-definition and motivation, people need enemies" (quoted Holmes, 3). Such claims are rarely made so baldly in academic analysis,[21] but they appear more frequently in fiction and popular culture,[22] and any audience trying to make sense of *Othello* needs to take them seriously — as the truth of the matter. Maybe hatred, resentment, and envy — all the emotions that Iago represents — *are* at the base of our identity, the center of our humanity. If not ontologically prior, once activated they seem impossible to control. "Hatred is always a sin," an Alice Munro mother tells her daughter. "Remember that. One drop of hatred in your soul will spread and discolor everything like a drop of black ink in white milk" (6). The trick, presumably, is not to let it into your system. But audiences of *Othello* do not have the choice. The play makes sure that Iago is injected into us right from the beginning, undiluted, not just before we know what is happening but as *the way* we know it is happening. Why should it do that?

No matter how irresistible Iago's qualities, they remain relatively inert or potential until they are transformed into action. Iago engages with the characters of the play and with us in three distinct performances in act 2: his manipulation of Roderigo, his witty improvising about women in 2.1.117–64, and his managing of Cassio's cashiering in 2.3. Let's consider them in that order.

The Roderigo business runs through not just all of act 2 but the whole play, but it tends to be taken for granted. Iago doesn't have to be diabolically clever to string Roderigo along and seems himself sheepishly apologetic about expending the considerable talents of his "own gained knowledge . . . with such a snipe" (1.3.383–384). At the same time, Roderigo's monumental self-absorption makes Iago's invitation for us to join in the pleasure of his gulling very difficult to refuse: it's a free ride. There are, to be sure, more sinister possibilities. In Jude Kelly's 1996 Washington production,

> we are encouraged to laugh when this pathetic clown crumples sobbing on the floor at the end of the senate scene and tries ineffectually to stab himself with the official paper knife. So what are we to make of the fact that Othello ends up in the same location, when he laments how it "pleased heaven to try me with affliction" and later stabs himself with what seem to be the same gestures? (Potter)

The fact is, there's a lot we can make of it: Roderigo and Othello are both (with Cassio) made fools of by Iago. If we laugh at the process in one case, we are guilty by association with the other, so that when Lodovico tries to concentrate responsibility onto Iago at the end — "This is thy work" — we have to acknowledge our share. ("If Iago is guilty," as Sheila Rose Bland puts it succinctly, "so is the audience" [37].) But this may be too abstract to get across in such a gestural echo (the reviewer, apparently, was just confused). Perhaps there are more accommodating theatrical possibilities. The dramatic writing may allow for some moments of sudden pathos, requiring us to acknowledge Roderigo's humanity — potentially awkward moments, considering the delight we have taken in Iago's manipulation. But there doesn't seem to be evidence in the theatrical or critical record of capitalizing on such possibilities. Besides, there are much better investment opportunities in the play for producing guilt, more than we need, beginning with the Iago-Desdemona exchange early on in the act.

This business has often been reduced, sometimes drastically, in the theater. The nineteenth-century theater was always looking to cut; the modern stage has usually eliminated the time-consuming changes of spectacular scenery, but still needs to cut, and quite possibly even the Globe couldn't manage the texts we have within the time constraints.

But the problem isn't just time: there's something unpleasant about the scene, partly a matter of an indelicacy offensive to earlier theatergoers (who were spared Bianca even though plot coherence really suffers in her absence). In short, this is a distasteful and expendable scene. Ridley, the New Arden editor, no doubt represents a lot of critical and theatrical sentiment over the play's long reception history in declaring it "one of the most unsatisfactory passages in Shakespeare" (54).

Honigmann quotes this remark and comments, "Yet it shows how Iago wins an ascendancy over others, his improvising skills (note how Cassio is overshadowed), and that Desdemona understands sexual innuendo." In part, Honigmann is quoting Ridley for the same reason Furness quoted Rymer: he is there. Editors cite their predecessors, especially Arden editors; it's their job. But something more complicated is involved. Honigmann wouldn't feel it necessary to refute Ridley unless he believed there was something to refute (Furness's disclaimer of such a need only made it more evident). Most of Ridley's commentary locates his sense of dissatisfaction in the action-retarding purposelessness of the episode, during which the play itself, like the characters on stage, seems to be marking time: "All we gain from it is some further unneeded light on Iago's vulgarity. . . . Perhaps the passage was just a sop to the groundlings" (54; a "sop to the groundlings," like its tonier counterpart, "playing to the King," is often a marker of critical desperation). Honigmann shows that the episode communicates a lot of significance; this, however, does not eliminate a sense of dissatisfaction, but rather transfers it from functionlessness (nothing's going on here) to a particular function (something's going on here, and we don't like it), namely, our being made to acknowledge that "Desdemona understands sexual innuendo." It is this, perhaps, that underlies Ridley's very long commentary, though he represents it as a secondary matter ("Then, it is distasteful to watch her engaged in a long piece of cheap backchat with Iago, and so adept at it"). Certainly this is what motivates Stanley Cavell, another troubled viewer of this scene, who, working out of Ridley's edition (though not referring specifically to it) worries about Desdemona's actively sexual nature "as the dimension of her that shows itself in that difficult and dirty banter between her and Iago as they await Othello on Cyprus" (136).

What is the matter here? Surely it is not "dirty" to understand sexual banter. A sexual nature doesn't make you a whore. As Othello says, resisting Iago's suggestions,

> 'Tis not to make me jealous
> To say my wife is fair, feeds well, loves company,
> Is free of speech, sings, plays and dances well:
> Where virtue is, these are more virtuous. (3.3.186–189)

It is true that Desdemona partakes of and in fact instigates Iago's performance: "What wouldst thou write of me, if thou shouldst praise me?"
(2.1.117–118); but she cannot know what she is getting into, and in case
we wonder about her vanity, the play goes out of its way to reassure us:

> *Desdemona:* Come on, assay. There's one gone to the harbour?
> *Iago:*   Ay, madam.
> *Desdemona:* I am not merry, but I do beguile
>   The thing I am by seeming otherwise.
>   Come, how wouldst thou praise me?

She is worried about Othello, and the aside at the beginning of the second speech makes it clear she is trying to distract herself. According
to Honigmann, "she is not asking for compliments, but wants to stop
the marital bickering and places herself in the firing line (as later with
Othello-Cassio)." This is plausible but highly speculative. Presumably
Honigmann feels compelled to reassure us about Desdemona's virtuous
generosity because he wants to prevent us from getting the wrong idea,
but the trouble is we've already got the wrong idea. The critical tradition
is the immediate antecedent, a perplexed Cavell, a dissatisfied Ridley,
and beyond them the "many readers" to whom Ridley refers, a long and
continuing line of interpreters who seem not just troubled but more or
less convinced that Desdemona is at least a bit of a whore after all (where
there's smoke, there's fire).[23] At the origin of this tradition is Rymer ("It
is difficult not to sympathize for once with Rymer," says Ridley, ending
his note with a long quotation from *A Short View* — why are we not
surprised?), and beyond the critical tradition is Iago himself, the origin,
the source of the nasty suggestion. Honigmann is right to want to deny
all this. The play has gone out of its way to disconfirm Iago's view in
the first act and is going out of its way even now to deny it again in
Desdemona's aside. But once the suggestion has been absorbed, these
denials have as much reinforcing as reassuring power ("it is wrong to
think that *women are whores*"; "at least it's wrong to think that *Desdemona is a whore*"), and it's the play that made us absorb the suggestion
to begin with.

What's more, Iago's "improvisational skills" are even now reinforcing it yet again. The game he plays with Desdemona requires him to work two sets of variables, foolish and witty, ugly and pretty (with the interesting racial resonances of "black" and "fair") into the same point of view. Iago rises to the challenge. On the spur of the moment, he invents four rhyming couplets to arrive at the same conclusion: women use whatever qualities they possess, intellectual or sexual, to get power over men. But it's variation as well as repetition. The last of Desdemona's variants, "foul and foolish," is the hardest. Can a woman without qualities gain power? Iago rises to the higher challenge: "There's none so foul and foolish thereunto / But does foul pranks which fair and wise ones do." Whether purposefully managed or not, potentially marketable or not, a nasty sexuality is the essence of female nature. Desdemona ups the ante again. In positing "a deserving woman indeed," she requires him to go outside the game to a place where his rule of a universally dirty female sexuality does not apply. Not one but five and one-half couplets follow this request, ending in a suspense-sustaining pause: "She was a wight, if ever such wights were — " and Desdemona has to prompt him: "To do what?" Iago's conclusion snatches victory from the jaws of defeat: "To suckle fools, and chronicle small beer." Babies and household accounts. Even supposing virtuous women really existed (and "if ever such wights were" is skeptical at best), the contemptibly trivial nature of female life makes exceptionality insignificant. All of his apparent labor trying to accommodate the game and the reality was a mockery. The game is all there is. There is nothing outside the game.

Even as Iago tells us where he's going, he manages to stay one step ahead of us. The mixture of predictability and surprise is timed brilliantly to make us laugh. As with the more outrageously Ovidian *jeux d'esprit* in Donne's *Songs and Sonets*, the improvisation occurs within and is made possible by very stylized rhetorical structures. The subject matter is also highly conventionalized. Iago's speech is a tissue of maxims, "old fond paradoxes to make fools laugh i'th' alehouse," as Desdemona says (138–139). Like Millman Parry's Homer, Iago is full of commonplace formulas. Instead of rosy-fingered dawn and wine-dark sea, he bases his invention on misogynous stereotypes:

> Come on, come on, you are pictures out of doors,
> Bells in your parlours, wild-cats in your kitchens,
> Saints in your injuries, devils being offended,
> Players in your housewifery, and housewives in . . .
> Your beds! (109–113)

Iago

Honigmann quotes a very similar entry in Dent's collection of Elizabethan proverbs, comments that there "were many variants before Shakespeare," and furnishes another one.

In this passage and elsewhere, Iago works out of the standard version of sixteenth-century misogyny, the destructive excess of uncontrolled female sexuality ("housewives" was pronounced "hussifs," that is, hussies). As a result of the changes in belief that constitute our own sexual stereotypes, Iago's main assumption may strike us as odd, but in other particulars (women are nags, they never shut up, they keep making incomprehensible demands), his banter needs no historical introduction. Its tone of fed-up irritation remains the standard fodder of standup comedy where, with or without a wit comparable to Iago's, it's almost always good for a laugh.[24] But if laughter is a kind of assent, what does it mean that we laugh at Iago's jokes?

According to Lisa Jardine's commentary on this scene, although "Desdemona takes" Iago's jokes "as a familiar type of game, a familiar part of the contemporary culture ('These are old paradoxes')," the audience "easily hears the exchange as impugning Desdemona's own modesty" with the consequence that what "provides a witty paradox for the jest books is, it appears, a source of serious confusion when it comes to our scrutinizing the activities of a particular woman" ("Cultural Confusion," 2). Jardine's commentary may seem to miss the joke. After all, Iago's just kidding; we don't *really* believe what he says. But are we sure we know what belief is and how we come to our opinions about the world? For Michael Neill the scene provides a temporary release in which "even Iago, playing with disarming insouciance the role of urbane jester in a lady's court, appears for a short time (however misleadingly) liberated from his claustrophobic hutch of resentment" ("Changing Places," 117). For the scene to work this way, we need to assume a two-tier model of belief, which allows us to keep our actual opinions separate from and untouched by other forms of assent.[25] This two-tier model has a lot going for it. It is the basis for many counters from esthetic theory — such as Coleridge's "willing suspension of disbelief for the moment, which constitutes poetic faith" (in *Biographia Literaria*, chapter 14; Engell and Bate, 6) or Sidney's assurance that the "poet never makes any circles about your imagination, to conjure you to believe for true what he writes" (35). The same separation allows us to claim that we are rational creatures; this claim stands behind the disconfirming interpretation of act 1 of the play and underlies the Miltonic distinction between what comes in and goes out of our minds. Only the latter counts, the words or deeds which are the consequence of conscious choice or rational consent.[26] Perhaps most important, a similar distinction helps to sustain us through the ordinary trials of life in the everyday world.[27]

But *Othello* does not take place in the everyday world. The persistence of our anxieties about Desdemona — the "ease of impugning" and "serious confusion" Jardine insists on in the interpretive traditions — show this to be Iago's world. Iago creates a chilly climate or marks the fact that it already exists. "There is a whispering," as Kenneth Burke says about the beginning of *Othello*; and Iago is the "voice at Othello's ear" and ours as well ("*Othello*," 169, 166), telling us what we already know ("What you know, you know" [5.2.300]): blacks are the devil, women whores, foreigners foreign, and they're all trying to get you; *it's a jungle out there*. His sententious generalizations, proverbs, good old jokes ("old fond paradoxes") or fashionably new claims ("likelihoods / Of modern seeming"), or both together like the "wise saws and modern instances" of Jaques's fat old justice (*As You Like It*, 2.7.156) function like the clichés and conventional commodities of Don DeLillo's "white noise": we don't even know we're hearing it but wind up reproducing it nonetheless, either unthinkingly (the first line of the Pope couplet Coleridge half-remembered about "most women" gets at this point: "Nothing so true as what you once let fall") or, in times of stress, when we fall back on anything that might seem to help. Brabantio's leap to the witchcraft conclusion is a good example: "Have you not read of some such thing?" For the sentimental equivalent: "I can't recall who said it / I know I never read it / I only know that falling in love is grand." Iago produces "a multitude of our tiny and unnoticed assents" (Hunter, 54); "his seductive power is situated in his ability to manipulate the sociolect, . . . the site of 'myths, traditions, ideological and esthetic stereotypes . . . harbored by a society,' as well as the site of 'ready-made narrative and descriptive models that reflect a group's idea of or consensus about reality'" (Fultz, 203, quoting Michael Riffaterre). To say we do not believe Iago may be true but misses the point. He subtends and determines belief.

All this should allow us to appreciate Iago's masterpiece, his transformation of Cassio at the end of the act. This is a major piece of business, sustained over the last half of act 2 and (unlike the praise of women) with crucial implications for the overall action of the play. "If

Act I of *Othello* could be called 'Iago Plans Vengeance'," Kenneth Burke suggests, then "Act II would be 'Cassio', or better, 'Cassio Drunk'" ("*Othello*," 171). Cassio drunk, however, is represented as a production of Iago, like act 2 as a whole. He starts on Cassio immediately they are left alone with suggestions about Desdemona's sexual appeal. Othello has "not yet made the night wanton with her," she is "full of game," her eye "sounds a parley to provocation," her voice "an alarum to love" (2.3.16–24). All of this is jokey suggestion, but the joke is on Iago. Cassio either does not hear these innuendos or refuses to respond in kind. He loves women and is invulnerable to misogyny (at least for now). But Iago soldiers on relentlessly. If "idle hands are the devil's work," this is because the devil himself is never idle: "Well: happiness to their sheets! Come, lieutenant, I have a stoup of wine, and here without are a brace of Cyprus gallants that would fain have a measure to the health of black Othello" (26–29). If Iago can't get to Cassio with women, what about wine — and song?

Iago gets Cassio drunk — what does this mean? "O thou invisible spirit of wine," Cassio says later, "if thou hast no name to be known by, let us call thee devil!" (277–279). He imbibes of the demon grape, so to speak, but the devil isn't just a metaphor in *Othello*. As the wine goes into Cassio's mouth — "O God, that men should put an enemy in their mouths, to steal away their brains! . . . transform ourselves into beasts!" (285–288) — so Iago's poison goes into his ears, chiefly in the form of song, a verse of "let me the cannikin clink" sandwiched between two calls for "Some wine, ho!" and "Some wine, boys!" (64–71). If Iago's jokes were just jokes, his song is just a song, meaningless but familiar and fun. "'Fore God, an excellent song!" Cassio exclaims, presumably because it makes him feel good, an old fond song to make you sing along. Iago's next song is more of the same, one of the many variants of an early ballad that "we may assume Shakespeare's audience was familiar with" (Honigmann, 377). This song, though, which a by-now-drunk Cassio declares "more exquisite . . . than the other!" (94–95), is (like Iago's woman-hating maxims earlier) far from meaningless.

It's about a king ("a wight of high renown") and a tailor ("but of low degree"), the prince and the pauper, and about the arbitrary privileges of wealth, power, and social position. When the king refuses to pay for his breeches and calls the tailor a "lown," there's not much the tailor can do about it. "'Tis pride that pulls the country down, / Then take thine auld cloak about thee." This is Iago's mixture of resentment and unillusioned acceptance ("Why, there's no remedy") a tone beautifully realized later in the Victorian music hall:

> It's the same the whole world over
> Ain't it all a bleedin' shame
> It's the rich that get the pleasure
> It's the poor that get the blame.

To this resentment of the rich, Iago adds xenophobia, the competitive hatred (who can drink more?) of "your Dane, your German, and your swag-bellied Hollander" (173–174), mixed with disgust for the flesh, the fat-gutted, swilling, and puking body. (He had already got racism into the mix with "black Othello" at the beginning of the scene — one hardly notices.) Cassio, who is hearing but not listening, picks up on these suggestions:

Cassio. Well, God's above all, and there be souls must be saved, and there be souls must not be saved.
Iago. It's true, good lieutenant.
Cassio. For mine own part, no offence to the general nor any man of quality, I hope to be saved.
Iago. And so do I too, lieutenant.
Cassio. Ay, but, by your leave, not before me. The lieutenant is to be saved before the ancient. (98–106)

Grace is not a finite commodity. Like Desdemona and Othello's love, there's enough of it to give the whole world comfort. But Cassio is now seeing the world through Iago's eyes — interpellated, one might say, by the class-envy apparatus. The murderous assault on Roderigo and Montano is a short and apparently inevitable step ahead.

From one angle, the scene requires us to make an unambiguously harsh judgment on Cassio. Some people just can't hold their liquor. We cannot all be drinkers; there are happy drunks and nasty drunks. Cassio knows himself to be one of the latter. He should have just said no. This is Cassio's own judgment. He is ashamed and self-disgusted, and in a way that immediately helps to redeem his tarnished image, he refuses to make excuses for what he considers inexcusable behavior. The play allows for less harsh responses as well. After all, he lets his guard down only once. Is it reasonable to expect anyone to sustain a lifetime of uninterrupted moral attention? Given a relentlessly busy devil (or a corrupt nature), relaxation is likely to have terrible consequences. (It lands Una and the Redcross Knight in the Forest of Error at the beginning of Spenser's *Faerie Queene*). But who would presume to be able to do better? "Use every man after his desert," as Hamlet says, "and who shall 'scape whipping?" (2.2.529–530).

The play gets at this in a somewhat different way. Cassio does try to say no and agrees only reluctantly on Iago's insistence:

> *Cassio.* Not tonight, good Iago, I have very poor and unhappy
> brains for drinking. I could well wish courtesy would invent
> some other custom of entertainment.
>
> *Iago.* O, they are our friends. . . . What, man, 'tis a night of revels,
> the gallants desire it.
>
> *Cassio.* Where are they?
>
> *Iago.* Here, at the door, I pray you call them in.
>
> *Cassio.* I'll do't, but it dislikes me. (30–44)

Cassio does not want to spoil the party. This may be heard as a lack of individual integrity, but also as a respect for social norms, the behavioral rituals through which comradeship is enacted. These are barracks norms, to be sure, but "courtesy," a term often on Cassio's lips, denotes his general affability and affectionate good nature. How can he be expected to transcend the norms of his society in favor of isolated purity? Cakes and ale are at the essence of his virtue. The trouble is that it's Iago who has come to stand for and fill the social norms of this play's world. Cassio's temporizing "Where are they?" is the voice of a man suffering from "serious confusion," like the audience of Iago's misogynous routines at the beginning of the act; it is the pathetic question of a man who senses — rightly — that he is trapped. He doesn't seem to have a chance against Iago, any more than we did earlier. Why should we expect Othello to fare any better?

The Fall of
Othello

At the end of act 2, Iago's plan has taken shape: Cassio will solicit Desdemona to argue for his reinstatement,

> Myself the while to draw the Moor apart
> And bring him jump when he may Cassio find
> Soliciting his wife: ay, that's the way!
> Dull not device by coldness and delay! (2.3.380–383)

Like Hamlet's sprightly couplet at the end of the soliloquy terminating act 2 ("the play's the thing / Wherein I'll catch the conscience of the King"), Iago's last words promise rapid purposeful action. Act 3 keeps the promise; everything begins to fall into place. Emilia tells Cassio that Desdemona has already been urging his suit: "The general and his wife are talking of it, / And she speaks for you stoutly" (3.1.44–45). After 3.2, a perfunctory six lines showing Othello taking care of business, we find Desdemona assuring Cassio that she will persevere in her advocacy, and Iago brings Othello on stage as planned. In fact, with Cassio's embarrassed-looking departure and Desdemona's unpredictably sustained and insistent advocacy, Iago's scheme seems to be working out better than he had hoped. This is one of those moments when audiences are driven mad by the play. We want Desdemona to stop (perhaps we feel like throttling her into silence). Yet all our anxieties turn out apparently to be groundless. Desdemona departs, leaving Othello alone on stage with Iago, and the episode ends with Othello's aside, "Excellent wretch! Perdition catch my soul / But I do love thee! and when I love thee not / Chaos is come again" (3.3.90–92). This is ominous, like Desdemona's assurance to Cassio just earlier that "thy solicitor shall rather die / Than give thy cause away" (3.3.27–28); but whatever our premonitions, Othello's speech is an unqualified effusion of contentment and trust.

Within a few minutes of this aside, however, Desdemona has been transformed in Othello's mind from the object of his affectionate delight into a whore. Thereafter, although the play offers us occasional prospects for Othello to come back to his senses, we know, even as we invest hope in these prospects, that Iago is right to see Othello's transformation as irreversible —

> Not poppy nor mandragora
> Nor all the drowsy syrups of the world
> Shall ever medicine thee to that sweet sleep
> Which thou owedst yesterday. (3.3.333–336)

— and that he is doomed to an appalling course of destructive and self-destructive action.

The Temptation Scene — Othello and Iago's sustained contest, Othello's transformation — is in every sense the play's center. The earliest audiences of which we have record thought so: "the top scene," according to Rymer's contemporaries, "the Scene that raises *Othello* above all other Tragedies on our Theatres" (Rymer, 149). Garrick thought it was the "single finest scene" in all of Shakespeare, although, as Carlisle points out, his own failure as Othello gave him "little cause to love this play" (173). When Bradley began with *Othello*'s "distinctive impression" as "the most painfully exciting and the most terrible" of "all Shakespeare's tragedies," this was the scene he thought of: "From the moment when the temptation of the hero begins, the reader's heart and mind are held in a vice, experiencing the extremes of pity and fear, sympathy and repulsion, sickening hope and dreadful expectation" (143). Even Welles's film, which used the playtext as little more than a jumping-off place, felt the need to foreground it.[1]

Bradley's "extremes" get us to something beyond the scene's pivotal place in the play's overall arc of experience. Describing an intensely contradictory engagement with the action, Bradley implies (though refuses to acknowledge or act on the implication) an investment not just in Othello's resistance to Iago but in Iago's success. If for no purpose beyond satisfying our appetite for developing the action, we continue to be complicit with Iago's schemes. As a result, the scene besets us with an excruciating contrariety of desires — desperately wishing Othello not to believe Iago, eagerly and appreciatively watching the moves by which Iago conducts Othello to the abyss. If the play as a whole asks us to respond to the action from a position shared with and fractured by Othello and Iago, this is indeed *Othello*'s "top scene."

Rymer intended the phrase ironically; he fiercely attacked contemporary taste for both the play and the scene, claiming that Desdemona's behavior would make anyone suspicious of her fidelity and thus that Iago's inducement of Othello's jealousy is anticlimactic and redundant:

> After forty lines more [of her pleading], they part, and then comes the wonderful Scene, where *Jago* by shrugs, half words, and ambiguous reflections, works *Othello* up to be Jealous. One might think, after what we have seen, that there needs no great cunning, no great poetry and address to make the *Moor* Jealous. Such impatience, such a rout for a handsome young fellow, the very morning after her Marriage must make him either to be jealous, or to take her for a *Changeling*, below his Jealousie. After this *Scene*, it might strain the Poets skill to reconcile the couple, and allay the Jealousie. *Jago* can now only *actum agere*, and vex the audience with a nauseous repetition.
>
> Whence comes it then, that this is the top scene . . . (148–149)

This is surprising. Most of Rymer's essay is devoted to cataloging *Othello*'s improbabilities, of which the protagonist's transformation has always been the main instance, beginning with the characters inside the play ("this would not be believed," "Is this the noble Moor . . . ?" etc. [4.1.241 and 264 ff.]). We might therefore expect Rymer to make much of Othello's transformation as inadequately rather than excessively motivated — incredible rather than predictable. In fact, he regularly does so elsewhere, but his discussion of the Temptation Scene itself inverts the problem from lack of probability to lack of suspense. Perhaps he is engaging in a willful perversity designed to entertain us or shock us into interest, but he may be genuinely convinced. The mugging histrionics he describes probably correspond to stage practice, and the effect of irritating repetition squares with theatrical response through the eighteenth century. We are a long way from the stunning brilliance Booth's and Irving's audiences found in the role. But whatever Rymer's intentions, his remarks focus our interest on the main questions of the scene (really two sides of the same question): how do we understand Othello's failure to sustain himself? how do we understand Iago's success in taking him apart? Since our answer shapes not just the meaning of what follows but retroactively determines our sense of the action that has brought us to this crucial point, this is the central question for any interpretation of the play.

Any answer depends on a sense of timing. For Rymer, the conclusion of the Temptation Scene was predetermined at least as early as its immediately antecedent action. The main traditions of nineteenth-century performance and commentary, however, opted to underplay such premonitions. In Fechter's 1861 production Desdemona's advocacy is played as "free from all misgiving": she "coaxes him like a child, kissing his black beard"; he "toys with her curls, and treats her as a father might treat a child who was asking for some favour." The delights of familial domesticity are typical not only of the more "refined" line of Victorian productions; the "passionate" Salvini was "equally playful" in his treatment of this episode and made use (as did Booth and Irving, among others) of the striking business usually attributed to Fechter (though apparently originating in Charles Dillon's Lyceum performance of 1856) whereby Othello sits at a desk doing paperwork, more of a modern bureaucrat than an Elizabethan general, and thus hardly pays attention to Iago's suggestions at the beginning of the Temptation Scene proper. Even those who objected to this business did so not because of its intention to gradualize Othello's transformation, but because the intention was not realized. Hence Lewes complains that Fechter, answering Iago "carelessly, for some time, playing with his pen as he spoke, . . . was at last '*suddenly* convinced.'" A similar complaint helps to explain Irving's problems with the role. "His jealousy was easily aroused, 'the mine of passion . . . sprung too soon and too suddenly.'"[2]

As Matteo sums up the situation, "Nineteenth-century actors laboured hard to make Othello one not easily jealous — when they didn't they were criticized for it. . . . On the other hand, when actors did exhibit the slow growth of jealousy within Othello, his reluctance to be suspicious, they were praised" (225–226). Whatever its internal differences, nineteenth-century stage practice seems to be agreed on this matter — "the Fechter-Salvini tradition," as Hankey somewhat oxymoronically calls it (217). In his note "Othello in the Temptation Scene," Bradley insisted on this performance consensus, referring to reports of Booth and Fechter and to his own experience of Salvini, who "played this passage . . . with entire understanding. Nor have I ever seen it seriously misinterpreted on the stage" — the argument being that those who think Othello "easily jealous" . . . completely misinterpret him in the early part of this scene. They fancy that he is alarmed and suspicious the moment he hears Iago mutter "Ha! I like not that" . . . in fact, it takes a long time for Iago to excite surprise, curiosity, and then grave concern — by no means yet jealousy — even about Cassio; and it is still longer . . . not until Iago hints that Othello, as a foreigner, might easily be deceived, that he is seriously disturbed about Desdemona. (*Shakespearean Tragedy*, 370).

The concept of a gradual process deferred until Iago focuses on Othello's foreign status allows us to understand Othello's alteration as a lucid sequence. Echoes of act 1 in the Temptation Scene contribute to this sense. Hence Othello's confidence at the beginning that "my demerits / May speak unbonneted to as proud a fortune / As this that I have reached" (1.2.22–25) now diminishes to a sense of "mine own weak merits" (190). This acknowledgment, trivial in itself, precipitates a rush of startling reversals. Brabantio's admonition, "Look to her, Moor, if thou hast eyes to see: / She has deceived her father, and may thee," had prompted a secure dismissal early on: "My life upon her faith" (1.3.293–295). Now in the face of Iago's reiteration, "She did deceive her father, marrying you," Othello becomes worried: "And so she did" (209, 211). The anomalous Irving characteristically intensified the anxiety in both instances. In the face of Brabantio's early warning in an 1876 performance, Irving "cried 'No' as though 'to banish a rising doubt.'" In his 1881 promptbook, his response to Iago's reiteration in the Temptation Scene was cued with underscoring and exclamation points: "*And so she did!!!!*" (Alan Hughes, 143, 149). Fechter's delivery of this line was closer to the norm, allowing for a sense of unhurried extension: "stands aside with his eye fixed on vacancy, as one reasoning out in contemplation the path shown him to the hell whither it leads" (Sprague, *Shakespeare and the Actors*, 195).

In the scene's apparent turning point a moment later, Othello suddenly takes the initiative, "And yet how nature, erring from itself — " and Iago, himself cautious so far, spots an opportunity so desirable that he interrupts Othello to seize it:

> Ay, there's the point: as, to be bold with you,
> Not to affect many proposed matches
> Of her own clime, complexion and degree,
> Whereto we see, in all things, nature tends —

> Foh! one may smell in such a will most rank,
> Foul disproportions, thoughts unnatural. (232–237)

Nature is the crucial idea here, and again we hear echoes of the beginning: "and she, in spite of nature, / Of years, of country, credit, everything, / To fall in love with what she feared to look on?" (1.3.97–99). For Brabantio, nature should have drawn Desdemona to young Venetians of her own rank, "the wealthy, curled darlings of our nation" (1.2.68), and her attraction to Othello, "against all rules of nature" (1.3.102), must be the perverse consequence of witchcraft. The intensely contradictory and incompletely resolved feelings raised by the opening action return here, clustered around the same concept of nature; they move Othello, who has finally got Iago to leave him alone with his own thoughts ("I once more take my leave"), to adopt the identical cultural stereotypes to define his own nature:

> Haply for I am black
> And have not those soft parts of conversation
> That chamberers have, or for I am declined
> Into the vale of years — yet that's not much —
> She's gone, I am abused, and my relief
> Must be to loathe her. (267–272)

On "nature, erring from itself," Junius Brutus Booth "glanced at his own hand 'as it passed down before his eyes from his forehead.'" The gesture, as Sprague remarks, redirects the reference from "Desdemona's adultery . . . to the fact of her marriage" (*Shakespeare and the Actors*, 195). Now this soliloquy seems to clinch the process whereby, in Arthur Kirsch's words, "Othello eventually internalizes Iago's maleficent sexual vision and sees himself with Iago's eyes," repellent in "his age and color," thus "becom[ing] convinced that Desdemona's manifest attraction to him is itself perverse" (31, 32). That this story has survived Bradley and is even now commonly held testifies to its plausibility;[3] but if it clarifies the meaning of Othello's transformation, the motive remains mysterious. Why should Othello, against all evidence and self-interest, buy into the view Iago offers of himself and Desdemona? Othello himself sees the foolishness — "Exchange me for a goat / When I shall turn the business of my soul / To such exsufflicate and blown surmises" (183–185) — but proceeds to make the investment nonetheless.

Othello's alien status furnishes a familiar current context — the immigrant novel — by which to naturalize his strange behavior. In Salman Rushdie's *Satanic Verses*, Saladin Chamcha experiences literally the metaphorical transformation suggested by Othello: he turns into a goat.

His thighs had grown uncommonly wide and powerful, as well as hairy. Below the knee the hairiness came to a halt, and his legs narrowed into tough, bony, almost fleshless calves, terminating in a pair of shiny, cloven hoofs, such as one might find on any billy-goat. Saladin was also taken aback by the sight of his phallus, greatly enlarged and embarrassingly erect, an organ that he had the greatest difficulty in acknowledging as his own. (157)

Finding himself in a kind of asylum along with other embodied clichés of an exotic colonial domain — a manticore, some water buffalo, slippery snakes, "a very lecherous-looking wolf" — Chamcha asks, "But how do they do it?" "They describe us," the manticore tells him. "That's all. They have the power of description, and we succumb to the pictures they construct" (168).[4] In *Othello*, this irresistible power is represented by Iago, Burke's "voice whispering at the ear," the unidentifiable origin of the cultural clutter — stories, superstitions, social stereotypes, clichéd aphorisms, vague memories, dreams, overheard aimless chatter, and snatches of old songs — by which belief is subconsciously determined and on which identity imperceptibly rests. In this context, Rushdie's description of *The Satanic Verses* — "the move from one part of the world to another and what that does to the various aspects of one's being-in-the-world" (Banville, 34) — can make Othello's transformation the centerpiece of an altogether plausible narrative. At first he has the power to describe himself, inhabits his own narrative, but upon moving to Christian Europe he becomes gradually displaced from his "perfect soul" and begins to occupy a different story, until finally his blackness serves to figure not a royal-heroic self but bestial sexuality.

But should we be reading Othello as the abject victim at the center of an immigrant novel? The play was produced in an early colonialist culture, substantially ignorant of much that we have come to know of colonial and postcolonial experience. And there are generic as well as historical problems in such a view. *Othello* lacks the accumulation of finely attenuated nuance required to work in the manner of an immigrant novel, the sense of "dilatory time" (2.3.368) that Iago, a master narratologist, understands as necessary for such a mode.[5] This problem is insoluble (plays are not novels), but *Othello* goes out of its way to exacerbate it, compressing the expansive source narrative in Cinthio into an action that seems to occupy a mere two days, beginning at night with the elopement, arriving the next day at Cyprus, proceeding to the Temptation Scene on the day after, and concluding with the murder that night. We have bumped into the famous "double-time" problem — "the gap," as John Bayley puts it, "between the swift dramatic time of the plot and the lingering fictional time of the domestic psychology . . . between the impact of the *coup de théâtre* on our emotions, and the effect of the analysis of love and jealousy upon our minds" (134).[6] It is possible to demonstrate that the impact of swift time is misleading, but the impression remains, and, as in Morgann's famous adage, "in Dramatic composition, the *Impression* is the *Fact*" (4).[7] From this perspective we should understand Othello's transformation not as the "*eventual* internalizing" of Kirsch's narrative, or as something that "gradually" or "finally" comes about, as in my own rewriting of the play, but as issuing from his experience in the very brief interval that seems to elapse since the beginning of the action.

It is here that the sexual interest of recent criticism seems to pay off. According to Stanley Cavell, *Othello* makes us think "not merely generally of marriage but specifically of the wedding night. It is with this that the play opens" (131). Despite Iago's graphic specificity, however, we are by no means certain whether the old black ram and the white ewe's coupling is taking place "even now, now, very now" — or has taken place at all. As many critics have argued, the uncertainty when or even whether Othello and Desdemona consummate their marriage serves to generate anxious speculation on our part, sustained by the pressure of a highly eroticized language which enacts to the mind's eye various images of the deed about whose actual performance we remain unresolved.[8] This irresolution lasts at least until Othello's invitation on the first Cyprus night: "Come, my dear love, / The purchase made, the fruits are to ensue: / The profit's yet to come 'tween me and you" (2.3.8–10); but even as Othello's disarmingly ingenuous couplet gives rest to one kind of anxious uncertainty — *have they or haven't they?* — its alarming specificity gives rise to another: *what now will it be like?* This interest is displaced by the flurry of business with Iago, Cassio, Roderigo, and Montano; but Cassio's story of a transformative descent into violent passion sustains as well as displaces our interest in Othello and Desdemona's lovemaking, occurring (presumably) "even now, now, very now"; especially when Iago's astounding simile to describe the disturbance re-evokes that opening image:

> friends all, but now, even now,
> In quarter and in terms like bride and groom
> Divesting them for bed; and then, but now,
> As if some planet had unwitted men,
> Swords out, and tilting one at other's breasts
> In opposition bloody. (2.3.175–180)

The Temptation Scene follows and the play gives us the dramatic impression — the fact — of occurring the next morning.

As a consequence of *post hoc ergo propter hoc*, a mode of narrative understanding implicit in Morgann's Law of Dramatic Composition, we are encouraged to locate the origins of Othello's transformation in his sexual consummation. The impression is powerfully confirmed at just this pivotal point of Othello's soliloquy, when his sudden loathing situates itself with specific reference to Desdemona's body:

> O curse of marriage
> That we can call these delicate creatures ours
> And not their appetites! I had rather be a toad
> And live upon the vapour of a dungeon
> Than keep a corner in the thing I love
> For others' uses. Yet 'tis the plague of great ones,
> Prerogatived are they less than the base;
> 'Tis destiny unshunnable, like death —
> Even then this forked plague is fated to us
> When we do quicken. (272–281)

For Cavell, "the thing *denied our sight* throughout the opening scene" (132) was an image of sexual coupling; but as Patricia Parker notes, the focus in the middle of *Othello* is much more concentrated upon "the 'privities' of woman" ("Fantasies," 87). The "corner in the thing I love" directs us to Desdemona's genitals. The forked plague alludes to the cuckold's horns, but its demonstrative specificity, "*this* forked plague," so soon after "keep a corner," summons the groin to the mind's eye, like the "bare, fork'd animal" in *Lear* (3.4.108–109). And like the "simp'ring dame, / Whose face between her forks presages snow" later in the same play (4.6.118–119), Desdemona's whole being seems for a bizarre moment drawn down and compressed into her private part: she is both the thing and the thing in the thing — as Neill puts it, "not merely the precious 'thing,' the stolen treasure of love's corrupted commerce, but herself the lost place of love" ("Changing Places," 128). A similarly bizarre compression is produced in temporal terms for Othello. Two distinct time frames inhabit the "when" of the last line: the moment of birth (quickening as the emergence into life) and the moment of desire (quickening as tumescence), both swallowed up at once in betrayal, as though the entire trajectory of the male affective career in the tragic (or satiric) mode is simultaneously present, from beginning to end, in this same loved and loathed thing.

Within twenty-five lines of Othello's soliloquy, Emilia gives the handkerchief to Iago in an exchange that recalls the corporeal specificity of "the thing I love": "I nothing, but to please his fantasy. . . . I have a thing for you." "You have a thing for me? it is a common thing" (303–306). Iago, though, is not echoing Othello but rather echoing Othello's echo of himself earlier in the scene, working as usual (to recall Neill's phrase) "close to the unstable ground of consciousness": "Look to your wife . . . look to't. / I know our country disposition well." "My lord, I would I might entreat your honour / To scan this thing no further" (200–204; 248–249). "Country disposition" is a version of Hamlet's pun on "country matters," "a fair thought to lie between maids' legs" (3.2.116, 118–119), and it may be said to originate the explicit focus upon female sexual parts. The double meaning — I know how our Venetian women dispose of their cunts; I know how our Venetian cunts dispose of themselves — substantiates the gross synecdoche by which "wife" becomes "it," resubstantiated a moment later in Othello's soliloquy, transforming women into the things that make them women.

The sexual disgust first made evident in the soliloquy dominates Othello's language for the rest of the play. In his speech to Desdemona in the "bordello scene" (4.2), "the imagery," as Honigmann says, "picks up from" the soliloquy in explicit iteration:

> *Oth.* But there where I have garnered up my heart,
>   Where either I must live or bear no life,
>   The fountain from the which my current runs
>   Or else dries up — to be discarded thence!
>   Or keep it as a cistern for foul toads
>   To knot and gender in! Turn thy complexion there,
>   Patience, thou young and rose-lipped cherubin,
>   Ay, here look grim as hell.
> *Des.* I hope my noble lord esteems me honest.

Oth. O, ay, as summer flies are in the shambles,
   That quicken even with blowing. (4.2.58–68)

Here again, temporal compression: life given and simultaneously denied
("discarded"), desire at once awakened, ripened, and repellently rotten
(the summer flies that quicken with blowing). And once again, the temporal concentration is registered in spatial terms. As Kittredge remarks
(211), *thence*, the repeated *there*s, and finally *here* emphatically situate our
attention. They serve as pointers (the notable image of a line earlier, "the
fixed figure for the time of scorn / To point his slow and moving finger
at," has to reinforce this sense), directing us to witness a sequence of
images that reduce Desdemona to an "it" ("look to't") at once vague
and, with the final image of the angel's rosy lips, grotesquely specific.

Despite all the critical attention understandably devoted to "ocular
proof" and "the gaze," the play's language here works by multiplying
and condensing incompatible images and contradictory significances to
produce an effect not of mastery — a privileged vantage from which to
fix meanings, as in a stable visual field — but of giddiness verging on
nausea.[9] The "mind now floods," as Graham Bradshaw says (179) of the
rapid sequence of images in the bordello-scene passage — "fountain,"
"cistern," "it" — unarrestably, until we are allowed (or required) to
pause at the climactic image of the copulating toads. The toad was regularly associated with lust in the period,[10] but the symbolic content of
the image depends on its structural instability: do we see a closeup of a
couple or a wide-angle shot of an orgiastic swarm? and what accounts
for their malignant metamorphosis — metastasis — from the solitary
toad in the soliloquy? Before we can assimilate, let alone answer, such
questions, the speech introduces a third performer, the rose-lipped
cherub. (Or rather, cherubin. "It is not to be supposed that either Shakespeare, or his contemporaries, knew or cared that this is a Chaldee plural," says Furness [261], trying belatedly to fend off a supposition that
has already risen against his better judgment, summoning with it the
transient image of a celestial host superimposed on the individual angel.) With the cherub comes a crowd of syntactic and semantic complications which effectively undermine and overwhelm any residual sense
of interpretive control. "Ay, here look" in Honigmann and most modern editions derives ultimately from Theobald's emendation in the eighteenth century. Both Q1 and F print "I here look." Since these same early
texts indiscriminately print "I" where the context clearly intends "ay"

("I, there's the point"), the emendation gives readers an otherwise un-available meaning, "ay" as interjection, but dispossesses us of "I" as subject. With both meanings present to the ear, we cannot determine whether Othello is commanding someone else's action (the cherub's? Desdemona's?) or indicating his own.[11]

This problem is compounded by the surprising shift from "there" to "here," which intensifies but also contradicts our sense of position. If we hear the words as an imperative addressed to Patience, then the rose-lipped cherub is now discovered looking out from the place he was look-ing *at* two lines earlier. Eighteenth-century editors emended "here" to "there" in order to avoid this inexplicably abrupt transposition. Modern editors generally reject this emendation (Sanders is an exception), but they frequently aim at the same reassuring effect by glossing "turn thy complexion" as "change your color," with "here" now abstract or tem-poral rather than spatial in significance ("at this point," "taking this into account"). Given the play's thematic context, "change your color" is an irresistible meaning (though as a blackening, surely, not the blanching these glosses often suggest for "grim as hell"); but the context of spatial direction is too emphatic to be displaced or eliminated from the phrase. The suggestion of color change thus compounds rather than solves the already compounded problem — adding an inexplicable transforma-tion of appearance to an inexplicable transposition, so that the cherub is discovered looking out, *now black*, from the place he was looking at, *then rose-lipped*, a moment earlier. The same compounded problem must characterize the other possibilities of Othello's address. If speaking of himself ("I here look"), then he too has changed color, at least symboli-cally (his face is already black); he will be seen both observing and oc-cupying the same place, looking perhaps like the hellmouth of Psalters and Books of Hours — a monster's gaping maw, sometimes duplicated in the middle of its body, generously dilated to accommodate the damned hordes awaiting entry to their eternal perdition. If Othello is addressing Desdemona, then we must for another monstrous moment behold her assuming the posture of *Lear*'s "simp'ring dame," her face between her forks, perhaps displacing the previous occupants, perhaps joining the crowd congregating and congregated at the same rose-lipped black hole that is herself (figs. 1–3).[12]

As distinct identities collapse into one another in this passage, so the distinction between observation and action collapses as well, for the in-habitants of the scene, who both perform and look at their performance, and for us, here and there at once — "here and everywhere," to recall

1. The Jaws of Hell, fastened by an angel, from the twelfth-century
Winchester Psalter. Courtesy of the Bridgeman Art Library.

Roderigo's words about the "wheeling stranger," Othello. We have returned to (not that we ever departed from) the nightmare of volatile
movement and monstrous undifferentiation at the beginning, but with
a difference. When Iago first oppressed Brabantio and us, anxiety concentrated chiefly on Othello as an object, "a thing to fear." By the middle
of the play, Othello has become subject to the same anxieties, now clustered around a different object, a new thing, Desdemona's thing: the
empty and crowded site of occupation to which all interest is irresistibly
drawn and on which all attention tries to fix itself (unsuccessfully, for as

2. "Ay, here look, grim as hell," the gaping mouth of hell,
from the French fifteenth-century *Hours of Catherine of Cleves*.
Courtesy of the Pierpont Morgan Library.

Othello tells Lodovico just earlier about the wheeling Desdemona, "she
can turn, and turn, and yet go on / And turn again" [4.1.253–254]); what
Edgar in *Lear* calls the "indistinguish'd space of woman's will" (4.6.271).

At the very beginning of the play, indistinction takes the form of
pronominal fluidity, our inability to determine whether "his delight"

3. Hellmouth, with face between forks, from the fifteenth-century French *House of the Virgin for Claude I Mole*. Courtesy of the Pierpont Morgan Library.

and "his joy" belongs to "her father" or "the thicklips" (chapter 1). As Edward Snow argues, these "ambiguous pronouns" serve to "connect Brabantio and Othello," thereby "making Othello see Desdemona's love for him through her father's eyes" ("Sexual Anxiety," 388–389). The slippage helps to account for (if not quite explain) the transformation in

The Fall of Othello

the Temptation Scene, when Othello's feelings for Desdemona begin to express themselves from inside Brabantio's proprietary discourse (in the soliloquy and in the second toad passage "keep" expresses the anxiety of ownership: whatever the legal arrangement, Desdemona owns her own appetite, her thing, over which Othello has only custodial rights). A similar slippage underlies the substitution of Cassio for Othello which derives from — that is, takes its first recognizable form in — the pronominal fluidity of Iago's first soliloquy:

> Cassio's a proper man: let me see now,
> To get his place, and to plume up my will
> In double knavery? How? How? let's see:
> After some time to abuse Othello's ear
> That he is too familiar with his wife. (1.3.391–395)

Who is "he" in the last line? When editors like Bevington and Honigmann feel obliged to identify "he" at the end as Cassio, they are trying to warn us off Othello, the closer antecedent; but as Stephen Greenblatt says, the "ambiguity is felicitous; indeed, though scarcely visible at this point, it is the dark essence of Iago's whole enterprise . . . to play upon Othello's buried perception of his own sexual relations with Desdemona as adulterous" (*Renaissance Self-Fashioning*, 233).[13]

Graham Bradshaw argues that "Greenblatt's extraordinary reading is altogether severed from any dramatic context. . . . Iago's speech occurs in the third scene, when the marriage has not even been consummated: Iago doesn't and couldn't see what he is said to be doing and playing upon" (198). Much the same argument could be made against Snow: how can Othello be made to "see Desdemona's love through Brabantio's eyes" as a result of a speech he never hears? But Bradshaw is arguing out of a normative idea of dramatic context — distinct beings performing particular actions at separate times — that doesn't work well for this play. Indeed, the double-time problem arises precisely because the actions of the play seem to inhabit two distinct temporal frames at once. Double time may be a production of Iago, yet another instance of his poisonous work, and from the perspective (just the wrong word) Iago makes us share with Othello in the middle of the play, the foundational stability on which concepts of proper knowledge might be sustained has disintegrated. To complain that Greenblatt's interpretation "leaves the conscious and the unconscious to play peekaboo" (Bradshaw 198) may be — for a play that (to recall Neill's phrase) works "close to the unstable ground of consciousness itself" — less an objection than a description.

Nonetheless, Bradshaw is on to a serious problem of theatrical realization. What kind of ocular proof is available for an absent scene limited not only to discourse but to primal fantasy? It is hard to see how an actor can represent "being made to see through somebody else's eyes," or find a performative equivalent for the textual instability and multiplicity I have described in Othello's speech. Yet it was an actor, or at least an actor-critic, who may be said to have originated this line of interpretation. Long before Stanley Cavell established the terms out of which contemporary discussion has been working, Robert Speaight suggested that Othello's "experience of consummation was so strong and . . . so startling" that the hitherto "chivalrous" Othello could never regard the "gentle" Desdemona in "quite the same way" again; there must have been "something in their mutual delectation which added fuel to his jealousy." Carlisle, who quotes the Speaight suggestion (211), does so only to reject it. "The only person who could possibly benefit . . . would be an actor who is trying to convince himself that Othello could *really* be as jealous as Shakespeare makes him. Perhaps such an actor should simply forget about playing Othello" (214–215; Carlisle's emphasis). From this perspective, such meanings are simply unperformable.[14] In a sense Carlisle is right: literal equivalence — a "muffin"-clutching or crotch-gazing Othello — is pretty clearly a bad idea;[15] but literal equivalence doesn't exhaust performance possibility. Over the long stage history of the play, actors have developed a much richer variety of verbal and especially bodily gestures by which to realize and connect with the kinds of meanings suggested by the text.

As an example, consider again the crucial moment in the Temptation Scene when Iago suddenly takes the initiative: "Ay, there's the point: as to be bold with you . . ." As Edwin Booth remembered it, his father delivered this line

> not as an apologetic parenthesis addressed to Othello, as it is usually printed, but as though catching up and pursuing Othello's own train of thought, and thus insidiously summoning to Othello's memory secret occasions when Desdemona had shown a "will most rank," and had been "bold" with him. I wish I could describe the white-lipped, icy smile, the piercing glance at Othello's half-averted face, and eager utterance, with which my Father said, "Ay, there's the point; as to be bold with *you*." (Furness, 187)

Booth's rendition picks up on a slippage in the line, the effect of which is similar to the pronominal fluidity elsewhere. The infinitive phrase, "to be bold with you," floats independently of a subject: whose boldness is at issue? The context is overloaded with echoes of Brabantio's speech at the beginning, including "a maiden never bold," and in Booth's emphasis, the phrase represents not just Iago's risky frankness but Desdemona's erotic energy as well. In effect, two substitutions are performed: Iago is superimposed over Desdemona (Cavell thought this was the key question, "How has [Othello] come to displace Desdemona's imagination by Iago's?" [130]), and aggressive seduction over affectionate encouragement. Both work "insidiously" to transform Othello's remembered experience into (or to recreate it as) Brabantio's horrified sense of betrayal at the beginning. Both are powerfully reinforced in the marriage parody at the end of the scene, not just in the ritualized language but in the bodily gestures of kneeling performed by the two celebrants.

Such substitutions of both person and affect proliferate in *Othello* (Neill, "Changing Places"), and nowhere more dizzily than in Iago's account of Cassio's dream. With its "strange layering of desire on desire" and "strange confusion of the sexes and sexuality (Cassio and Desdemona, Cassio and Iago, Iago and Othello, Othello and Desdemona, Othello and Cassio)" (Greenberg, 24), the dream represents a volatile scene where "no identity is certain, and no one irreplaceable" (Calderwood, 101). And here another Booth performance, this time Edwin's, discovers an arresting physical gesture to embody the idea. At the line "And then, sir, would he gripe and wring my hand" (3.3.423), Booth "holds Othello's hand, which Othello draws with disgust from his grasp" (Furness, 207). Edwin Booth was not an aggressively physical actor, and his Othello was inclined to underplay the flesh, both its delights and its disgusts: "I think their *heart-throbs* are better than kisses," he declared (Furness, 113), spiritualizing the greeting kisses on Cyprus ("And this, and this") into nothing more than an affectionate embrace. As Iago, however, Booth seemed able — or felt required — to perform with more bodily presence. Cassio's courtly greeting of Emilia is (as it were) despiritualized:

> Kiss her face; not, as is frequently done, her hand. Iago winces slightly, for he "suspects Cassio with his nightcap." I was once so irritated by Cassio's kissing the hand of Emilia, despite directions at rehearsal, that I said "If she would give you so much of her *hand*," &c., which staggered Cassio and set all the actors giggling. (Furness, 105)

The wincing represents Cassio's kiss as an assault on Iago's own body, experienced again in the dream ("and then kiss me hard / As if he plucked up kisses by the roots" [3.3.424–425]) and reproduced as a contaminating assault by Iago himself on Othello's body. Booth's action, like his father's tonal emphasis ("bold with *you*"), helps give a particular immediacy to the familiar Pauline idea that, as Hamlet says, "man and wife is one flesh" (4.3.51).

The surprising physicality of Iago is not limited to Booth, or to this moment in the play.[16] A strong tradition of theatrical practice discovers bodily assault as central to the role's performance, going back at least as far as George Frederick Cooke very early in the nineteenth century who, playing Iago to John Philip Kemble's Othello,

> refused Kemble's summons to rehearsal. "Let *Black Jack*" — so he called Kemble — "come to me." So they went on the boards without previous rehearsal. In the scene in which Iago instils his suspicion, Cooke grasped Kemble's left hand with his own, and then fixed his right, like a claw, on his shoulder. In this position, drawing himself up to him with his short arm, he breathed his poisonous whispers. Kemble coiled and twisted his hand, writhing to get away — his right hand clasping his brow, and darting his eye back on Iago. (Sprague, *Shakespeare and the Actors*, 194)

There are two assaults here — one on Kemble and one on Othello. The effect of violence is intensified by the element of surprise in both the dramatic action and the theatrical situation (no rehearsal). Though no stage direction exists to justify it, the action seems appropriate to the part as written: Iago sets the play in motion with a graphic representation of the sexual act and drives the action relentlessly to an inevitably "incorporate conclusion" (2.1. 260; Finlay's Iago "wiggled his finger" with this phrase [Wine, 61]). Wherever it originates, this tradition carries on to more recent Othellos — Plummer, Finlay, McKellen — whose performances have similarly emphasized a busy and unwanted bodily contact, frequently in the context of a perverse eroticism.[17]

Othello's role too has been particularly rich in significant bodily contact. In his showdown with the elder Booth (described in chapter 1), "Kean upon his entrance 'spontaneously took Booth *by the hand*,'" and the audience "applauded wildly" (Sprague, *Shakespearian Players*, 77; quoting Macready, who emphasizes "by the hand"). This is the Cooke-Kemble story over again, with the roles reversed: another histrionic-cum-dramatic contest, decided with an improvised and unexpected assault, but this time the Othello actor triumphs. More usually, Othello's strong corporeal actions occur during or after the Temptation Scene, by which point, possessed by Iago, his identity has disintegrated into a frenzy of sexual anxiety. Two such episodes deserve special consideration in terms of theatrical performance — the "Collaring Scene" and the trance.

The "Collaring Scene" is the designation given to the fillip of action just after Othello's farewell to his occupation, when the tone changes suddenly to rage and violence:

> Oth. Farewell: Othello's occupation's gone.
> Iago. Is't possible? my lord?
> Oth. Villain, be sure thou prove my love a whore,
>   Be sure of it, give me the ocular proof, [*Catching hold of him*]
>   Or by the worth of man's eternal soul
>   Thou hadst been better have been born a dog
>   Than answer my waked wrath!
> Iago.   Is't come to this? (3.3.360–366)

The stage direction goes as far back as Rowe in 1709. Sprague thinks that it "may record the stage practice of his time," adding that Barton Booth, whose Othello predates "the death of Betterton, is described as having caught Iago by the throat," and that the business is "in all probability as old as the play itself." By the mid eighteenth century, the episode was so familiar "that it could be glanced at, effectively, in a farce." It was a high point of many nineteenth-century stage productions, including Kean's, Macready's (this was the moment of that notable intervention in Liverpool, "Choke the devil! choke him!" — see chapter 1), Salvini's, and others', and it is "a piece of stage business still regularly used today," where it continues to produce powerful theatrical effects (*Shakespeare and the Actors*, 198, 199, 197).

The stage direction, Sprague declares, "is appropriate to the lines rather than implied in them" (*Shakespeare and the Actors*, 198). Honigmann makes a similar claim in his note on "*Catching hold of him*" as "authenticated by" Othello's suicide speech: "I took by th'throat the circumcised dog / And smote him thus!" (5.2.352–353). A sense of this verbal echo of the physical action seems to have motivated Fechter's unusual business at the end. He "dragged Iago to Desdemona's bedside and forced him to kneel; at the words 'circumcised dog' he seemed ready to stab Iago but stabbed himself instead" (Carlisle, 203). Edwin Booth's Othello also connected the collaring with the suicide, though less coercively. He "snatched Iago's own dagger and threatened to stab him with it," as he will later threaten to stab the circumcised dog who is also himself (Sprague, *Shakespeare and the Actors*, 200). Olivier picked up on this business, consciously or not, and made the connection more explicit. "On 'Villain, be sure thou prove my love a whore,'" he "locks Finlay by the throat and hurls him to the ground, threatening him with a trick knife-blade concealed in a bracelet (he will later — in V.2. — use the same weapon to cut his own jugular vein)" (Tynan, 8).

Such enactments help to give bodily specificity to the idea of lost occupation, the fragmentation of Othello's identity as Iago, like perdition, takes possession of his soul. But the Collaring Scene looks forward to the "incorporate conclusion" even more directly, for it is of course Desdemona whom Othello finally strangles. Wilson Barrett made the connection explicit in his version: "after hurling the villain across the chamber," he "suddenly turned to the picture of Desdemona . . . and vented his rage upon it, knocking it down, or even hacking the canvas into pieces" (Sprague, *Shakespeare and the Actors*, 200). Even without such telegraphing, the central idea of Desdemona's displacement by Iago is bound to be present to any audience of the scene, where it will be reinforced by the physical enactment. Consider the performance of Salvini, with whose "animal ferocity" and "colossal physique" the "'Collaring Scene' will always be associated": "Having taken Iago by the throat, shaken him, and dashed him to the ground, he lifted his foot as if to trample on him. . . . Then he recoiled. Iago flung up his arm, as if to protect himself from a fresh attack; but instead, the Moor took his hand and 'penitently, yet with a species of loathing,' helped him to his feet" (Sprague, *Shakespeare and the Actors*, 200). In his sudden withdrawal from rage Salvini replays an action from the beginning of the play, threateningly pursuing Brabantio off stage and then turning gently to the kneeling Desdemona and elevating her into his embrace — a gesture to be repeated yet again in the elevating of Iago to his new status as Othello's lieutenant and his "own forever" at the end of the Temptation Scene (Sprague, *Shakespeare and the Actors*, 188, 201). Such abrupt transformations of identity and feeling are at the heart of Salvini's performance. Passionate desire, as in the lovers' greeting embrace in Cyprus, and murderous assault, as in the Collaring Scene, echo and merge with each other to produce the same "shiver" in their audiences.[18]

Playing in Italian, Salvini seems nonetheless to have found his way into the perverse center of feeling in the play's text — the exciting and appalling identity of killing and kissing, doubly emphasized in Othello's final couplet. In this respect, Salvini's heir is Olivier, who also performed the part with an aggressively sexual and assertively foreign body.[19] In "the stark violence of the brothel scene [4.2]," Olivier revisits with Maggie Smith the perverse eros acted out in his assault on Finlay in the Collaring Scene: "even as he threw Desdemona to the floor again and again, leaving her finally in a stupor, he also wept and embraced her" (Wine, 52). In Tynan's description, Olivier "crawls across the stage and lies on top of Desdemona: for a moment, desire almost overcomes disgust: or rather, both emotions coexist. Othello comes close to committing the crime of which Brabantio accused his daughter: he nearly 'falls in love with what he fears to look on'" (11; this is one way to perform Snow's putatively unplayable idea that Othello comes to "see Desdemona's love for him through her father's eyes"). In what Wine calls "the most memorable moment" of this production, "Othello lifts the slain Desdemona from her death bed and rocks her back and forth with her locked in his arms," in an echo of the Temptation Scene when, "as the ensign inflames the general's imagination with a verbal picture of Desdemona 'naked with her friend in bed / An hour or more', 'the two men even begin to sway gently from side to side, locked together in the rhythm of Othello's pain'" (72, quoting Tynan). In this final embrace, Othello, Desdemona, and Iago merge into a shared identity, constituted out of pleasure and pain, marriage and murder, kissing and killing — the happiness of death. This is the ominous and unintended pun with which Othello greets Desdemona on Cyprus, "If it were now to die / 'Twere now to be most happy," reverberating at the end, as Booth astutely recognized (Carlisle, 262–263), in his defeated acknowledgment of Iago's survival: "I am not sorry neither, I'd have thee live: / For in my sense 'tis happiness to die" (5.2.286–287). The pun is realized — embodied — in the final object that "poisons sight."

Othello's paroxysmal fit is the episode where bodily action is most unspeakably present on the stage. "I tremble at it." Othello's shuddering frame and his collapse into stupor are the primary facts of the scene, and they resonate with other climactic actions: his suicidal collapse at the end ("Should Othello's fall here remind us of his fit?" Honigmann asks); the incorporate sexual climax we are made in our mind's eye to witness over and over again in the play. In the Olivier production, "after Othello breaks down and 'falls' to the ground in a trance," Finlay's "Iago straddles him and thrusts the handle of his dagger into his victim's mouth" (Wine, 61). In the Sam Mendes–David Harewood production at the RNT (1997), "the struggling of Desdemona while being strangled in her bed recalled the motions of the fit" (Dessen, "Postcards," 6). The trance episode seems bound to evoke such images, which is probably why the eighteenth- and nineteenth-century stage refused to play it.[20] But its meaning finds its way back into the play in other forms and at other moments. Hence Kean's first accession to Iago's poisonous slander: "there was a sudden spasmodic contraction of the body, as if he had been abruptly stabbed; his hands were tightly clenched, his features were horribly contracted, his eyes rolled, his shoulders were drawn up, and his frame writhed" (Sprague, *Shakespeare and the Actors*, 195; cf. *Shakespearian Players*, 82). The Collaring Scene itself may be one such moment, to judge from contemporary reports of Kean's performance: his "rage was 'nothing less than convulsion'; it was 'a frantic assault'; and 'the feebleness which followed' gave evidence 'of the intensity of suffering that had consumed him'" (Sprague, *Shakespearian Players*, 84). This description of a spasmodic loss of control followed by depletion, all passion spent, seems equally appropriate to the expense of aggressive and erotic energy. Perhaps the Collaring Scene became invested with such disturbing power partly as a compensation for the loss of the trance episode.[21]

The trance episode is the one where substitution proliferates most promiscuously in the play:

Iago. Lie.
Oth.   With her?
Iago.   With her, on her, what you will.
Oth. Lie with her? lie on her? We say lie on her when they belie her!
Lie with her, zounds, that's fulsome! — Handkerchief!
confessions! handkerchief! — To confess, and be hanged for
his labour! First to be hanged, and then to confess: I tremble at
it. Nature would not invest herself in such shadowing passion
without some instruction. It is not words that shakes me thus.
Pish! Noses, ears, and lips. Is't possible? Confess! handkerchief!
O devil!
                    [He] falls in a trance. (4.1.34–44)

In the various possible actions designated by "lie with," "lie on," and "belie," distinct meanings disappear into a rapid sequence of contiguous postures and punning conceptual connections: lying as slander or mendacity and as inhabitation, as in the clown's explosive quibbling at the beginning of the previous scene: "To tell you where he lodges is to tell you where I lie."[22] Whatever these actions are, who performs them?

What and how many individuals comprise the "we" that lie on her? the "they" that belie her? Distinct identity, dispersed into multiplicity at the beginning of the passage, implodes at the end into separate and sexualized bodily parts — "noses, ears, and lips." An individual seems to emerge for a moment in "his labour." Othello is presumably thinking of Cassio: "lie with . . . lie on" reproduces the sequence of actions reported by Iago of Cassio's dream: "I *lay with* Cassio lately . . . / And then, sir, would he . . . *lay* his leg *o'er* my thigh" (3.4.416–426). But Iago's scurrilously brilliant "with her, on her, *what you will*" requires us to recognize this labor as a production of Othello's desire, reenacting the reenactment of his own labors. He is "absorbed," as Snow argues, "in a fantasy that makes him the guilty and at the same time punitive onlooker in the primal scene of his own marriage" ("Sexual Anxiety," 395), playing Brabantio to his own Cassio.[23]

In conjunction with the intensity of its physical presence, the kaleidoscopic volatility of reference in the trance episode makes it impossible to arrest the flow of signification in a stable interpretation. What does the shuddering mean? To which of the various scenarios performed by these shifting dramatis personae does it belong? All of them make sense, in the manic way that belief achieves oppressive mass in *Othello*.[24] But perhaps the most important substitution acted out in the trance passage — as in the other passages, though I've so far tended to ignore it — is with Desdemona. Othello understands the shuddering as proof, experienced in his own bodily nature, that his anxieties are justified; but "nature" is feminized here, as always in the play, and insistently identified with Desdemona. When Othello "shakes . . . thus," he is reenacting the excitement associated with Desdemona's desire, as Iago described it: "And when she seemed to shake, and fear your looks, / She loved them most" (3.3.210–211). The echo is reinforced by Cassio later, in the trance scene, describing the sexual boldness of Desdemona's substitute, Bianca: "So hangs and lolls and weeps upon me, so shakes and pulls me!" (4.1.138–139). As a reenactment of Desdemona's desire from within himself, Othello's spasm expresses the loss of manly self-command, absorbed by and transformed into passionate abandon — the dispossession he assures Iago, still later in the same scene, that he will not allow her to repeat: "I'll not expostulate with her, lest her body and her beauty unprovide my mind again" (201–203). Othello has become one flesh with his wife, not in the enriching exchange he imagined ("the sea's worth"), but as part of the nightmare shadowed in Iago's first speech, "If ever I did dream / Of such a matter, abhor me" (1.1.4–5), within which

The Fall of Othello

he finds himself abhorred and abwhored, transformed to a contaminated femininity.[25]

For Freud, according to Leo Bersani, sensations are

> experienced as *sexual* pleasure when they are strong enough to shatter a certain stability or equilibrium of the self [and] when the organization of the self is momentarily disturbed by sensations somehow "beyond" those compatible with psychic organization. Sexuality would be that which is intolerable to the structured self.[26]

Othello's shattering abandonment of self into the empty space of female will is evoked throughout the latter part of the play in sexual terms, as the secretion and exchange of bodily fluids. Othello's last words before the murder scene, "Thy bed, lust-stained, shall with lust's blood be spotted" (5.1.36), call attention to themselves as contradicting his earlier resolve to strangle Desdemona; but Honigmann's question, "Is it Shakespeare or Othello who cannot decide how she should be killed?" responds to the suggestion that something deeper is involved.[27] "The interlocking symmetry," as Snow says, "reinforces the sense of confusion in Othello's mind between blood stains and lust stains," part of a process by which various expressions of male and female bodies flow into one another: a "tendency to fantasize both sides of the sexual exchange at once, and interpret each in terms appropriate to the other. Thus Desdemona's virginal blood can become in Othello's fantasies a lustful orgasmic discharge, the female equivalent of his semen."[28]

There may be no way for an actor to represent such a meaning literally on stage, but there are theatrical equivalents nonetheless. Finlay's Iago solicitously "wipes the spittle from Othello's tongue" when Lodovico is announced shortly after the trance. Bob Hoskins in the 1981 BBC version "cups in his hands water from a fountain and sprays Brabantio with it" in the play's opening scene. According to Wine, the gesture merely conveys a jokey insolence: "the enjoyment of mischief for its own sake. No deep passion or emotion troubles him" (61, 77); but in this play, lethal contamination is from the beginning transmitted through liquid and through touch. Hence Boose sees the fountain as

> a cistern, into which Iago gleefully splashes his hands. Besides anticipating Othello's later "cistern for foul toads / To knot and gender in" . . . the prop provides an immediate visual metaphor that allows us to see Iago as moving from cistern to cistern across the city, the source whose poisoning of Brabantio's and later Othello's delight is

visually suggested to us as the poisoning of the city's life fountain. ("Grossly Gaping Viewers," 188)

Even without any actor's gesture, an audience may well wonder, when Iago tells Othello he saw "Cassio wipe his beard" with the handkerchief (3.3.442), what it was he wiped. Fluidity of self is not just a metaphor in the language but a bodily fact of the play. Becoming nothing by becoming one with Desdemona, Othello liquidates by liquidizing his identity. If "matter" means "pus," as elsewhere in Shakespeare, then the matter dreamed of in Iago's first speech, and anxiously sought in the question "What is the matter?" reiterated throughout the play, is the action by which distinct selfhood is expressed — disseminated, wasted, vaporized — into what Othello at the end of the play describes as the "slime that sticks on filthy deeds" (5.2.145).[29]

Sexual repulsion is evoked so intensely and overwhelmingly in the latter part of *Othello* that we risk exaggerating its explanatory power. These abhorrent feelings help to account for Othello's transformation only in the sense of location; the marriage bed is the site where meaning is revealed in the play, not where it is produced. Othello's horrified disgust with Desdemona's body is the consequence rather than the origin of his transformation, not the cause but the effect — and specifically, an effect of discourse. Despite Othello's claim to the contrary, it *is* "words that shakes" him thus. In "we say 'lie on her' when they belie her!" at the beginning of the trance episode, he seems to be sounding out acoustic images, as though testing their effect in the world: like a child acquiring speech or a foreigner a new language, Othello is finding his verbal place in the collective order of knowledge represented by "we." The plural pronoun first replaces the singular for Othello in the Temptation Scene soliloquy, when he has come to understand his particular experience as typical of all married men ("that we can call these delicate creatures ours") and to assume the generalized authority of aphoristic worldliness ("yet 'tis the plague of great ones"). This is the sententious and insouciant tone of the canny insider, Iago-speech ("I know our country disposition well"; "why there's no remedy, 'tis the curse of service"), a "fellow . . . of exceeding honesty," as Othello describes him at the beginning of the soliloquy, who "knows all qualities, with a learned spirit, / Of human dealings" (262–264). Speaking from the cultural center, Iago is the source of the "instruction" by which Othello becomes "invest[ed] in such shadowing passion," the author of the narrative — woven of social, racial, and sexual stereotypes — in which Othello's knowledge (of himself, Desdemona, everything) has become embedded.

The manticore was right; Iago has "the power of description," and Othello "succumbs to the pictures" Iago constructs; in Rushdie's Heideggerian phrase, he reconstitutes his "being-in-the-world" to accord with Iago's. We are back to the unwritten immigrant novel in *Othello*. The play does not record the process of transformation by which Othello comes (as Kirsch says) to "see . . . with Iago's eyes." It provides a beginning, up to and including "Perdition catch my soul / But I do love thee," and an ending, starting with "O curse of marriage," separated by only a few minutes' playing time. In lieu of an extended narrative middle, the play gives us intensely charged erotic images, allowing (or requiring) us to register Othello's transformation as a dramatic fact, but one whose explanation and origins remain painfully obscure.

There is, finally, no satisfactory explanation for the fall of Othello: we "cannot speak / Any beginning to this peevish odds."[30] Not that we therefore abandon the quest for this absent origin; quite the contrary, as witness the massive monuments of interpretation on *Othello* and *Paradise Lost*. As Empson says about the "tension" among different impressions produced by Shakespearean character, if "the dramatic effects are heightened to the verge of paradox," it doesn't follow "that the audience is not meant even to *try* to resolve the contradiction" ("Honest in *Othello*," 240; Empson's emphasis). The question is what sort of attempt is made, what assumptions guide this impossible interpretive enterprise, and what we can use from the various strategies that have been developed among different interpreters at different times.

Bradley offered an eclectic and probably inconsistent assortment of explanations — a not easily jealous Othello, nonetheless vulnerable in his very innocence ("his whole nature was indisposed to jealousy, and yet . . . unusually open to deception" [151]) and an irresistibly clever Iago — each of which may seem more or less convincing but together adding up to less than the sum of their parts and reproducing the problem they were designed to resolve. With Eliot's "*bovarysme*," however, and Leavis's projection backward of an Othello who "has from the beginning responded" with self-dramatizing egotism, a new interpretive mode was initiated, which dominated *Othello* commentary until roughly midcentury.[31] For if "the essential traitor is within the gates" from the outset, then there is no problem of trying to explain Othello's transformation because there is no transformation to explain.[32]

For current critics too, Othello is vulnerable from the beginning —
not, though, because of some peculiar (and presumably corrigible) failure on his part but as the necessary consequence of a general condition. The essential traitor is now "always already" within the gates. In
the dominant version of the current story, we focus on the inherent
vulnerability of Othello's alien status, the "self-doubt of this displaced
stranger" which "opens him so fatally to Iago's attack" (Neill, "Changing
Places," 127), the "precarious entry into the white world" of "a colonised
subject existing on the terms of white Venetian society and trying to
internalise its ideology" (Loomba, 48). From another angle, Othello suffers not from his cultural background but his gender. According to Janet
Adelman, "the impossible condition of male desire, the condition always
already lost," "inevitably soils that object" in which it invests itself and
therefore "threatens to 'corrupt and taint' [Othello's] business from the
start" (69, 63, 67). In the Lacanian description, Othello's fate is determined by desire itself, irrespective of gender. "If language is born of
absence," Catherine Belsey tells us, "so is desire, and at the same moment. This must be so. . . . Desire, which invests the self in another,
necessarily precipitates a division in the subject" ("Desire's Excess," 86,
95). In Stephen Greenblatt's strong and influential version, Othello's
transformation is simply the "clearest and most important" example of
social construction as a general condition: "In *Othello* the characters
have always already experienced submission to narrativity" (*Renaissance
Self-Fashioning*, 237).

This shift in contemporary criticism — from a focus on character to
the ontologically prior formations (social, psychosexual, linguistic) by
which subjectivity is constructed — is clearly a matter of some consequence. Indeed, according to Perry Anderson, writing about theory
since World War II, "the nature of the relationships between structure
and subject in human history and society" is the "one master-problem
around which *all* contenders have revolved" (33, Anderson's emphasis).
From this angle, the current *Othello* may be understood as exemplifying
the further evolution of a process begun in the early part of this century, by which critical commentary distanced itself from the nineteenth-
century habits, epitomized in Bradley, of reading Shakespeare novelisti-
cally for the characters. But the concept of character as a fundamental
premise for literary and theatrical analysis has not vanished; it persists
broadly in contemporary practice, even among those practitioners committed most deeply in principle to its eradication. The evidence for this
claim as well as some speculations about its significance are produced

elsewhere (see appendix); here I am interested in the practical consequence of the persistence of character, which is, I take it, that we ought to locate the decisive move in the interpretation of *Othello* earlier rather than later, between Bradley and Eliot rather than (say) between Heilman and Greenblatt. In conceptual terms: the determining transition occurs not in the shift from one to another conception of the "structure-subject relationship," but from one to another understanding of Othello: the noble vs. the feeble Moor; a protagonist of "perfect soul," whose disintegration is puzzling and painful, or one who is anxiously vulnerable and radically flawed from the beginning, proceeding inevitably to utter collapse.

In the action leading up to the Temptation Scene, the play continually confronts us with problematic passages that seem to demand an interpretive choice between these contradictory views of the protagonist. Especially important are those premonitory moments in the play — "If it were now to die" in Othello's delighted greeting of Desdemona in Cyprus, "when I love thee not / Chaos is come again" at the cusp of the Temptation Scene — which require a strenuous effort of adjustment between our sense of foreboding and the protagonist's evidently happy imagination of his own future. Perhaps the most heavily interpreted of these problematic passages is Othello's Senate speech supporting Desdemona's request to accompany him to Cyprus (1.3.261–275). As Kenneth Muir remarks (190), "Those who think that Othello is deceived about himself fasten on" his claim to be motivated "not / To please the palate of my appetite, / Nor to comply with heat, the young affects / In me defunct" (263–265). "What cloudy irresolutions trouble his awareness of sex?" Robert Heilman asks from a position of superior knowledge that continues even now to be the generative site of critical understanding.[33]

There are, though, other ways of hearing these speeches and of negotiating the distance between the protagonist's and the audience's understanding. According to James Bulman, "if *we* are made aware, through those images, of a possible impending tragedy, so much the better for Shakespeare's art, but it does not necessarily follow that Othello is aware of it or that he must be held accountable for the resonance of every image he uses" (113; Bulman's emphasis). Here difference is just difference, with no necessary superiority on either side. Graham Bradshaw goes further along this line, sensing the distinction as working to Othello's advantage rather than our own. Like Heilman et al., Bradshaw begins with "cloudy irresolutions," acknowledging "some qualm, some tremor of misgiving that I think Othello's speech produces in us," but then (like Bulman) locating these anxieties in the play's audience. The protagonist himself is "so touchingly, magnificently ardent that it seems almost gross to reflect that this marriage has still not been consummated." Reflecting similarly on Cassio's speech imagining Othello and Desdemona's lovemaking, Bradshaw remarks that the "frank and forward, happily human quality in Desdemona, to which fair young Cassio is responsive," is something that Othello in the "palate of my appetite" speech "seems both above and below. Again the question that might be stirring in our mind seems coarse" (186–187). Bradshaw is uncertain which is superior, the spectator's knowledge or the protagonist's. Perhaps Othello is not naive but innocent, in which case we are left feeling not sophisticated but "gross" and "coarse": embarrassed in the face of a nobility that shames us into acknowledging our own meanness of spirit. As Bradshaw understands them, these problematic speeches have the effect of turning us into something like the "guilty reader" in Stanley Fish's version of *Paradise Lost*, "forced to admit that the evil he sees under everyone's bed is his own" (102), or like Hamlet's guilty creatures sitting at a play, driven to proclaim their malefactions. It is no wonder the play's stage history is so rich in anecdotes of resistant audiences crying out in the midst of performance. We are back to the process of guilt-inducing disconfirmation of the play's opening action, which serves to endow Othello with "the glamour of an innocent man that *we* have wronged, and an admiration stronger than he could have achieved by virtue plainly represented" (Hunter, 46; Hunter's emphasis). The same passages which have produced an insecure and vulnerable protagonist become in Bradshaw the basis for a return to the "all in all sufficient" protagonist of the Bradleyan tradition.

Othello is very accommodating of interpretive difference. The feeble and the noble Moor are both theatrically and critically available; both have been played and justified with interpretive argument.[34] The text seems to thrust a choice on us but leaves us free to make the choice: "what you will," to recall the festive subtitle of *Twelfth Night* (or the differently festive phrase with which Iago precipitates Othello's fit). As usual, Shakespeare seems to give us the play we want. At the same time, the choice has real consequences for the kinds of dramatic experience that ensue, producing two fundamentally different plays.

The heroic Othello is built on critical traditions going back beyond Bradley to the Romantics and on theatrical traditions extending considerably further back than this. Hazlitt inaugurates his commentary on

Othello by declaring that "tragedy purifies the affections by terror and pity. That is, it substitutes imaginary sympathy for mere selfishness. It gives us a high and permanent interest, beyond ourselves, in humanity as such. . . . It makes man a partaker with his kind" (200). Hazlitt's emphasis on the strenuous interpretive effort required to engage with a transcendent text ("imaginary sympathy . . . beyond ourselves") survives in a post-Bradleyan afterlife as late as Helen Gardner: "In *Othello* the heroic, as distinct from the exemplary and the typical[,] directly challenges the imagination" (192). This tradition is richly responsive to Othello's nobility but much less so to Iago's malignity, unable or unwilling to recognize the intimacy the play creates between Iago and the audience. Iago is the cause of Othello's fall in Bradley but only in the sense of an abstract evil, separated out from the dramatic action. One consequence is that Iago is rendered incapable of interfering with our admiration for Othello, but another is that we are rendered incapable of understanding Othello's fall. By interpreting us into a position independent of Iago, the Bradley tradition tends to produce a dramatic experience that is fundamentally incoherent. For it is only when we can acknowledge possession of and by Iago's abhorrent dream that Othello's fall turns from a mystery into a simple matter of fact: *these things happen*. Written as we are into Iago's perspective at the beginning, sustained in this alliance, no matter how unholy we know it to be, who knows better than we that these things happen?[35]

It is here that modern and contemporary commentary is most useful. Consider the tone of normative certainty dominant in contemporary views: "always already," "inevitably," "necessarily," "this must be so." *Cosi fan tutti*. These critics are worldly and insouciant; they know their culture disposition well. As I have joined others in remarking (see chapter 1), the antiheroic reading of the play is performed in Iago's voice.[36] This is potentially a good thing. By helping to account for precisely that sense of guilty complicity refused by the heroic reading, twentieth-century interpretation restores the voice that makes for *Othello*'s coherence. But the coherence comes at a price. By treating Othello as an exemplary subject, trapped in the prisonhouse of language or the impossible condition of male desire, current versions leave only his alien status as extraordinary. Once this status is defined as the immigrant protagonist's inherent and necessary vulnerability, we are left with nothing more than abjection: *l'homme moyen sensuel* — not a transcendent "humanity as such" but an unillusioned "human, all too human." A fall from this height, like Gloucester's from what he supposes to be Dover

Cliff, evokes some pity, perhaps, but no fear, and (since we see it coming) not even much surprise. As Rymer said, predictability induces a vexatious and nauseating repetition. The sharp clarity of focus in the current *Othello* is the result of diminished size. Eliminating all traces of what we take to be Victorian sentimentality, we have also drastically reduced the play's capacity to evoke direct sentiment of any kind. Unwilling to respond to Othello's existence at the beginning with "imaginary sympathy," with affection and wonder to a marvelous strangeness emanating from a world elsewhere, a different bodily place, black or tawny but in any case "beyond ourselves" — unable, that is, to see Othello's visage in his mind, we have emptied the play of its tragic power.[37]

According to Helen Gardner, Othello's collapse is not made "ultimately explicable" by "searching for some psychological weakness in the hero which caused his faith to fail, and whose discovery will protect us from tragic experience by substituting for its pleasures the easier gratifications of moral and intellectual superiority to the sufferer" (198). The modern refusal of Othello's heroism may indeed produce anodyne consequences, but the guilt-denying refusal of Iago is a roughly equal though opposite way of anesthetizing us to the play. That Bradleyan and anti-Bradleyan approaches arrive at similar positions is another piece of evidence to suggest that theoretical and epistemological assumptions are less than fully determining. The convergence also serves as further testimony to the assaultive nature of this play, against which such powerful defenses need to be built. And it allows for a return to the proposal I made at the start: that we should try to unite the contradictory interests motivating *Othello*'s interpretive traditions into a position that responds equally to Othello's and to Iago's voice.

I have already acknowledged conceptual and methodological problems in such a project, but there are historical constraints as well, and these make the endeavor not just problematic but impossible. The issue is first of all race. For nineteenth-century audiences, Othello's blackness was an insurmountable obstacle to engaging with the protagonist; embodied in the performer, it constituted an intolerably disgusting assault on their racialist beliefs and led to the "tawny Moor" and to claims of the superiority of the read text to the performed play.[38] Current postracialist beliefs result in a different but equally unendurable situation, for which no accommodation, however compromised, seems to be available. A white actor performing Othello is bound to provoke intense resistance. Miller's attempt to downplay race with Anthony Hopkins as a Hashemite warrior didn't work. On the other hand, Olivier's assertive blackness, risky at the time, is probably so offensive to current sensibilities, not just among right-minded academics, as to be unthinkable.[39] Ruth Cowhig offers what seems like an obvious solution. "There can still be an infinite set of variations in the interpretation of Othello; but for myself, I only want to see black actors in the part (23–24). But a black actor simply transfers the problem to an audience for whom heroic blackness may now be as much of an impossibility (though for very different reasons) as it was for the nineteenth century.[40]

The problem of race may be understood as a particular inflection of a more generally insurmountable problem. We simply can't do the heroic mode; it is fundamentally alien to contemporary sensibilities and beliefs. As Lois Potter remarks, this is not just a problem of theatrical talent. "It is often said that Othello has become an unplayable role because it demands something that no longer exists: a tragic, heroic actor. But a tragic actor needs an audience capable of admiring heroes, not one which, like Iago, is 'nothing if not critical'" (17). Bradley-talk is just not available any more, still less Hazlitt-talk; "humanity as such" is a category quite seen through: the transcendental signified of essentialist humanism. For theatrical interpretation, the heroic Moor is even more impossible (so to speak) than for critical discourse, owing again to the physical immediacy of theatrical experience. Even if we somehow magically transcended the problems of race, a heroic Othello on the contemporary stage would still be unendurable; it would probably generate not so much disgust as embarrassed laughter.[41]

Feminism has a lot to do with this (does *Othello* make woman a partaker with her kind?), and the next chapter will be concerned with the play's highly problematic relation to current feelings about gender. But the current distaste for the heroic goes back further, to the post-Victorian disillusion with "a century of hero worship" (Bentley). There were and are many good reasons for this; a roundup of the usual suspect images would include Passchendaele, Nuremberg (the triumph of the will, the trial of the camp commanders), My Lai. Against this background, our connection to the heroic Othello is bound to be tenuous and ironic. For some time, we've been with Holly and Harry Lime on top of the Ferris wheel in *The Third Man*, looking down at the bombed-out buildings and the tiny creatures. Even if we could by a simple act of will return to an enchanted world, who wants to go back to Empire and Jubilee, especially when such sentiments seem to sign us on to Wyndham Lewis's politics? We probably shouldn't try to retrieve the heroic Othello. We make fools of ourselves when we do, as in those desperate efforts I described at the beginning, trying to read the play and the Simpson case in each other's terms. For better or worse or both, we've lost the noble Moor, but we've got Iago better than ever and perhaps, like Harry Lime, a sour stomach. This may not be the play we want (*Othello* never really has been the play we want), but it's arguably the play we deserve.

5

The "Pity" Act

In his essay "The Women's Voices in *Othello*," Eamon Grennan calls the Willow Song scene (4.3) "one of the most dramatically compelling scenes in Shakespeare."

> To account for the perfection of the sequence one could point to its intimacy, the quotidian familiarity of its action, its unhurried simplicity, its willingness to be ordinary. One might also refer to the atmosphere of private freedom within this protected feminine enclosure[,] an interlude suggesting peace and freedom, within the clamorous procession of violent acts and urgent voices. (277)

Grennan emphasizes the difference of the scene, its felt presence as an interlude closed off from the aggressive anxiety of the male-dominated action on either side. Kenneth Burke understood the scene in much the same way and recognized it as a characteristic performance within the affective economy of Shakespearean tragic practice in general: "*Act IV*: 'The Pity of It.' Indeed, might we not, even as a rule, call this station of a Shakespearean tragedy the 'pity' act? There can be flashes of pity wherever opportunity offers, but might the fourth act be the one that seeks to say pity-pity-pity repeatedly?" ("*Othello*," 174). Burke gives many examples — Cordelia's reunion with Lear, Ophelia's death, Mariana at the grange, etc. — working out of similar material: a quiet lull in the action, women's voices and vulnerabilities, songs, pathos.

If the scene is a crucial contributor to *Othello*'s emotional effects, it is surprising to discover how consistently it has been cut or very substantially reduced in performance. The song itself — "what most moves us . . . the brief, beautiful pause in the center of action" (Grennan, 277) — is absent in the first Quarto. Perhaps it was added in revision or, more likely, cut when the company lost the boy's voice required to bring it off.[1] We might want to join Helena Faucit's lament: "How sad it is that the exigencies of our stage require the omission of the exquisite scene . . . so important for the development of [Desdemona's] character, and affording such fine opportunities for the highest powers of pathos in the actress!" (quoted Carlisle, 182). Of course, Faucit was speaking about the "theatrical exigencies" of a later stage — chiefly (it may be assumed), the extensive script-cutting required to accommodate the elaborate and time-consuming scenic spectacles of nineteenth-century production. Since the Willow Song scene wasn't needed for the plot, it must have been a prime candidate for elimination.

But more is involved than the material demands of Victorian *mise-en-scène*. The scene was cut from the eighteenth-century stage as well, going back at least to Addison's time. Francis Gentleman, writing in the *Dramatic Censor* (1770), suggests the reasons. "If Desdemona was to chaunt the lamentable ditty, and speak all that Shakespeare has allotted for her in this scene, an audience . . . would not know whether to laugh or cry, and Aemilia's quibbling dissertation on cuckold-making, is contemptible to the last degree" (quoted Carlisle, 181). Gentleman takes us beyond strictly theatrical exigencies to more broadly cultural determinants. Like Ophelia's songs, which were similarly censured at the time, the Willow Song scene was felt to diminish the dignity of tragedy with domestic female babble, thereby disrupting or contaminating the norms of at once genre and gender. Too much womanly presence interferes with the appropriate effects (laughter instead of tears, pathos instead of fear, chronicles of small beer instead of the history-making of politics and war); it demands restriction ("guardage"), if not elimination. And here Bianca's particular form of female presence becomes especially interesting. Bianca was absented altogether from the eighteenth- and nineteenth-century stage. This was a more radical and invasive surgery than excision of the Willow Song scene. Since Bianca "subtly affects many episodes, involving the working up of the jealousy of Othello" (Odell, 34), her elimination risked rendering the plot even more "improbable" than Rymer claimed it to be. That prior interpretive tradition felt it necessary to take this risk suggests the extent of the threat Bianca must have represented.[2]

How do we explain this felt need? Writing about the exclusions from F1 to the Shakespeare canon over the centuries based on the changeable criteria of what "sounded right," Stephen Orgel remarks that the early "texts may, of course, be unauthentic, but they may also be evidence that Shakespeare had a greater range of styles than we care for" ("The

Authentic Shakespeare," 3).[3] Diana Henderson expands on the point: "During the nineteenth century, the heyday of a gendered ideology of separate public and private spheres, the generic tag *domestic tragedy* developed as a way of acknowledging these classically improper or 'impertinent' plays" (174). Renaissance audiences seemed to think of genres less as fixed and rigorously distinct categories and more as a set of generative possibilities, and may have thought of gender and sexual difference in a similarly fluid way (Laqueur). When at the end of *Othello* Lodovico exhorts us, with Iago and the others onstage, to "look on the tragic loading of this bed" (5.2.361), he points to the bodies of Othello, Desdemona, and Emilia. That the women share space with the protagonist, not just as adjuncts but as presences who have earned their own place in the story, presumably didn't jar on the sensibilities of the original spectators as it did on the nineteenth-century interpreters, theatrical and critical, who (as we shall see in the next chapter) labored diligently to erase them from the final picture.

The restoration (and even highlighting) in our time of the Willow Song scene and of Bianca is an extraordinary accomplishment. Whether or not it constitutes a recovery of Shakespearean intentions, it does seem to have opened up more interesting literary and theatrical possibilities than the ones transmitted to us by the interpretive tradition. About Emilia, whom I shall turn to first, this seems to be specially true. But tradition is not always obedient to the reformative will. It is shaped often by the irreversible and recalcitrantly material accidents I have mentioned: an adolescent boy actor's voice cracking in the ring, an author's or somebody else's second thoughts, changing theatrical technologies; and by others I will get to: the development of print culture, an aggressive scribe's invention of a dramatis personae list, the Victorian star system. And then there are still others that are unmentionable because, like Althusserian ideology, they cannot be externalized into perception. Some objects poison sight. Even the visible ones are not necessarily changeable as a consequence of critical understanding. The sheer immovable mass of inertia accounts for a lot in history, theatrical and critical and otherwise, and in *Othello*, where inertia is named Iago, the potentially emancipatory and clarifying efforts of innovation are brutally frustrated. From this perspective, we might be skeptical about the new forms of prominence given to the women in *Othello*: are they really so radically discontinuous with the old forms of erasure? Perhaps current attentiveness to the women's voices in the play is, willy-nilly, just a subtle way of silencing them yet again.

"Alas! she has no speech" (2.1.102), says Desdemona, dismissing Iago's nasty complaints about Emilia's noisiness. Desdemona seems right, until the middle of the play. Emilia has no existence apart from her instrumentality to the plot. She passes the handkerchief to Iago but doesn't know what she is doing: "what he will / Heaven knows, not I, / I nothing, but to please his fantasy" (3.3.301–303). We need a verb here. Whatever we supply — do, know, am — seems less consequential than the absence itself. Emilia fills a place in the plot, but the play doesn't encourage any deeper interest on our part. Like "most women" in Pope's couplet, Emilia has "no character at all."

In the context of these expectations, her sudden eruption into prominence is remarkable. It begins, perhaps, with her disgusted generalization about men:

> 'Tis not a year or two shows us a man.
> They are all but stomachs, and we all but food:
> They eat us hungerly, and when they are full
> They belch us. (3.4.104–107)

The intensity comes out of nowhere, and the lines invite us to look toward a substantial personal history, more than "a year or two," from which it has been produced. (Toward it, but not into it. We don't want to fabricate a detailed girlhood for Shakespeare's heroines, like Mary Cowden Clarke; but the sense that it's there is important for the dramatic effect.) Soon after this, she delivers the remark on jealousy, "They are not ever jealous for the cause / But jealous for they're jealous. It is a monster / Begot upon itself, born on itself" (160–162), which has become so familiar because it resonates with what sounds like the play's own authority: she's right, we are made to feel, "speak[ing] true," as she says in her dying speech (5.2.248).

These impressions of sensibility and intelligence, far exceeding mere plot function, emerge into full prominence by the Willow Song scene. The speech about the double standard is a major part of this, but so is the affectionate wit of her rejoinder to Desdemona's idealism: "I do not think there is any such woman." "Yes, a dozen, and as many to th'vantage as would stock the world they played for" (4.3.83–84). By the final scene, her persistent unwillingness to shut up, like Cleopatra's in the midst of Antony's efforts to achieve the heights of heroic demise, requires Othello to share space with her at the center of our concern. Bradley sensed this and saw the pattern of emerging prominence:

Towards few do our feelings change so much within the course of a play. Till close to the end she frequently sets one's teeth on edge; and at the end one is ready to worship her. . . . From the moment of her appearance after the murder to the moment of her death she is transfigured; . . . who has not felt in the last scene how her glorious carelessness of her own life, and her outbursts against Othello . . . lift the overwhelming weight of calamity that oppresses us, and bring us an extraordinary lightening of the heart? (196–198)

Bradley must have been reading his way out of the theatrical tradition; Victorian productions drastically cut her part (they probably recognized and wished to avoid the risk of an upstaged protagonist). But Bradley, though he couldn't have known it, was also reading his way into future performances through to our own time. On the twentieth-century stage, Emilia's enraged refusal to be silent — "like a bellow from the mouth of Melpomene herself," in Herbert Farjeon's description of Edith Evans; "I don't believe Mrs Siddons could touch her" — can "come to dominate the play."[4]

Emilia's most impressive quality in the context of the dramatic action is a pragmatic common sense. Responding to Desdemona's difficulty in imagining infidelity, "Wouldst thou do such a deed for all the world?" Emilia insouciantly points out that "the world's a huge thing: it is a great price / For a small vice. . . . the wrong is but a wrong i'th'world" (4.3.67–69, 79). Sex is just sex, marital fidelity is marital fidelity; they aren't the essence and totality of experience. This is Iago's tone, "the wine she drinks is made of grapes" (2.1.249–250), but without cynicism or malice; the words take us out of the claustrophobic intensity of the play's world into the larger space of the real world — or maybe just the different space of comedy. As Burke says, "Emilia here utters the basic heresy against the assumptions on which this play is built." Given the intolerable experience of a beleaguered audience, such apostasy must seem like an attractive possibility.

Burke's point, though, is that Emilia ultimately serves the purposes of the tragic engagement she seems to undermine. Since "many average members of the audience might be secretly inclined to resist" the "*excessive* engrossment" of high tragedy, it might seem "unwise of the dramatist to let their resistance be expressed on the stage." The effect, however, at least according to Burke, is the reverse: "*her* voicing of our resistance" acts as a lightning rod; by absorbing and redirecting such feelings away from the action, Emilia therefore "protects, rather than endangers, the tragic engrossment" ("*Othello*," 185, Burke's emphases). This shrewd and powerful analysis is particularly applicable to the finale, where Emilia's mockery of Othello's stupidity, by externalizing our own feelings, may seem designed to write us into a more appreciative response to the Moor's greatness of heart.[5] But there are no guarantees that performers and theatrical audiences will stay within the enclosure of (an assumed) original intent. If writing is an "essential drifting . . . cut off from all absolute responsibility, from *consciousness* as the authority of last analysis, orphaned, and separated at birth from the assistance of its father" (Derrida, 316), how much more so is theatrical writing, especially centuries after the original productions? Emilia's power at the end can be made to serve the interests of a heroic protagonist but may also assert her own interests, taking over the place made available by his evacuation. (Hankey's twentieth-century examples are frequently of Emilia's adding vitality to otherwise dull productions.) Even in the original productions, Emilia may have earned her place in the story as more than a surrogate or foil; her transformation at the end of the play is potentially interesting in its own right.

It is, for all her roaring, a quiet change, taking place under the diversely inflected reiterations of "my husband" (5.2.138–150). The play is smart enough not to specify what is going through her mind; audiences can be counted on to endow Emilia with something like their own thoughts, reviewing her actions and their contribution to the catastrophe. Whatever she comes to realize, Emilia's commits herself to resistance:

> *Oth.*   Peace, you were best!
> *Emi.* Thou hast not half the power to do me harm
>   As I have to be hurt. O gull, O dolt,
>   As ignorant as dirt! Thou hast done a deed
>   [*He threatens her with his sword.*]
>   — I care not for thy sword, I'll make thee known
>   Though I lost twenty lives. (156–162)

This should sound thrilling, the stoic self-affirmation heard by editors from Dr. Johnson ("I have in this cause more power to endure than thou hast power to inflict" [quoted Ridley, 186]) to Honigmann ("She can endure more than he can inflict" [*harm* = hurt]). But Shakespeare (and other Renaissance writers) tend to treat Stoic claims with skepticism,[6] and "harm" does not quite equal "hurt." The difference is unelaborated but arresting; it points to an order of sensibility separate from Othello's murderous rage. Ridley heard the distinction: "Emilia is not saying anything about her endurance; she is speaking of her capacity for feeling pain, in her distress for Desdemona, which is far beyond anything Othello can inflict" (186). To Othello's rage she remains vulnerable, and it would be self-deluding to assert otherwise: but if he can indeed harm her, he cannot hurt her, because the hurt derives from Desdemona's death. The power she claims then takes the form of the affectionate loyalty she feels for her mistress, which is hers quite independently of the consequences (almost inevitably lethal, to be sure) of expressing it.

This may be more than we, hearing her speech, can know at this point. It is certainly more than Emilia knows; she still hasn't figured out the narrative facts, let alone their meaning. But even before the handkerchief becomes an issue, she seems to intuit the truth:

> Villainy, villainy, villainy!
> I think upon't, I think I smell't, O villainy!
> I thought so then: I'll kill myself for grief!
> O villainy, villainy! (5.2.187–190)

Despite these exclamations, her next speech is suddenly quiet and reflective, as though the quality of her voice has caught up with the inaudible mental processes that have been propelling her forward: "Good gentlemen, let me have leave to speak. / 'Tis proper I obey him — but not now. / Perchance, Iago, I will ne'er go home" (192–194).

The thoughtfulness here is directly opposite to the thoughtlessness — indeed, mindlessness: "I nothing, but to please his fantasy" — at the beginning of her story. Absorbed then into the conventional narrative of wifely obedience, she now seeks to do something Othello himself (and Cassio) couldn't, find a position of her own outside the space defined by Iago's malignant norms — in her case, literally outside Iago's home. Even now she accepts the conventional story as "proper"; she understands her greater loyalty to Desdemona and to the truth as transcending but not undermining the law. Her deference, requesting the "gentlemen" to let her speak, echoes Desdemona at the beginning, submitting to the Senate's authority. The extraordinarily intimate direct address, "Perchance, Iago, I shall ne'er go home," managed only once earlier in the play (4.2.117), makes it clear that she is still inside his home. (The effect is like Othello's heartbreaking "uncle" to Gratiano four lines later and at 252: at last he's part of the family [Honigmann, *Shakespeare: Seven Tragedies*, 94].) Emilia isn't sure what she's doing or where she's going;

she's making it up as she goes along, feeling her way into a new selfhood, or into selfhood at last. Modern audiences will probably see her on the path to Nora's exciting exit from Torvold's home at the end of *A Doll's House*. People sometimes wonder where Nora is going, and it's even less clear where Emilia can go, given the limited possibilities for women in the Renaissance. Before we can begin to consider such possibilities, Iago abruptly — so Finlay: "a brisk and business-like stab in the back" (Tynan, 19) — kills her.

Desdemona's is another voyage. Unlike Emilia, Desdemona begins with a powerful voice, trumpeting her love for Othello to the world, but she seems to dwindle away during the course of the play, and "Nobody. I myself" (5.2.122) in her final speech seems to constitute an act of self-erasure, an accession to nullity. This quality — or absence of qualities — made her of little interest to eighteenth-century interpreters: "a part of 'unvarying gentleness'" with "'no shining qualifications,'" according to Gentleman, Desdemona "is sufficiently characterized by terms like 'fond' and 'simple'" (Carlisle, 240, 241). Coleridge's sustained reflection on Desdemona's characterlessness (quoted in chapter 2) said much the same thing but made a virtue of defect. Recessiveness was precisely the source of her power as a profoundly moving object of desire. Coleridge's description established the terms for nineteenth-century response. Hazlitt, who brought a different set of critical and political concerns to Shakespeare, nonetheless says of Desdemona that "her whole character consists in having no will of her own, no prompter but her obedience" (205). Anna Jameson acknowledges a "transient energy, arising from the power of affection" but insists that the "prevailing tone of the character" is "gentleness verging on passiveness — gentleness, which not only cannot resent — but cannot resist" (245). Bradley at the end of this line recognized that Desdemona changes during the course of the action, beginning with "the active assertion of her own soul and will" and "showing a strange freedom and energy, and leading to a most unusual boldness of action" (165–166). But like Coleridge and Hazlitt, Bradley understood the later absence of will as Desdemona's essential quality ("Desdemona is helplessly passive. She can do nothing whatever. She cannot retaliate even in speech; no, not even in silent feeling" [145]), and it was this condition which inspired his own deeply affectionate response: "the 'eternal womanly' in its most lovely and adorable form, simple and innocent as a child" (164) and full of "heavenly sweetness and self-surrender" (165).

Such dissent as there was in the nineteenth century came mostly from the theater. The Booth edition (1881) records Ellen Terry's remark that although "my appearance was right" for Desdemona (that is, "a poor wraith of a thing"), "it took strength to act this weakness and passiveness of Desdemona's. I soon found that like Cordelia, she has plenty of character" (quoted Siemon, "Nay," 44). Later on, Terry complained that "no character in Shakespeare . . . has suffered from so much misconception," as "a ninny, a pathetic figure"; in fact, Desdemona "is strong, not weak" (Terry, 128–129). Helena Faucit reflected similarly on Desdemona's appeal for her as a young woman growing up early in the century: "I did not know in those days that Desdemona is usually considered a merely amiable, simple, yielding creature, and that she is generally so represented on the stage. This is the last idea that would have entered my mind" (246). Both Faucit and Terry could build on a performance tradition dating back to the late eighteenth century (Hankey, 52 ff.), when "the awesome, majestic" Sarah Siddons "surprised" and "amazed" audiences "at the transition from her erstwhile tragic majesty to sweet tenderness. The part even seemed to change her physically, 'absolutely [lowering] the figure of the lovely being which had been so towering in Euphrasia, or terrific in Lady Macbeth'" (Rosenberg, 51). But Siddons's performance did not establish either a norm or an ideal for the part on the nineteenth-century stage. For Elizabeth Inchbald, writing at the beginning of the century, "her face can never express artless innocence, such as the true representative of the part requires: her features are too bold, her person too important for the gentle Desdemona." As Carlisle wryly comments, "too much tragic majesty remained" (241). At the beginning of the next century, William Winter made much the same complaint, describing Siddons's performance as "greatly overweighting a part the predominant and essential characteristic of which is gentleness" (*Shakespeare on the Stage*, 250). Unlike Inchbald, who could well have seen Siddons's performance, Winter was working only with hearsay; but his very willingness to trust in such reports testifies to the established stability of the nineteenth-century consensus.

One way to measure the power of this consensus is to focus on the question of Desdemona's resistance in the murder scene. Othello's "Down, strumpet!" and "Nay, if you strive — " (5.2.78, 80) are textually embedded stage directions that call unambiguously for Desdemona's physical struggle. George Swan understood as much in his advice to Garrick: "He was convinced [that] Desdemona should so effectually resist Othello's efforts to smother her that he would be forced to use the dagger after all. Swan interpreted the text to imply that Desdemona twice struggles from Othello's grasp." But Swan's advice, however, was only hypothetical, probably not deriving from theatrical practice and almost certainly not leading to it.[7] In a similar way, a strongly resistant Desdemona on the nineteenth-century stage remained only an un- or under-represented possibility. Though his acting edition called for fierce struggle, "Fechter's performances apparently did not enact" them fully if at all (Siemon, "Nay," 43), for reasons that were suggested by Sir Theodore Martin:

> These stage directions make one think rather of the murder of Nancy by Bill Sikes, than of Othello and Desdemona. Even now there is too much violence. Why should Desdemona spring out of bed, to be brutally thrust back into it? . . . "Tradition" was right in confining Desdemona to her couch: Mr. Fechter is wrong in hazarding the ludicrous effects of the opposite course. (Quoted Sprague, *Shakespeare and the Actors*, 214)

Or consider the case of Fanny Kemble. Playing the role for the first time in 1848, she determined to "make a desperate fight of it . . . for I feel horribly at the idea of being murdered in my bed. The Desdemonas that I have seen, on the English stage, have always appeared to me to acquiesce with wonderful equanimity in their assassination. On the Italian stage they run for their lives." But she was thwarted on the one hand by an apparently edited script ("Shakespeare's text," she worried, "gives no hint of any such attempt . . .") and on the other by the material realities of costume and taste: "against that possibility was the 'bedgown' she was wearing" (Sprague, *Shakespeare and the Actors*, 213; Carlisle, 259). When Kemble revisits the question in 1884, she thinks differently. She

> berates Salvini for failure to follow the stage tradition and the manifest "intention of Shakespeare" . . . for a passive Desdemona . . . : "The terrified woman cowers down upon her pillow like a poor frightened child. Indeed, the whole scene loses its most pitiful elements by allowing Desdemona to confront Othello standing, instead of uttering the piteous pleadings for mercy in the helpless prostration of her half recumbent position. (Quoted Siemon, "Nay," 43)

Kemble's change of mind probably had something to do with the weight of contemporary opinion against making a fight of it. Siemon quotes an "outraged response" in midcentury "to Brooke's Desdemona [Sarah Anderton] having 'struggled in almost an erect position' as 'out of character'" ("Nay," 43). It most probably had something to do as well with the sheer power of the normative tradition — the "unalloyed delight," as Charlotte Vandenhoff's 1851 performance was described, "to see her sad, fearful, yet gentle as a bruised dove bend meekly to the implacable jealousy of the swart Othello, and receive her death, while kissing the hand which gives it" (quoted Carlisle, 244). Sustained exposure to this sort of thing must have been very difficult to resist.

This is not to say that resistant Desdemonas did not appear: Gustavus Brooke's and Salvini's (as well as the other Italians'), as we have seen; Madge Kendal opposite Ira Aldridge, and Faucit and Terry as well. But these possibilities too were underrepresented. Faucit "fell as a victim to the star system," which required that a leading actor, "whether woman or man, had to shine as the dominant light in a play, not merely contribute to the effect of chiaroscuro." As a consequence, "she rarely acted the role during her touring days, the longer and much the finer part of her career." As for Terry, though "she gave a memorable interpretation, spirited as well as pathetic," her "theatrical fortunes were bound up with" Irving, and when he abandoned Othello after 1881, Terry's "Desdemona was lost to the stage from that time. [Hence] the two actresses who should have been most identified with the role actually performed it for relatively brief periods" (Carlisle, 249–250). Like the dramatic character, the role itself on the pre-twentieth-century stage is saturated with the pathos of defeated potentiality.

Maggie Smith, who performed opposite Olivier in the premier production of our time, suggests how far we have come from the nineteenth-century theatrical tradition. Smith of course is not "a poor wraith of a thing," like Ellen Terry; her body type didn't predispose her to representing a bruised dove, and she played Desdemona out of her own strength.

The milksop Desdemona has been banished from this stage and a girl of real personality and substance comes into her own. Fighting back, not soppily "hurt," but damned angry, she makes the conjugal battle less one-sided and so more interesting and certainly more exciting. When these two throw the book at each other bodies come hurtling after it; and what a relief it is not to see two high-bred ninnies bleating reproachfully at each other from opposite sides of the stage but actually striking each other to the floor in the grandeur of their agony. (Tynan, 16)

But in modern criticism, as distinct from theatrical interpretation, the image of Desdemona's self-surrendering sweetness has managed to sustain itself, though at an increasing distance from the veneration of earlier response. Burke says that "in her preparations for Othello's return . . . there are strong forebodings (making her rather like a victim going willingly towards sacrifice). She seems doubly frail, in both her body and her perfect forgiveness" ("*Othello*," 174). This sounds surprisingly like residual angel-in-the-house sentiment, but Burke's locus is ritual enactments rather than gender norms or marital relations. Whether or not every man wants a woman like Desdemona, as Coleridge claimed, every sacrificial plot does, and "the willow song casts her perfectly in the role of one preparing meekly for sacrifice" (184).

This relocation of affect portends a more radical change in recent criticism — a withdrawal or even reversal of affect. Jane Adamson is struck by "Desdemona's strange passivity in the face of the violence that assails her" (236). Where nineteenth-century audiences delighted in Desdemona's prostrate speechlessness, for Adamson "her peculiar passivity" is "most disturbing" (220): "what we find hardest to bear" in the murder scene is Desdemona's "terrible silence. . . . She has no strength or will to resist it or even to cry out for help" (257). More recent criticism, motivated by an augmented methodological and ideological self-consciousness, has nonetheless experienced a similar discomfort.[8] Ania Loomba recalls that "as undergraduates at Miranda House, Delhi[,] . . . who were 'dissatisfied' with Desdemona's silence in the face of her husband's brutality, we were told that we did not 'understand' her because we had never been 'in love.'" Loomba acknowledges Desdemona's self-assertiveness early in the play, but laments that "she then betrays it by her submissiveness. Discussions with my own students located such a betrayal as the source of our own uneasiness" (39).

Whether celebrating or deploring it, the critical tradition has been remarkably consistent for two centuries in describing Desdemona as silent, submissive, and in a sense even complicit in her own murder. It is therefore worth noticing on what an unsubstantial foundation this massive interpretive edifice has been constructed. Despite Adamson's "terrible silence" and Loomba's "silence in the face of her husband's brutality," Desdemona vigorously protests her innocence in the murder scene

(5.2.58–61, 66–68) and, finally desperate, looks for any expedient to protect herself against Othello's murderous assault: "O, banish me, my lord, but kill me not! . . . Kill me tomorrow, let me live tonight! . . . But half an hour! . . . But while I say one prayer! . . . O Lord! Lord! Lord!" (77–83). This is not merely speech; it seems to be the powerfully sustained eloquence Henry Jackson heard in 1610 ("she pleaded her case very effectively throughout," *optimè semper causam egit*). As Anthony Dawson argues, "Jackson's account . . . puts into question the reading of the victimized, subjected Desdemona that some recent critics have seen as central to the cultural work the play is said to have performed" (35). To be sure, these lines can be delivered in the manner Kemble recommended, as "piteous pleadings for mercy" (Shakespeare's dramatic writing is infinitely appropriable); but the embedded stage directions, "Down, strumpet!" and "Nay, if you strive — " are a different matter. The words nineteenth-century script-doctors cut away, strong twentieth-century interpreters seem to have erased.

Such extraordinary reconstructions of the murder scene can't have been created out of nothing, but if we look backward over the action of the play it is hard to find the evidence of acquiescent self-surrender on which they would be based. Perhaps the earliest relevant episode shows Desdemona, just before the Temptation Scene, acceding to Othello's request to cease soliciting for Cassio and "to leave me but a little to myself": "Shall I deny you? No, farewell, my lord" (3.3.85–86). But this is hardly a defeated submission. Othello has apparently already informed Desdemona that he intends to reinstate Cassio (3.1.45 ff.), and he promises as much here again: "I shall deny thee nothing" (84). Moreover, Desdemona's exit speech, "Be as your fancies teach you? / Whate'er you be, I am obedient" (88–89), makes obedience sound like self-affirmation, almost bravado. The obvious analogy with Emilia's "I nothing, but to please his fantasy" is primarily a contrast. Unlike Emilia, Desdemona manifests a distinct and even freely critical identity, implying perhaps that Othello is caught up in silly obligations of military protocol ("your fancies"), while she at least is holding up her end of the bargain. Indeed, commentators are sometimes irritated by her needling here, although Othello's "Excellent wretch!" just after confirms the context of affectionate delight within which he has understood the exchange.

With the first signs of Othello's madness, Desdemona maintains this tone, meeting his insistence head on with her own ("The handkerchief!"

"I pray, talk you of Cassio" [3.4.94]) and resistance ("I'faith, you are to blame" [98]). Her first instinctive reaction to the slap is a protest, "I have not deserved this" (4.1.240). After the appalling "rose-lipped cherubin" speech, when Othello accuses her of being a "strumpet," she is again angrily assertive in denying the charge: "By heaven, you do me wrong" (4.2.83). This isn't "peculiar" or "strange passivity in the face of violence" — it isn't passivity at all; and in the context of the Renaissance theatrical practice, audiences of *Othello* would have much more likely been impressed by Desdemona's self-assertion than by her passivity.[9] Even at the end of the bordello scene, although she is by now almost fully traumatized ("Do not talk to me, Emilia; / I cannot speak, nor answers have I none / But what should go by water" [104–106]), Desdemona nonetheless generates an impressively sarcastic anger: "'Tis meet I should be used so, very meet. / How have I behaved that he might stick / The small'st opinion on my greatest misuse?" (109–111). These lines are delivered on an empty stage, Desdemona's only soliloquy; the play seems to be going out of its way to foreground an emphatic resistance in the face of inexplicable hostility — which is just what Henry Jackson heard.

That this resistance seems to diminish in the course of the dramatic action is certainly true, but the question is, what should we make of its diminution? About her request to Emilia, "Lay on my bed my wedding sheets: remember" (4.2.107), Neill says that "Desdemona shrouds herself here in a narrative of eroticized self-immolation as self-consciously as Othello in his final speech will dress himself in the narrative of heroic self-conquest," pointing to "the fashion, increasingly popular amongst aristocratic women in the early seventeenth century, for having one's corpse wound in the sheets from the marriage night" (*Issues of Death*, 165). But Desdemona is not acting with coherently self-conscious purpositivity, and in its immediate context her request seems to be a hopeful gesture, designed to "win my lord again" (151), presumably by reminding him of what she remembers about the shared delight in their original union. By the Willow Song scene, she has abandoned protest (at least temporarily) for acquiescence. "We must not now displease him," she tells Emilia (15), acceding to Othello's request for Emilia's dismissal. We know that the accession has the effect of facilitating the murder, but is this her intention?

This question focuses on character, the effect of Desdemona as a developing consciousness within the dramatic action and affective economy of the play. If we want to ask it (and not everyone does),[10] then a

good place to look for an answer is the long and tortuous speech, addressed to Emilia or herself or both, with which Desdemona first reflects
on the meaning of Othello's transformation:

> Something sure of state
> Either from Venice, or some unhatched practice
> Made demonstrable here in Cyprus to him,
> Hath puddled his clear spirit, and in such cases
> Men's natures wrangle with inferior things
> Though great ones are their object. 'Tis even so,
> For let our finger ache and it indues
> Our other healthful members even to that sense
> Of pain. Nay, we must think men are not gods
> Nor of them look for such observancy
> As fits the bridal. (3.4.141–151)

Desdemona begins with an attempt to account for Othello's inexplicable harshness as a displacement of political irritation ("something sure
of state"). In effect, she buys into a distinction between the male public sphere and the female domestic sphere ("inferior things"), thereby
abandoning her earlier desire to share the totality of Othello's life. This
distinction between male and female nature is almost immediately negotiated with a sense of shared bodily existence: "our finger" is not a
peculiarly female possession. But then bodily existence seems to have
become gendered female, as in the next lines "we" is clearly limited to
women in contrast to the men as "them." In acknowledging the inevitable abatement of love from "the bridal," Desdemona picks up on
Emilia's speech just a minute or two earlier, "'Tis not a year or two . . . /
They belch us." She lacks Emilia's disgusted abhorrence but moves in
that direction — which is to say, toward the origin of such beliefs in
Iago's voice. As Othello himself had succumbed to a generalizing misogyny, "that we can call such delicate creatures ours," so Desdemona
begins apparently to settle into a generalizing misandry, us and them.
She echoes his acquiescence to necessity ("'Tis destiny unshunnable,"
"Nay, we must think"), both of them echoing Iago at the very beginning
("Why, there's no remedy. 'Tis the curse of service"). Who can blame
her? She has more of a cause and, after all, the wine she drinks *is* made
of grapes. Maybe Auden was right to think Iago was right: "Given a few
more years . . . and she might well, one feels, have taken a lover" ("The
Joker in the Pack," 269).

This entire process is abruptly reversed, however, in the extremely

awkward and complicated set of reconsiderations at the end of Desdemona's speech:

> Beshrew me much, Emilia,
> I was, unhandsome warrior as I am,
> Arraigning his unkindness with my soul,
> But now I find I had suborned the witness
> And he's indicted falsely. (151–155)

Turning on the earlier self who was arraigning Othello's unkindness, she
tries to recapture the feelings of their reunion on the beach when Othello had addressed her as "my fair warrior." Her status as an "unhand-
some warrior," though, seems still to occupy the present ("as I am"),
and it is difficult to sort out the putatively real Desdemona at the end of
the speech from a variety of superseded voices earlier on. Can "my soul"
be totally recreated into a new "I" that now suborns its own earlier position? The attempt at a willful self-reconstruction is rendered suspect
by the oddly passive "find"; from this position, the different beliefs at
the end of the passage are not so much affirmed as observed in a way
that renders them problematically abstract, maybe even dissociated.

It is possible to understand this speech as "a nervous *refusal* to acknowledge — even to herself — that Othello could possibly be jealous or
suspicious" (Adamson, 225; Adamson's emphasis). Desdemona is then
pathologically self-deluding, deliberately disconnecting herself from the
truth of her situation in a way that abandons self-protection. If "Nobody. I myself" constitutes self-cancellation, then this speech seems to
be the place from which she embarks on the course that reaches that
termination. But is Desdemona refusing the truth of what Othello has
become or affirming the reality of what he was when she saw his visage
in his mind, and further affirming the value of her continuing response?
"Unkindness may do much, / And his unkindness may defeat my life /
But never taint my love" (4.2.161–163). Like Emilia at the end, Desdemona asserts her own power here. Othello's unkindness may defeat her
life, but it's her choice to love him. Julia Genster is one of several recent commentators who hear in Desdemona's "last words," asking to be
commended to her kind lord, "not an act of submission but a challenge"
(804–805).[11] From this perspective Othello was right (though he had the
wrong word for it) to say "that we can call these delicate creatures ours
/ And not their appetites" — sensing in Desdemona a powerful energy
that he would never fully own, and that was Desdemona's own self.

In the beginning of the Willow Song scene, responding to Emilia's

"Would you had never seen him!" Desdemona once again reaffirms her choice: "So would not I; my love doth so approve him / That even his stubbornness, his checks, his frowns / — Prithee unpin me — have grace and favour" (16–20). In the way "my love" is represented as acting independently of and in contradiction to the self-preserving "I," Desdemona strikes a note of passivity and self-exposure that may seem to verge on masochism. But the song that follows, for all its plaintive pathos, moves into a stronger and more assertive tonality. According to Joel Fineman,

> the central, we can say the most Shakespearean, fact about this "Willow song" is that it is *not* by Shakespeare, and would have been recognized as such, i.e., as non-Shakespearean, by the original audience for the play. What is called Desdemona's "Willow song" is, in fact, a traditional ballad, reproduced in miscellanies, that appears to have captured Shakespeare's aural imagination. ("The Sound," 94; Fineman's emphasis)

But the even more important fact is that ballads in the play are part of the anonymous tradition by which Iago acquires power over people's souls. If he performs his cultural work "close to the unstable ground of consciousness itself," this is precisely the place from which Desdemona's discourse is generated in the scene. Like Brabantio at the beginning ("Have you not read . . . / Of some such thing?"), she is traumatized to the point where anything comes out of her mouth that has found a place in her mind ("Mine eyes do itch, / Doth that bode weeping? . . . I have heard it said so" [57–59]), including especially the song: "That song tonight / Will not go from my mind" (28–29).

In this context, the remarkable thing is that the song doesn't take possession of Desdemona's soul; she takes possession of it. She substitutes a female singer, and her affection for "Barbary" is clearly a displacement of her affection for Othello. The play goes out of its way to emphasize her transformative power by calling attention to her mistake: "Let nobody blame him, his scorn I approve — / [*Speaks.*] Nay, that's not next" (51–52). The words pick up on her own claim at the beginning of the scene, "My love doth so approve him," now establishing "I" and "my love," problematically disconnected earlier, as an absolute identity. Revising herself, she also revises tradition. The "right" line in the versions that survive is "Let nobody blame me, her scorns I do prove."[12] The original audiences wouldn't have focused on the details but might well have sensed the fundamental difference between the tradition, which emphasized the passive suffering of unrequited love, and Desdemona's version, which proclaims even in the midst of such grief a continuing affirmation of her own power to love. "O, you are well tuned now: but I'll set down / The pegs that make this music, as honest / As I am" (2.1.198–200). Honest Iago keeps his promise for everyone in the play, with the partial exception of Emilia. But Desdemona sings her own song.

The interpretive tradition has been generally unwilling or unable to hear Desdemona singing her own song. During the period between Coleridge's claim that "Desdemona has no character at all" and Sinfield's that "Desdemona has no character of her own" (54), we have been consistently replacing Desdemona's voice with silence and transforming her presence into absence. The nineteenth century doted on its own created emptiness, and now we deplore it; but the tenacity with which the basic structure has sustained itself is remarkable — and perplexing. The adorably prostrate Desdemona served the nineteenth century in ways that look either silly to us now (Lillian Gish tied to the railroad tracks) or pornographic. The objectionably prostrate Desdemona of contemporary opinion must also be serving important cultural needs, but it's difficult to be sure what they are. Robert Brustein once said that "the passive, virtuous, all-suffering Desdemona is a part . . . difficult to cast in an age of women's liberation" (quoted Wine, 67); but feminist criticism has constructed, or at least generally cooperated in maintaining the construction of, Desdemona in terms of such qualities. It is one thing to emphasize that "Desdemona only invokes the right to owe duty to her husband and not her own autonomy"; even the strongest theatrical Desdemonas have represented the character as fundamentally unwilling and almost unable to imagine selfhood in terms of an exclusively self-enclosed or self-contained space.[13] But to conclude from this that Desdemona therefore doesn't serve the interests of "our critique of the silencing of women in literature and in the classroom" (Loomba, 40) moves into much more speculative territory. It assumes — unnecessarily if not wrongly — that Desdemona's affectionate generosity necessarily constitutes an acquiescence to her own victimization, and (a sort of reverse Falstaff) contributes to witless self-destruction in at least some members of the audience.

Henry Jackson's response — not only moved to tears by the pathos of Desdemona's situation, but impressed with the power of her performed selfhood — is an intriguing exception to subsequent interpretation. There is no reason to believe that Jackson was a protofeminist, but as Paul Yachnin points out (26–31), his rhetorical training seems to have predisposed him to an appreciative response to theatrical performance independent of his own particular opinions. Yachnin argues that Renaissance theater negotiated a "powerless" position for itself — meeting the audience in a space outside the normalizing structures of real belief and action (1–24). This is not the space within which most current interpretation wishes to engage with Renaissance drama. We're interested in role models; maybe we have to be.[14] However we explain it, the fact of Desdemona, "subdued to the very quality" of Othello rather than committed to her own autonomy, is simply an intolerable prospect, not to be endured. Like Othello's heroism, it so violates fundamental convictions about the world that it has been rendered invisible. We see instead the passivity and prostration inflicted on us by a perverse interpretive tradition, thereby reinforcing this tradition in a way that, like Desdemona herself as we fabricate her, seems to cooperate with the forces that defeat desire. O the pity of it. But that's just the way it is; as Iago says, "there's no remedy."

Shakespeare invented Bianca out of almost nothing, two widely separated sentences in Cinthio which refer in passing to two apparently distinct women, neither of whom is named or speaks or contributes to the action, one of whom is designated "*una meretrice*" (Furness, 385). For a long time, as we have seen, nothing came of nothing. There was no place for Bianca on the eighteenth- or nineteenth-century stage. She isn't mentioned in Bradley, the summa of nineteenth-century critical traditions. *Shakespearean Tragedy* is mostly a male preserve, but Bianca is unrepresented among Anna Jameson's heroines and Helena Faucit's female characters as well, and her girlhood never fired Mary Cowden Clarke's imagination. Like their theatrical counterparts, nineteenth-century critics were not fondly overcome by Bianca's particular kind of female charm.

She came into view mostly in the middle of this century. More relaxed beliefs about female propriety and critical decorum must have had a lot to do with this. But Bianca's emergence corresponded to a shift in critical method and assumptions as well, away from dramatic characters conceived as though their speech and action were generated from particular desires and histories, and over to the concept of a unified design, to which the characters were only contributory effects. Unity took different forms — author, thematic coherence, world picture, spatial form, poetic language — but all could serve to make Bianca a prominent constituent. In one influential version, Maynard Mack offered Bianca as a "mirror" image contributing to structural integrity. "At the point when, in Othello's mental imagery, Desdemona becomes the soliciting whore . . . Bianca enters in the flesh [and] flourishes the magic handkerchief, now degenerated [to] the subject of jealous bickering" (252). The powerful achievement of such criticism is impressive. It contributed significantly to the creation of Bianca out of almost nothing into an important dramatic presence. At the same time (as with Desdemona), we might wonder whether this creation is also a fabrication in the pejorative sense, and (if so) what factors have contributed to the distortion.

The trajectory of Bianca's career is much like Emilia's. She is clearly functional to the plot in the middle, but she emerges into prominence at the end, in her case flaring up for a very brief but quite spectacular moment in the play's penultimate scene. "O fie upon thee, strumpet!" Emilia's cry, provoked by Iago's "This is the fruits of whoring," reiterates the false accusation at the play's center. For this reason, Bianca's immediate denial, "I am no strumpet / But of life as honest as you, that thus abuse me" (5.1.116–123), earns respectful attention. It "rings with simple dignity as well as indignation," Jane Adamson says; Bianca "is *emotionally* no more a 'strumpet' than Emilia (whom Iago accuses of promiscuity) or for that matter Desdemona, who has also beguiled many men in her time, including . . . a man who in turn calls her a 'strumpet'" (*"Othello" as Tragedy*, 242, Adamson's emphasis). By insisting on the *honesty* of her life, Bianca's denial draws us into the energies of an extraordinarily overloaded term. Empson claimed about the "fifty-two uses of *honest* and *honesty* in *Othello*" that "there is no other play in which Shakespeare worries a word like that . . . as a puzzle" ("Honest" in *Othello*," 218). Emilia's own denial just after adds to the intensity of this moment: "As I?" she wonders, in response to Bianca's "honest as you." Then, "Foh, fie upon thee!" (5.1.123). Emilia may be recalling her earthy, pragmatic arguments about marital fidelity just earlier; we probably are. The exchange is charged with a sudden anxiety about innocence and guilt, resonating (like so much in *Othello*) on a sexual register.

Or so it might be argued; but neither theatrical nor critical interpretation has been interested in pursuing such implications. For at least one spectator, Kate Skinner's Bianca in Jude Kelly's 1997 Lansburgh production evoked the kind of complicated and affectionate interest I suggest above.[15] Nonetheless, on the stage, as Adamson remarks, "Bianca is generally played as a (rather sluttish) whore" (242), an effect to which skin color has often contributed. The very sexy and very black Bianca in the

The "Pity" Act

recent Branagh-Fishburne movie may well owe something to Trevor Nunn's deliberate decision in 1989 to cast Bianca as black in order "to show "Cassio's double standard in sexual matters — he idealises the divine Desdemona, but relieves himself with a harlot" (quoted Vaughan, 229); and behind both of these may be Mary Miller's "swarthy local whore . . . spat upon by her compatriots for fraternizing with the occupying troops" in John Dexter's 1964 production (Tynan, 14). Kate Skinner's Bianca was white, but the Kelly production was a "photo-negative" — everybody of consequence was black except for Skinner and Patrick Stewart as Othello, so the casting was "appropriate" for "a role that these days is usually given to African-American actors" (Johnson-Haddad, "The Shakespeare Theatre *Othello*," 10). Perhaps the most remarkable inflection of Bianca's powerful strangeness occurs in George Tabori's 1991 production for the Akademie Theater in Vienna, where she is "dressed as an Arab woman in flowing black robe and head-covering, her face and hands a deathly white, her lips and eyes outlined in black," visible at the very beginning of the action, shaking a "mysterious rattle that was echoed elsewhere in the auditorium at the end of each act." She neither speaks nor is spoken to, but "throughout the evening, this menacing shadow could be glimpsed moving quietly in the peripheral darkness or even creeping about under the stage itself," suggesting "some external dark power controlling the actions of the play" (Carlson, 228). A stage tradition seems to have emerged to play Bianca as a mysteriously dark lady, a thing of darkness.

Critical interpretation has proceeded along similar lines. At least one earlier critic, Kenneth Muir, puzzled over the passage ("Bianca is perhaps more honest, in one sense of the word, than Emilia" [214]) but without elaboration. Empson himself, commenting on the "divergent uses of the key word" by even the minor characters, notes that "the unchaste Bianca, for instance, snatches a moment to claim that she is more honest than Emilia" (218). But by abstracting the puzzling qualities of the speech from the speaker, Empson makes clear his conviction that whatever uncertainty is attached to the concept, "honesty" is something his "unchaste Bianca" does not possess; whatever whores are, Bianca really is one — "in" (to recall Mack's phrase) "the flesh."

In the last quarter of this century, criticism has cashed in esthetic coherence for the contingencies of history and (most recently) culture. We are still interested in Shakespeare's structural relations, but these tend now to be characterized as asymmetrical power relations, based on gender and social difference. With the ascendency of feminist and materialist assumptions, our beliefs and their critical deployment have changed profoundly since the time of Mack and Empson and Muir. We might expect Bianca to look different as a consequence, but not so. Although *Othello* is now routinely held to represent pathological male debasements of a healthy female sexuality,[16] nonetheless even critics who interrogate the process by which women are called whores reproduce it almost without exception in the case of Bianca.[17] Thus according to Michael Neill, the play world's "whispering can . . . make 'the fair Desdemona' seem indistinguishable from the prostituted Bianca (whose own name, ironically enough, means 'white' or 'fair'). It is a place where no one is truly at home, and where the only native Cypriot we meet is, significantly, the jealous camp-follower, Bianca" ("Changing Places," 118). A Cypriot camp-follower: where does such detailed assurance come from? James Calderwood and Douglas Bruster offer strong materialist arguments about property as the unstable basis for identity in *Othello*, yet (inconsistently) stabilize Bianca's identity as (in Calderwood's words) "that mortal enemy of all virtuous wives, the whore" (55) or (in Bruster's) "a once-dependent prostitute whom [Cassio] has jilted" (84) — all because she is the handkerchief's final custodian. Maynard Mack all over again. How to explain this? To adapt Emilia's question about Desdemona, why should we still call her whore?

According to Valerie Traub, "although *Othello*'s Bianca and *The Comedy of Errors*' 'courtesan' are ostensibly courtesans, they are treated as common whores by the other characters" (158); but in a play centered in misprision, we should be skeptical about "the other characters." Adamson is justified in her insouciant general dismissal of Iago; "we need not accept *his* pejorative meaning" (242). Moreover, the peculiar terms he uses to describe Bianca — "A housewife that by selling her desires / Buys herself bread and clothes" (4.1.95–96) — should reinforce our suspicion. The designation "housewife" ("huswife" in the original texts) floats ambiguously between pejorative (hussy, whore) and favorable meanings, an effect reinforced by contradictory signals about Bianca's position in the overall action and reflected in editorial and critical uncertainty.[18] Similar questions might be asked about "selling her *desires*" as well. Strictly construed, Iago's words define prostitution as marketing not attractiveness but attraction, as though it is the whore who is aroused, rather than her clients. This slippage seems to have provoked no editorial or critical commentary, but in a play whose final action is driven by the projection of men's guilt onto the women who arouse sexual interest, Iago's substitution of desire for desirability should be worth at least a passing nod.

Even more striking than Iago's loaded words is the sententious tone with which he goes on to assure us that whores regularly fall in love with one of their clients: "it is a creature / That dotes on Cassio — as 'tis the strumpet's plague / To beguile many and be beguiled by one" (4.1.96 – 98). On what experience or data (or narrative convention) is this implausible stereotype based? Bianca herself had appeared a few minutes earlier without benefit (so to speak) of Iago's mediating description, and although her affectionate relation to Cassio includes a clearly sexual charge, her wit and charm (not to mention computational skill: "eight-score eight hours . . . O weary reckoning!" [3.4.174 – 176]) should make Iago's contemptuous characterization sound like gross misrepresentation. Why has it stuck? Presumably because Iago speaks with the authority of the canny insider, the resonant generality that convinced Othello in the Temptation Scene. But once burned, twice shy — or so we might think. We have seen through Iago's strategies with Othello earlier. Why should we believe him now?

This is where Cassio's testimony in the overhearing scene comes into play: "I marry! What, a customer!" (4.1.120) Cassio is, clearly, more reliable than Iago; he if anyone should know what to call Bianca. But the designation of "customer," absent from the Quarto, is puzzling. Buyer or seller? — it is the same slippage as in "selling her desires." By glossing the word as "seller = whore," modern editors tend to suppress the doubt that should characterize our response. In contrast, earlier commentators offer evidence to suggest that "customer" in the sense of "seller" was very likely an obsolete or peculiar usage even for the play's first audiences.[19] In any case, the most substantial basis for skepticism about this description of Bianca is the striking structural analogy which asks us to see Iago, before leading Othello to exchange himself for a goat, turning Cassio toward a drunken violence that Cassio himself characterizes as bestial. In the overhearing scene, Iago confirms Othello's transformation by making him witness a repeat performance in the figure of Cassio, whom he now metamorphoses into a misogynist. Iago's success now is demonstrated in Cassio's newly contaminated speech: "'Tis such another fitchew; marry, a perfumed one" (4.1.145 – 146). Like Othello in act 3, Cassio, who was earlier impervious to Iago's innuendos about Desdemona and who seemed only moments ago to delight in his "sweet love" as "my most fair Bianca" (3.4.170 – 171), now reproduces Iago's nauseated, corporeally specific hatred of "our country disposition": "Foh! one may smell in such a will most rank." In fact, the "perfumed fitchew" line is attributed to Iago in the Quarto. Even taken as Cassio's designation, "a customer" is reliable evidence not of Bianca's occupation but of Iago's — poisonously transmitting (in the play's pun) the abhorrence of women.[20]

But again, since we need no more evidence of Iago's true nature, why do we believe him? Because, it may be said (getting now to the crux of the matter), she is identified as "a Curtezan" in the Folio character list, an identification more or less reproduced in all modern editions. In short, our designation derives from the accumulated authority of textual scholarship;[21] but as Random Cloud points out, the tradition "of editorial dramatis-personae lists" isn't very reliable. "No Shakespeare text published before his death has such a list, and only a handful exist in the folio tradition after his death. [Yet it] has insinuated itself between the title page and the opening of Act 1 [and] now become as sacrosanct as the very body of Shakespeare's playtext" (95). Even more "sacrosanct": its privileged position at the beginning seems, especially for first-time student readers, to accord a kind of ontological priority. Like the textual apparatus into which it tends to be merged, the character list is treated not as the product of interpretation but as its ground. Empson once said that "all the characters are on trial in a civilized narrative" (*Milton's God*, 94), but as part of the textual apparatus, the character list seems to embody legal civility itself, the evidentiary and procedural rules with which the characters' and our own interpretive voices are tried. Illegitimately, it might be claimed. These lists, systematically included first by Rowe, not only postdate Shakespeare: their presence even in the "folio tradition" is suspect, since it seems likely they were included for plays that happened, by the accidents of the printing process, to end at the top of a page.

All this lets us finally answer the original question: we call Bianca a whore *because of a scribe's, compositor's, or editor's sense of the esthetics of the printed page.* This in turn lets us restate the question to conform to Othello's own version, addressing Desdemona in (where else?) the "brothel scene": "Was this fair paper, this most goodly book / Made to write 'whore' upon?" (4.2.72–73). But before jumping to the *no* to which my argument seems to be heading, consider that this anonymous Folio worker, call him Ralph Crane, however motivated to devise a character list, did not invent the details out of nothing.[22] His designation of Montano as "Governor of Cyprus," for instance, may be based on a stage direction in Q1 (or some related text or manuscript). "A Curtezan" has no comparable textual foundation, but something in the available texts must have led to the designation. As a contemporary witness, Crane's interpretive actions merit some speculation. Why did he call her "curtezan"?

The textual absence of "curtezan" may suggest not arbitrariness but conscientiousness; Crane goes outside the playtext (let us speculate) in response to signals within that playtext about the need for independent judgment. By not calling Bianca "a whore" or "Cassio's strumpet," or for that matter "a huswife" or "a customer," Crane seeks a more reliable basis for identifying Bianca than any provided by the characters. Crane knows enough not to trust Iago, whom (in the same character list) he calls "a villain." But why not identify Bianca as "Cassio's friend" or "Cassio's love" or "in love with Cassio"? Such terms would correspond to the characters' own sense of their relation as they appear prior to Iago's descriptions:

> *Bian.* Save you, friend Cassio!
> *Cas.*   What make you from home?
>   How is't with you, my most fair Bianca?
>   I'faith, sweet love, I was coming to your house.
> *Bian.* And I was going to your lodging, Cassio. (3.4.169–172)

Presumably, the same independent judgment that prevents Crane from taking Iago's word makes him wary of taking Bianca at her own estimation. But Crane is not evenhanded in his final judgment. However we distinguish "courtesans" and "common whores," the term is much closer to Iago's view than to Bianca's own.[23] Crane reproduces Iago's basic view even though he knows that Iago is "a villain."

His reasons (I further speculate) are implicit in the passage just quoted, which provides the only information about Bianca independent of Iago or the character's own self-representation. We learn here that Bianca is economically and sexually independent. She governs her own life apparently without father or husband; she has amatory interests which she actively pursues, coming out from the domestic space of her own house to look for Cassio (who himself has only a "lodging" as the place "where he lies" — a very *loaded* set of terms in the play). Of course, to suggest that an autonomous, sexually active woman is necessarily a whore, selling her desires for bread and clothes, does not follow. It is one of the "preposterous" conclusions Joel Altman and Patricia Parker describe at the center of Iago's contaminating villainy. The information in this passage, then, does not so much corroborate Iago's view as resonate with and activate a predisposition to accept Iago's view. And this, I think, is the point. Crane may know Iago's views are villainous, but he believes him anyway. Iago, as we have seen, represents the invisible and inaccessible assumptions on which belief rests ("Belief of it oppresses me already"). Burke's "voice whispering at the ear," Iago is already there, like "ideological interpellation," or what Renaissance commentators understood, from inside a theological rather than sociological lexicon, as diabolical possession. Crane believes Iago *because he has no choice.*

Neither do we. Complaining about the way editors "read and crib from . . . other editors," Cloud imagines the prospect of "read[ing] Shakespeare's text afresh" (96), as though we can simply efface the contaminating mediations through which the original text has been transmitted; but since the contamination exists in the Folio at the origin of this transmission, such a prospect, desirable or not, is impossible.[24] Cloud's funny and disingenuous puzzlement "why editors should inflict dramatis-personae lists on plays, and not novellae-personae lists on novels or sonnetae-personae lists on sonnet sequences" (95), points to the special problem of transmitting plays as reading texts. But we should resist any implication about bypassing textual transmission in favor of an antecedent in theatrical performance. The original performance is accessible only through textual transmission; and performance itself, as W. B. Worthen argues, is mediated by historically and culturally specific conventions and beliefs — is itself textual (151–170). Like the literary text, the performance has its determining pretext, Iago again, whose position at the beginning, as we have seen, is equivalent to that of the dramatis personae ("Thou art a villain!" "You are a senator"). We may have doubts about his designations ("old black ram," "white ewe," "beast with two backs"), but he is our gatekeeper and welcomer, the first insider we meet. Honest or not, he doubtless sees and knows more, much more, than he unfolds. Thrown into the midst of this bewildering action, we have no choice but to adopt him, however provisionally, as our guide.

We never cease trusting him; or rather, never clean our minds wholly of the filthy slime stuck there by that initial supposition. This, I take it, is the meaning of the charged Emilia-Bianca exchange about honesty at the end. It occurs as part of a *da capo*, recalling the nocturnal confusion of the play's first action.[25] Iago is still master of ceremonies; now, though, we know him for what he is. The scene emphasizes our knowing detachment by contrast to Lodovico and Gratiano's almost comic caution: standing apart, inert amid the cries for help until Iago comes and works them into his darker purposes, they seem designed to echo our own perplexed dependence at the beginning. But if Lodovico and Gratiano serve as a contrast to what we now know, the Emilia-Bianca exchange diminishes or eliminates the meaning of any such contrast; for whatever we have come to understand in the course of this painful play's long experience does not seem to have done us any good. For Adamson, the exchange confirms our belief in Bianca's essential honesty, but Bianca's proclamation of her own honesty is no more disinterested than Iago's accusations.[26] The critical and theatrical traditions that play her as a whore may be vile, but they cannot simply be wrong. "Behold her well, I pray you, look upon her: / Do you see, gentlemen?" (5.1.108–109). We took her for that cunning whore of Cyprus. This exchange should disconfirm our belief, reveal it as unjustified assumption, but cannot erase it or replace it with any alternative. Her name is neither ironic nor emphatic — or maybe it is both: whiteness as emptiness, absence, the blank page before cultural inscription. Whatever is there, we cannot know it.

This has not stopped speculation. Editors and critics have fabricated many interesting stories about Bianca's moral and social status, her financial and/or affectionate arrangements with Cassio, her real-estate holdings or lack of same, her origins (Venetian or Cypriot).[27] These stories stop short of inventing a girlhood for Bianca, though there seems to be no matter of principle preventing it. The reinvention of Bianca testifies to the durability of character, but more interestingly to the way all questions of motivation in *Othello*, for audiences and characters alike, seem to go back to Iago; he determines our speculations about Bianca as about everything else in the play. When Grennan refers to the "circumstances" that "can alter" Cassio "from Petrarchan idealist to sexual cynic" (276), he is vague and evasive, but he is altogether specific in echoing, probably unconsciously, the play's language — Bianca's complaint to Cassio that she "must be circumstanced" (3.4.202) and, the originating instance, Iago's evocation of the "strong circumstances / Which lead directly to the door of truth" where "satisfaction" may be found (3.3.409–411; cf. Jachimo in *Cymbeline*, 2.4.61). Like the obsessively reiterated "matter," "circumstance" is functional in its vagueness. It seems to demand the very specificity — social, economic, sexual, moral — that the play withholds, driving us to the desperate expedient of constructing some pretextual basis — any pretextual basis — to make sense of the dramatic action. Bianca enters the play at a particularly stressful point, the moment of Othello's and our own interpretive crises, when the "double-time" problem is especially perplexing (Bradshaw's Venetian Bianca is part of an attempt to solve this problem [147–168]). Never since the beginning of the play has our need been so desperate for a plausible temporal scheme and narrative structure as a way of at least provisionally organizing an understanding. As always since the beginning of the play, the name for this necessary pretext — the circumstance, the matter — is Iago: honest, honest Iago.

In disabusing us of our preconceptions, Bianca's "I am no strumpet / But of life as honest as you, that thus / Abuse me" shows us that we are still being abused; Iago's poison is still working. You cannot kill the devil; ourselves are ideology, nor are we out of it. The jarring disconfirmation of this exchange should precipitate a recognition of Iago's continuing influence in shaping our beliefs. It may therefore serve to narrow the distance that has grown since the middle of the play between us and the protagonist: can we find Othello merely ridiculous when we have been believing Iago as well? But in this play, pity isn't the main effect, not even with the women. The Bianca-Emilia exchange works to produce an appalled guilt, the stunned realization how fundamentally complicit we are — even now, now, very now — with the malign and contaminating motivations driving us on to the terrible catastrophe just ahead.

6

Death without Transfiguration

When he enters to Desdemona, sleeping in bed, Othello is a man on a mission:

> It is the cause, it is the cause, my soul!
> Let me not name it to you, you chaste stars,
> It is the cause. Yet I'll not shed her blood
> Nor scar that whiter skin of hers than snow
> And smooth as monumental alabaster:
> Yet she must die, else she'll betray more men. (5.2.1–6)

He identifies himself with his soul and the chaste stars, claiming a disinterested commitment to an unspecified cause. This is presumably the purgation of sexual impurity, and he declines to name it in order to avoid offense; but the very referencelessness of "it" — incapable of definition, only of reiteration — contributes to the claim of dispassionate abstraction.

For Bradley, this Othello is an exalted figure who has transcended the "ravenous thirst for revenge" of his earlier self (160):

> The Othello who enters the bed-chamber . . . is not the man of the Fourth Act. The deed he is bound to do is no murder, but a sacrifice. He is to save Desdemona from herself, not in hate but in honour, in honour, and also in love. His anger has passed; a boundless sorrow has taken its place; and
>
> > this sorrow's heavenly:
> > It strikes where it doth love.
>
> Even when, at the sight of her apparent obduracy, and at the hearing of words which by a crowning fatality can only convince him of her guilt, these feelings give way to others, it is to righteous indignation

they give way, not to rage; and, terribly painful as this scene is, there is almost nothing here to diminish the admiration and love which heighten pity. (161)

This is one of the passages in *Shakespearean Tragedy* that has not weathered well. As Honigmann points out, with "Had all his hairs been lives / My great revenge had stomach for them all" (5.2.73–74), "Othello relapses into anger almost immediately." Even Samuel Foote, who as we shall see stands near the origin of the view generating Bradley's commentary, has to acknowledge the power of passion in Spranger Barry's delivery of these words: "We see Mr. Barry redden thro' the very black of his face; his whole visage becomes inflamed, his eyes sparkle with successful vengeance, and he seems to raise himself above the ground" (quoted Carlisle, 199). As Honigmann argues, "Bradley accepts Othello's self-justification too readily"; the claim to be performing a "noble action, . . . a sacrifice, not a murder," is evidently a "self-deception" (84).

This self-deception resonates, like so much else in the play, on a sexual register. Even as Othello claims to regard Desdemona as a statue on a funeral monument, his terms betray a far from disinterested sensitivity to her smooth white skin. ("This is flesh, and blood, sir," as Webster's Duchess says in a play dense with *Othello* echoes; "'Tis not the figure cut in alabaster / Kneels at my husband's tomb" [1.1.369–372].) By the end of the speech, his passionate involvement is rendered explicit:

> I'll smell thee on the tree;
> O balmy breath, that does almost persuade
> Justice to break her sword! Once more, once more:
> Be thus when thou art dead and I will kill thee
> And love thee after. Once more, and that's the last.
> *He* [*smells, then*] *kisses her.* (15–19)

By identifying himself with a female Justice (more emphatically in Q's "Justice herself"), Othello presumably claims an androgynous or sexless identity, but he has to acknowledge a vulnerability to Desdemona's sexual presence that "almost" destroys the claim. The actions that follow, smelling and then kissing her, destroy it utterly. Honigmann's "smells, then" is, as far as I can tell, without precedent; the words aren't in the original texts, but the interpolation may well be justified. Shakespeare frequently embeds stage directions in the speech of his characters; "smells . . . her" corresponds to what Othello says he will do; and, as Honigmann says, "the sense of smell is so important" to Othello —

arguably the most important register of erotic interest in the play (Pechter, "'Have you not read of some such thing?'" 209–212). Possibly Othello means "I'll smell thee" metaphorically, as in plucking the rose just earlier, but these metaphors insistently evoke the language of his sexual obsession, even more strongly in Q's "I'll smell it on the tree," where the reiteration of "it" ("look to't," "keep it as a cistern for foul toads / To knot and gender in," "it is the cause") produces a disturbing retrospective suggestion about the unnamed thing to which this whole speech refers.[1]

Like the editors, actors have not been eager to represent the action. The earliest exception seems to be Olivier in the Dexter production (see the photograph in Tynan, 86), where "smells . . . her" is set up with the protagonist's stunning first entrance: "Out of the dark strolls a young-ish, slimmish black man in a short, casually-tied white gown. In one hand he carries, stalk erect, a red rose," or in another version, "a long-stemmed pink rose," which "he sniffs at and toys with" as "a foreshad-owing of the lines in V.2" (Alan Seymour, quoted in Tynan, 13; and Tynan, 6). But then Olivier's performance was the centerpiece of a pro-duction noted for its erotic intensity, the power of which was derived in part from its consistent emphasis on smell as central to the emotional experience. "When Othello returns ('Ha! ha! false to *me*?' [3.3.336]), he has been unable to make love to Desdemona; he sniffs his fingers as if they were tainted by contact with her body" (Tynan, 8). Patrick Stewart picked up on this gesture in the Jude Kelly production at Washington: "In the middle of 3.3, when Othello exits with Desdemona, he took her hand and began to kiss it, then stopped suddenly and pulled back, look-ing briefly nauseated and confused. When he re-entered later in the scene, he was coughing and gagging into a handkerchief" (Johnson-Haddad, "The Shakespeare Theatre *Othello*, 10). Like Olivier (and these seem to be the only two) Stewart smells Desdemona at the end — part of a smell-conscious performance that, consciously or not, works out of Olivier's.[2]

Critics have been similarly unwilling or unable to respond to Oth-ello's gesture. Maurice Charney is one characteristically acute exception: "Othello comes as a lover, and the death scene is charged with powerful erotic imagery. . . . Othello smells the sleeping Desdemona, as if she were a rose. . . . He smells her and he kisses her and then he weeps" (253). Graham Bradshaw is another exception, but the alliterative jollity of his reference to "that final sniffing and snuffing" (167) suggests embarrass-ment. Perhaps this explains the general avoidance of the implications of Othello's words among editors, actors, and critics alike: it is hard to imagine without embarrassment the performance of such actions.

But avoiding embarrassment won't get us far with *Othello*, especially not with this passage, which requires us to sustain an excruciating focus on an Othello utterly deluded about the nature of his own feelings. "I will kill thee / And love thee after" may be intended as testimony to his sacrificial rather than murderous motives, but the statement is overtly necrophiliac. He hasn't transcended eros and aggression but perversely combined them. As Desdemona says, "That death's unnatural that kills for loving" (42). The embedded stage directions, "your eyes roll so" (37) and "some bloody passion shakes your very frame" (44), return us to Othello's spastic trance in act 4, as does all the language of confession and guilt. Although Othello focuses on Desdemona's guilt, it seems rather to be a confused sense of his own that propels him onward. By not scarring her, Cavell speculates, Othello engages in "a ritual of denial" (133), seeking to reverse the polluting act by which he had previously shed her virgin blood, and thereby not only contaminated her innocence but discovered his own towering passion. Such speculation helps with the difficult exchange precipitated by Othello's "Think on thy sins." "They are loves I bear to you." "Ay, and for that thou diest" (40–41). Commentators are hard-pressed to determine what guilt Desdemona acknowledges here (loving Othello more than God? disobeying Brabantio?), but in view of her later claim to die a "guiltless death" (121), the words seem rather to deny the existence of her sins than to specify their nature. She is reaffirming the purity of her affection for Othello. This is not what he understands, of course. Taking her words as confirmation, he presumably hears "bear" as "bare," an evocation of their naked revelations and self-discoveries on the wedding night: after such knowledge, to his crazed imagination, what forgiveness?

In his discussion of the very end, Bradley sustains his indifference — even resistance — to the play's representation of the protagonist:

> Love and admiration alone remain, in the majestic dignity and sovereign ascendancy of the close. Chaos has come and gone; and the Othello of the Council-chamber and the quay of Cyprus has returned, or a great and nobler Othello still. As he speaks those final words in which all the glory and agony of his life . . . seem to pass before us, like the pictures that flash before the eyes of a drowning man, a triumphant scorn for the fetters of the flesh and the littleness

Death without Transfiguration

of all the lives that must survive him sweeps our grief away. (*Shake-spearean Tragedy*, 161)

But chaos has come and stayed. Bradley's own words, "pictures that flash before the eyes," testify unconsciously to the fact of Othello's disinte-gration, not the fiction of his "ascendancy." As Calderwood astutely observes about the paratactic or cataloglike quality of Othello's suicide speech:

> What emerges is not the image of a unique and essential self but a series of generic snapshots: The Soldier-Servant ("I have done the state some service"), The Unfortunate Lover ("one that loved not wisely but too well"), The Jealous Avenger ("being wrought, per-plexed in the extreme"), then more ambiguously The Unlucky Indian or The Villainous Judean, and finally a fusion of The Infidel Turk and The Venetian Christian. Instead of a core-self discoverable at the cen-ter of his being, Othello's "I am" seems a kind of internal repertory company, a "we are." (103)

Where Othello was his story, he now has his stories: a variety of selves among which he is dispersed and from which he is, at the same time, irredeemably alienated; an unstable admixture of subject and object, past and present ("That's he that was Othello? here I am" [281]), that finally splits or implodes into annihilation ("I . . . smote him — thus!"). The play surely wishes us to recall the original Othello here at the very end, as Bradley suggests — not, though, by way of restoration, still less of augmented nobility, but of irretrievable loss.

Bradley is usually responsive to textual details; the *longueurs* in *Shake-spearean Tragedy* result from irrelevance, when he is talking in a way that no longer seems interesting, but rarely from such evident insensibility. The assumptions working to make Bradley turn a deaf ear and blind eye to the play must be deeply entrenched. They are fully in place as early as the mid eighteenth century, when Samuel Foote describes what he takes to be the "essential task" of performing Othello as the ability

> to excite in the audience a "Compassion for himself" even greater, if possible, than they would naturally feel for Desdemona; "and for this Purpose, the Strugglings and Convulsions that torture and distract his Mind, upon his resolving to murder her, cannot be too strongly painted, nor can the Act itself be accomplished with too much Grief and Tenderness [so that it will] appear as a Sacrifice to the Hero's

injur'd Honour, and not the Gratification of a diabolic Passion."
(Carlisle, 198)

Seven years after *Shakespearean Tragedy*, William Winter was looking at
the same play. Describing an undated Booth performance that both he
and Booth regarded as particularly fine, Winter says that in

> the killing of *Desdemona*, which, terrible though it be, is, in her hus-
> band's belief, a righteous immolation, *Othello* is like a priest at the altar.
> There is then no anger in his conduct . . . at last he is calm, in the con-
> centration of despair. *Desdemona* must die, because, as he believes, it is
> necessary and right. He is not doing a murder; he is doing what he
> thinks to be an act of justice. He confidently supposes himself to be ful-
> filling a sacred duty of *sacrifice*. He is the wretched victim of a horrible
> delusion, but in that awful moment he is a sublime figure, an incarna-
> tion at once of rectitude and misery. (*Shakespeare on the Stage*, 268)

Unlike Bradley, Winter recognizes that Othello is deluded, but this
doesn't seem to matter.

In more general terms, the assumptions driving the Bradleyan view
may be located in Hegel's claims about tragedy on which Bradley acknowledges his own work to be based.[3] Bradley takes from Hegel the
idea that tragedy is grounded in a deep and fundamental conflict within
the order of unified spirit. He modifies Hegel to emphasize the subjective basis of modern (including Shakespearean) tragedy, where the locus of the conflict is internalized in the protagonists. "The real subject,
the impelling end or passion, and the ensuing conflict, is personal —
these particular characters with their struggle and their fate" ("Hegel's
Theory," 77). Above all, Bradley insists, with Hegel, that tragedy ends
not just with suffering and loss, but with an affirmative renewal of the
unified spirit. Since in "modern" tragedy the "reconciliation is imper-
fect," and since modern audiences concentrate their "interest on in-
dividuality as such," this sense of affirmation is also focused on the
protagonist: "we desire to see in the individual himself some sort of
reconciliation with his fate [to] show us that, in face of the forces that
crush him to death, he maintains untouched the freedom and strength
of his own will" (79). It is this sense of transcendence that accounts for
"that strange double impression which is produced by the hero's death.
He dies, and our hearts die with him; and yet his death matters nothing
to us, or we even exult. He is dead; and he has no more to do with death
than the power which killed him and with which he is one" (91).

Bradley is not altogether comfortable with his Hegelianism. He believes that the effect of "reconciliation" produced by Shakespearean tragedy is more qualified than Hegel's theory allows, and in the specific case of *Othello* he is given to awkward retreats from his own claims about the protagonist's transfiguration.[4] Nonetheless, the power of the Hegelian machinery driving *Shakespearean Tragedy* is irresistible, in part because it was so generally dispersed throughout nineteenth-century belief and reinforced, often unconsciously and anonymously, through a variety of cultural practices, including earlier interpretive commentary going back to Hazlitt and Coleridge and, at least equally important, traditions of theatrical interpretation. As James Siemon demonstrates, "the evasions, embellishments, and outright contradictions of Shakespeare's text that win acceptance in the late eighteenth- and nineteenth-century performances of the final scene of *Othello* suggest a coherence of interpretation" (38), the main effect of which is to enact the Hegelian-Bradleyan scenario I have synopsized here: to eliminate, more or less systematically, those dramatic presences that might compete with a sustained focus on the protagonist's transcendent nobility.

Desdemona's reduction to prostrate passivity, the process described in the last chapter, is arguably the foundation of this interpretive system. As Burke says, acquiescence makes her "rather like a victim going willingly towards sacrifice." To put it the other way around, the reality of Desdemona's active resistance is problematic: it might produce a response like Henry Jackson's, deflected from the desired object of attention, focusing on her pain and courage rather than on Othello's spiritual struggle. The play writes the problem into Othello's own speech: Desdemona's resistance is inconvenient because it "makest me call what I intend to do / A murder, which I thought a sacrifice!" (64–65). By transforming Desdemona into compliance, nineteenth-century performances tend, like Bradley, to buy into Othello's delusions.

Distancing the murder, one way or another, is also a crucial part of this interpretive process. Othello's own words, "There lies your niece / Whose breath, indeed, these hands have newly stopped" (5.2.199–200), seem unambiguously and emphatically to refer to an act of strangulation — "these hands" even now ("newly") on that neck ("there"). Nonetheless, a pillow had been established as the standard prop as early as the beginning of the eighteenth century, and most nineteenth-century audiences had difficulty with those exceptional performances where it wasn't used. Sprague cites a Philadelphia newspaper in 1806: "If anything like a real *smothering* were to be exhibited, the audience, unable to contain themselves, would rush upon the stage to stop the murder." When Rossi strangled his Desdemona in an 1881 performance, "murmurs of dissatisfaction were audible in the house" (*Shakespeare and the Actors*, 212). A similar intention to reduce the effect of violent bodily contact seems to lie behind the practice, which originated in the eighteenth century and became conventional by the nineteenth, of Othello's administering the *coup de grâce* with a dagger. This is quicker and neater than strangulation, but it is precisely the length and messiness that the play insists on, the sheer physical exertion required to strangle Desdemona — flesh on flesh — and then to strangle her again.[5]

Both original texts provide a stage direction: "*smothers her*" in F, "*he stifles her*" in Q. As Hankey suggests, "the method of killing her would scarcely have been specified if the deed was not to be done in full view" (316). Nonetheless, nineteenth-century productions normally hid the action behind bed linen, for reasons suggested by a spectator's lament about a production that failed to do so: "You promised, Frank, that you would strangle her behind the curtains," said Benson's father "tearfully at the end of the play. 'I cannot bear it on the stage'" (quoted Hankey, 317). The bed's placement onstage is another part of the interpretive structure. Siemon remarks on "the consistency with which the period keeps the bed approximately centered and as far upstage as possible"; the "distance and symmetrical setting," he thinks, must have contributed to the desired "sacrificial" effect ("Nay," 40). When Fechter moved the bed downstage and to the side, Sir Theodore Martin complained that "'Tradition' was right in placing Desdemona's couch at a remote part of the stage: Mr. Fechter is wrong in bringing it so far forward that every detail is thrust painfully on our senses" (quoted Sprague, *Shakespeare and the Actors*, 214).

Fechter may have been reacting in part to the practical theatrical difficulty of hearing and seeing Othello so far upstage: solving one kind of problem had created another. Booth, who also moved the bed downstage and to the side, understood the unconventional placement in a way that reinforced the conventional meaning: "I prefer the bed at the side of the stage, with the head towards the audience; it is of more importance that Othello's face should be seen than Desdemona's dead body" (quoted Furness, 292). But an audience's gaze isn't as controllable in the theater as in film, say, and this decision may have had unforeseen consequences. Such consequences may also be relevant to Irving's performance of the murder. He returned the bed Booth had moved to its central position upstage (this was during the role-swapping engagement with Booth in 1881) and played the scene for sacrifice: "Othello's manner justified the assertion, '. . . nought did I in hate, but all in honour' . . . To him the murder seemed 'a just and necessary execution'; his jealousy was forgotten." But the extended pause when he closed the curtains behind himself and Terry produced a different result:

> The curtains were traditional, but Irving turned them to advantage with a characteristically bold stroke: there was a long silence, "broken by a loud knocking at the door, of which no notice is taken for a time." . . . The audience sat gazing at the empty stage, nerves harrowed by the knocking, full of the knowledge of what passed behind those enigmatic curtains, waiting through the interminable seconds for the Moor to draw them aside. (Alan Hughes, 149–150)

The sustained concealment and silence here don't distance horror; they insist on the working of our imaginary forces (do we really know exactly what is happening, even now, in that hidden place?) and thus render horror more intense. Salvini subsequently made use of a similar "long pause," creating "tension" that was "almost insufferable" (Sprague, *Shakespeare and the Actors*, 216), and Salvini played the scene not for disinterested sacrifice but for passionate violence. Perhaps Irving didn't appreciate the effect of what he was doing; as several commentators have remarked, the more nineteenth-century theatrical and critical practice tried to obscure the horrific action at the end of this play, the more they foregrounded it.[6] Then again maybe Irving knew what he was doing; theatrical savvy can sometimes produce more interesting results than conscious agendas.

The reduction of Emilia is much more straightforward in purpose and effect. Her lines are trimmed, frequently pruned, as a way of diminishing a presence potentially competitive with the protagonist's. The "incredulous iterations" of "my husband" are "curtailed from Bell's edition onwards during the nineteenth century," and Fechter's text "cut the whole idea" (Hankey, 311). The significance of her death is minimized. Shakespeare's play calls for her body to be placed with Desdemona's and then joined by Othello to make up "the tragic loading of this bed" (5.2.361); but in the fifty-two promptbooks Siemon examined for performances between 1766 and 1900, "Emilia is never granted her wish to be laid by Desdemona" ("Nay," 49). Indeed, the usual nineteenth-century practice calls for her either to be "carried off immediately" or (as in

Fechter) hidden behind a curtain. Forrest's Emilia was wounded but not killed and "supported off stage" (Hankey, 327). De Vigny and Salvini simply eliminated Iago's assault on her altogether.

For the very end of the play, nineteenth-century productions developed various strategies to isolate Othello as the object of our attention. "In Bell's acting edition," Iago "exits *guarded*, a little before the beginning of Othello's apologia, the words 'Away with him' being interpolated" as a way "to get him off" before the protagonist's suicide (Sprague, *Shakespeare and the Actors*, 222). This became general practice on the nineteenth-century stage, adopted by Kean, Kemble, the elder Booth, Phelps, Cooke, Young, Salvini, Forrest, and others (Siemon, "Nay," 50). As a consequence, Lodovico has no one to address in the play's final words, "O Spartan dog, . . . / This is thy work" (359–362). Hankey suggests that "perhaps he gestured in the direction of his [Iago's] exit" (334), but in the main, such confusion was avoided simply by jettisoning Lodovico's speech as well. "From Macready onwards, up to the early twentieth century, it was usual to bring the curtain down" after Othello's "smote him — thus!" eliminating all subsequent speech in favor of a silent terminal tableau (Hankey, 335). Among the cuts is Othello's dying couplet. In "45 of the 52 promptbooks . . . the lines about having kissed Desdemona before he killed her are missing" (Siemon, "Nay," 49). Instead, we get versions of a practice apparently first developed by Macready: "after falling 'he motions to be raised, his wish being complied with he hastily staggers towards the bed . . . supporting himself by the walls and furniture of the room, ejaculates faintly her name, just gazes on her face and falls dead upon the floor'" (Hankey, 337). Othello's couplet and Lodovico's "Look on the tragic loading of this bed" (361) together constitute an unambiguous direction that he dies on the bed with Desdemona and Emilia, but the nineteenth-century stage preferred a heroic aria — either the powerful rhetoric of Othello's "last great speech" (to use Eliot's ironic and inaccurate phrase[7] ["Shakespeare and the Stoicism of Seneca," 111]), or the Macready-inspired agonized pantomime — focused exclusively on the noble protagonist.

After Bradley, the Hegelian apparatus ceased to be a dominant force in critical response to *Othello*, but it sustains itself in a long afterlife. According to Tillyard, *Othello* "pictures through the hero . . . the birth of a new order. Othello in his final soliloquy is a man of a more capacious mind" (16–17). He "recognises his errors and transmutes them into his new state of mind" (21). Helen Gardner asserted of Desdemona's murder that the "act is heroic because Othello acts from inner necessity"

(200), and that the "revival of faith in Othello which rings through his last speech overrides . . . his own guilt" (202). Such claims about final transcendence survive in criticism to our own day, as they perhaps do in attenuated forms in theatrical interpretation as well.[8] They tend, however, to be withdrawn from the protagonist and reinvested in a political or collective idea. Hence G. M. Matthews:

> Othello's final speech, therefore, though it cannot mitigate what he has done, demonstrates the complete recovery of his integrity as a human being. . . . All that Iago's poison has achieved is an object that "poisons sight": a bed on which a black man and a white girl, although they are dead, are embracing. Human dignity, the play says, is indivisible. (145)

The most recent and perhaps strangest residue of nineteenth-century tradition is observable in Mitchell Greenberg's discussion of the play as a ritual purgation in which "the convoluted theme of scapegoating, sacrifice, and redemption is repeatedly acted out" (5). In this enactment, Othello is assigned the role of "the *pharmakos* victim" whose "sacrifice signals the originary act of a new moment in history: the state is instituted, but as an invisible distant power," the "transparent order of 'raison d'Etat,' . . . the evolving order of absolutism" buttressed by the "patriarchal ideology . . . that finally the tragedy espouses" (30–31). Matthews's claim about "human dignity" was substantially continuous with the interpretive system he transmuted: from the dialectic to Marxist humanism isn't an unbridgeable rupture. But when the Hegelian vocabulary of ultimate renewal (a "redemption . . . that finally the tragedy espouses") is enlisted in the service of the antihumanist Foucauldian thematics of concealed power, the effect is truly peculiar.

The Hegelian apparatus has great explanatory power, and its residual survival, even in such attenuated and contradictory manifestations, provides another piece of evidence for the force of inertia in cultural history. But it's not so easy to understand how this machinery was installed with the status of truth to begin with. The nineteenth-century *Othello* must have been serving some not wholly pathological purposes for its audiences, and it may even stand in some meaningful relation to the very different ways in which we try to make sense of the play in current interpretive practice. One place to look for clarification is Tillyard, precisely because of his position at or perhaps beyond the edge of tradition. (Minerva's owl, as they say, flies at twilight.)

Writing about the pattern of "regeneration," "re-creation," and "vital change" he sees enacted in Shakespearean tragedy, Tillyard focuses on the beneficial effects of this process for the audience:

> Those who witness tragedy are encouraged to heighten their own vitality by re-enacting the same process in themselves. In this sense tragedy goes outside drama. It is to be found in the last book of the *Iliad* and in *Lycidas*, as well as in Shakespearean tragedy. Put in these very simple terms, the notion of tragedy as implying regeneration may commend itself to some who might object to it in a more dogmatic or moral form. Anyhow, I postulate some such notion for my present purposes. (17–18)

This passage is remarkable for its unassertiveness. Tillyard seems almost indifferent to his own claims: you can take them or leave them, he implies at the end, they're only heuristic. The claims themselves are extraordinarily vague ("some such notion"), almost apologetically so ("these very simple terms"). Tillyard seems to be not only detached from his own beliefs but almost driven by embarrassment to dramatize his own distance from them. Hence, introducing his central idea that "the tragic pattern . . . implies destruction and recreation," he notes that this "theory . . . can be put in the simplest terms of everyday speech and can be applied to the most general human experiences" in a way "so simple and obvious as to be almost embarrassing to mention" (17).

To some extent, this is the genial *sprezzatura* of midcentury British criticism (in the non-Leavis mode), but something more is at work. The displacements and attenuations with which Tillyard represents his claims are especially noteworthy in view of the fact that the claims themselves are based on attenuation and displacement. Tillyard is recycling the Arnoldian idea of poetry as a replacement for religion, as Bradley was forty years earlier, perhaps with more conviction. Bradley, too, would make and then retreat from his claims about tragic reconciliation and was consistently vague in his discussions of transcendence. Over and over, Bradley tells us what the transfigured virtue at the end of Shakespearean tragedy is *not* — namely its equivalent in religious doctrine, legal morality, systematic philosophy, and so forth. Negativity doesn't merely characterize transcendence in Bradley; it defines it. The concept, like Iago, is nothing if not critical. It's hard not to be skeptical about such willful nebulousness: the refusal of specificity may be a way to disguise the embarrassment of nothing to see beyond the banalities; what passes as *je ne sais quoi* is actually *sauve qui peut*. But Bradley and Tillyard have a real purpose in refusing specificity; audiences "do not

Death without Transfiguration

heighten their own vitality" as an act of conscious will. An explicit understanding that we are participating in a sacrificial ritual empties the process of its purgative power. As René Girard says repeatedly, "In order to be effective, the reconciliation must not be perceived as a mimetic phenomenon. The only good scapegoats are the ones we are unable to acknowledge as such" ("An Interview," 202).[9] Say it and you lose it.

Perhaps there are no really good scapegoats anywhere in Renaissance tragedy. The playwrights, not just Shakespeare, effectively detached themselves from ritual foundations, psychologizing and estheticizing their practices for spectators increasingly conscious of their own obligations to what they recognized as a fiction.[10] But the detachment in *Othello* is peculiarly overt. Despite Tillyard's claim that "*Othello* is typical of Shakespearean tragedy in merely hinting at a rebirth" (18), *Othello* is atypical and probably unique among Shakespearean tragedies in wearing its purgative function on its sleeve.[11] Othello's opening speech establishes the idea of a generalized cleansing ("lest she betray more men") with extraordinary clarity. He returns to the idea repeatedly throughout the scene, juxtaposing murder with sacrifice, and alluding to the cosmic reverberations that occurred at the crucifixion: "Methinks it should be now a huge eclipse / Of sun and moon" (98–99). No wonder Burke chose *Othello* to illustrate the method of Shakespearean tragedy; the play is itself a kind of *discours de la méthode*. Othello himself is conscious of his role and increasingly skeptical about its realization — perhaps inevitably so. Not only does Desdemona make him suspicious that his action is murder and not sacrifice, but the eclipse never comes. Toward the end of the scene, the (absent) thunder is deprived of its appropriately cosmic significance — "Are there no stones in heaven / But what serves for the thunder?" (232–233) — and Iago's symbolic role is emptied out: "I look down towards his feet, but that's a fable" (283). Whether Othello is deluded and dies in a state of disenchantment are endlessly debatable questions, but our own disenchantment would seem to be guaranteed: by transferring its putatively purgative intention onto the protagonist, the play has crystallized a potentially diffused presence into visible form, given it a local habitation, "Othello's cause." He refuses to name it, but the play names it for us, and therefore empties it of its cleansing potential. *Pharmakos* revealed is *pharmakos* denied; it is said, therefore lost.

Nineteenth-century productions frequently performed the play's final scene to the accompaniment of thunder and lightning (Siemon, "Nay," 40), putting back the universal resonances that the play empties out of its own action in an attempt to give their audiences what critics like Hazlitt and Bradley sought to furnish the play's readers: "a high and permanent interest, beyond ourselves, in humanity as such," "reconciliation," and the exultant intuition of renewal in the fulfilment of a transcendent world order. Such efforts cannot have been fully successful. The more explicitly that nineteenth-century interpreters proclaimed therapeutic effects for *Othello*, the less power they had to deliver a healing that depends above all on implication and suggestion, perhaps even on mystification and ignorance, rather than on conscious assertion. Even if they managed to fill the play's vacancies with the gestures and sounds of transfiguration, these signs must have testified to their own conspicuous status as rhetoric in the pejorative sense — the will doing the work of the imagination.

From this angle, the loud and heroic affirmations of nineteenth-century interpretive traditions begin to look like denial, refusal, and resistance — overcompensatory strategies to deal with a dramatic experience that was simply unbearable. Dr. Johnson's anguish in the face of 5.2 as a "dreadful scene" that was "not to be endured" developed in fact out of perplexity in the face of Othello's perplexed distinction between murder and sacrifice ("this line is difficult" [Vickers, 5.165]). A century later, Halliwell-Phillipps confirmed Johnson's sense of intolerable pain in a way to suggest that this response was generally felt:

> Many readers will probably sympathize with Dr Johnson's concluding observation. Without disputing the masterly power displayed in the composition of the present tragedy, there is something to my mind so revolting, both in the present Scene and in the detestable character of Iago, which renders a study of the drama of *Othello* rather a painful duty than one of pleasure. (Quoted Furness, 300)

Halliwell-Phillipps locates the problem where it surely existed for nineteenth-century interpreters of the play — in "the detestable character of Iago."

Iago's detestability as such couldn't have been the problem (Dr. Johnson loved a good hater, nineteenth-century audiences loved Dickens's hateful villains); it must have been his triumphant power. About his ultimate invincibility as the "eternal villain," the play is suggestive throughout and, by the end, relentlessly insistent. Othello's first attempt on him achieves nothing — or rather, it results in Emilia's murder, and leads to the protagonist's bleak recognition that there are "no stones in heaven / But what serves for the thunder." [12] His second attempt produces the same meaning even more emphatically: an intuition of futility, "If thou be'st a devil, I cannot kill thee. [*Wounds Iago*.],'' followed immediately by unequivocal confirmation, "I bleed, sir, but not killed" (284–285). The effect of this is shockingly conclusive, not unlike the sequence "The gods defend her! *Enter Lear with Cordelia dead in his arms*," which generated Bradley's "we might almost say that the 'moral' of *King Lear* is presented in the irony of this collocation" (*Shakespearean Tragedy*, 272). In such a context, the assurances of Iago's imminent torture seem empty against his own claim that he will not provide satisfaction, "From this time forth I never will speak word" (301), and against the fact of his survival to see with us, at the very end, the object of his own work, in which he is presumably well pleased.

The *Lear* analogy is worth pursuing, especially because its ending impelled Dr. Johnson to an almost identical confession: "I was many years ago so shocked by Cordelia's death, that I know not whether I ever endured to read again the last scenes of the play till I undertook to revise them as an editor" (Vickers, 5.140). There is one apparently salient difference in the interpretive history of the two plays. "Unlike *King Lear*," Siemon remarks, "*Othello* was not rewritten for the stage with a more acceptable ending" ("Nay," 39). Presumably, the constricted plot and setting made revision of such magnitude impossible;[13] they did not, however, prevent less radical revision — getting Iago offstage to allow Othello the last word, among the many other things we have seen. Revision, anyway, is just one particularly striking form of interpretation; to put it the other way around, interpretation is a form of rewriting. When Salvini performed "[*Wounds Iago*.]," Henry James declared that the effect was

> "ineffaceable": the "tigerlike spring with which, after turning, flooded and frenzied by the truth, from the lifeless body of his victim, he traverses the chamber to reach Iago, with the mad impulse of destruction gathered in one blow . . . the manner in which the spectator sees him — or rather feels him — rise to his avenging leap is a sensation." (Quoted Hankey, 331)

Shakespeare's perplexed and defeated protagonist metamorphoses here into a heroic athlete, Othello *agonistes*, his sudden and pathetically ineffectual gesture transformed into a thrillingly sustained achievement. Transporting us in effect to the final scenes of *Hamlet* or *Macbeth* (or *Richard II* or *Richard III*), Salvini's performance allows us (to recall

Bradley) to "sweep . . . our grief away" into a "triumphant scorn for the fetters of the flesh and the littleness of all the lives that must survive him." The *Othello* of nineteenth-century theatrical and critical interpretation is a text fundamentally rewritten in order to deny the unbearable fact of Iago's controlling power.

Johnson himself didn't explain the unendurable quality of *Othello* in this way, or in any other, but we may assume that the amplification of his response to *Lear* is relevant to *Othello* as well: if "all reasonable beings naturally love justice" (Vickers, 5.139), then Desdemona's death, like innocent Cordelia's murder, frustrates a fundamental human need. Johnson is unambiguous in his abstractions and universals: reason, nature, all beings. He is similarly unequivocal in his attitude toward Iago: "There is always danger lest wickedness, conjoined with abilities, should steal upon esteem, though it misses of approbation; but the character of *Iago* is so conducted that he is from the first scene to the last hated and despised" (Vickers, 5.166).

Nineteenth-century interpreters couldn't manage such absolute decisiveness, either in criticism or on the stage. Although great pains were taken, as we have seen, to subdue Iago's power at the end, there was a persistent undertone of exception. A number of Iagos — Kean, the elder Booth, Forrest, Cooke, Phelps, et al. — have moments of impressive and memorable triumph on being led away before Othello's suicide. Then there are two Iagos who actually stayed onstage, as the text indicates they should. Fechter's 1861 acting edition provides one, with its surprising business whereby Othello drags him to the bed, forces him to kneel, and seems about to stab him at "uncircumcised dog." There are no doubt lots of reasons to suggest that this wasn't a good idea; Macready delivers his from the normative position we might expect, emphasizing Othello's transcendence: a "complete blindness as to the emotions of his character" in "the demission of his lofty nature to bestow a thought upon that miserable thing, Iago, when his great mind had made itself up to die!" (quoted Sprague, *Shakespeare and the Actors*, 221). The most powerfully exceptional performance was that of Edwin Booth, who

> gave up the un-Shakespearean exit and the added words . . . to stand
> waiting beside Emilia's body, "*at the window.*" But when he sees his
> enemy fall, he "*starts forward*" to gloat over him [and] in London,
> with Irving, the same Iago "brought down the final curtain standing
> over Othello, pointing . . . at the dead body and gazing up at the

gallery with a malignant smile of satisfied hate." (Sprague, *Shakespeare and the Actors*, 223)

A witness complained that Booth's performance was "not in harmony with the rest of the picture, not in sympathy with the dominant mind. It was as though a splash of crimson had been introduced in a delicate nocturne by Whistler" (quoted Alan Hughes, 150). The complaint itself, predicated on two different senses of esthetic effect, delicate harmony and shocking dissonance, acknowledges the power of Booth's exceptional performance even as it objects to it.

In critical discourse, too, the stark clarities of Johnson's contrasts begin to blur. Lecturing in Bristol in 1813, Coleridge assured his audience that Shakespeare's "purity . . . carried on no warfare against virtue, by which wickedness may be made to appear as not wickedness, and where our sympathy was to be entrapped by the misfortunes of vice; with him vice never walked, as it were, in twilight" (Foakes, *Coleridge's Criticism*, 57). But when he descends from generality to describe Iago's "motiveless malignity" a few years later (I reproduce the passage in chapter 3), Coleridge's sense of absolutely clear coordinates has disappeared; with "next to the devil, only *not* quite the devil," Coleridge seems to have walked with Iago into a twilight zone, and the excited assurances that Shakespeare has managed to pull off such a risky endeavor may betray an element of uncertainty. In a more or less contemporary comment about the villains in *Lear*, Coleridge developed his position more fully:

> For such are the appointed relations of intellectual power to truth, and of truth to goodness, that it becomes both morally and poetic[ally] unsafe to present what is admirable — what our nature compels to admire — in the mind, and what is most detestable in the heart, as co-existing in the same individual without any apparent connection, or any modification of the one by the other. That Shakespeare has in one instance, that of Iago, approached to this, and that he has done it successfully, is perhaps the most astonishing proof of his genius and the opulence of its resources. (Foakes, *Coleridge's Criticism*, 98)

This passage is structured by contrasts similar to Johnson's — between intellectual power and truth, what the mind admires and the heart hates. But unlike Johnson — who hates Iago from first to last and never senses a real conflict between "wickedness" and "abilities" or "esteem" and "approbation" — Coleridge acknowledges a response to Iago that is beset with a contrariety of desires. Although Coleridge again assures us that Shakespeare manages to avoid the risk of "poetical unsafeness" (the "danger" Johnson worried about), the basis for this assurance is not explained adequately — or indeed, at all.

Coleridge was not a systematic thinker, and the fragmentary and reported text from which we try to determine his ideas further complicates matters.[14] But consider Bradley, writing at the end of the Coleridgean line and in the much more coherent and finished product of *Shakespearean Tragedy*. About Iago, he asks:

> How is it then that we can bear to contemplate him; nay, that, if we really imagine him, we feel admiration and some kind of sympathy? . . . We are shown a thing absolutely evil, and — what is more dreadful still — this absolute evil is united with supreme intellectual power. Why is the representation tolerable, and why do we not accuse its author either of untruth or of a desperate pessimism?
> To these questions it might at once be replied: Iago does not stand alone; he is a factor in a whole; and we perceive him there and not in isolation, acted upon as well as acting, destroyed as well as destroying. But, although this is true and important, I pass it by and [continue] to regard him by himself. (190–191)

All the topoi going back to Johnson are here, unendurability attached to the figure of Iago, and to a by now quite explicitly acknowledged incongruity of response, divided between intellectual power and truth. At risk is Shakespeare himself, an author open to accusation who is not just an author but an idea: the "real Shakespeare," as Bradley says elsewhere, what Coleridge called "the poet for all ages" (I will return to these terms in the afterword). Like Coleridge, Bradley affirms his conviction that Shakespeare has not truly crossed over into the dangerous territory where accusation might be justified, and he even asserts his capacity to demonstrate why his conviction of Shakespeare's "purity" is justified. For some reason, however, he chooses not to do so ("I pass it by") and instead gives us a footnote, attached to "destroyed as well as destroying," which refers us to yet another footnote ("Cf. note at end of lecture") where he talks about the "feelings . . . which mitigate the excess of pain" at the end of the play, and which "lift the overwhelming weight of calamity that oppresses us, and bring us an extraordinary lightening of the heart" (198).

"Reconciliation" again, and again Bradley's rhetorical jitters betray a profound sense of discomfort and uncertainty, perhaps hinting at the intuition that Burke would make explicit: not just of Iago's triumphant power but of our complicity with Iago for having "goaded (tortured) the plot forward step by step, for the audience's villainous entertainment and filthy purgation" ("*Othello*," 170). Coleridge's hesitations imply something like his famous confession about Hamlet: he has a smack of Iago in himself. If *Othello* has written him into that position, then Shakespeare might be accused of having done what nature never yet has done, betrayed the heart that loved her. The nineteenth-century *Othello*, an increasingly inflated apparatus celebrating a final nobility and transcendence shared out between protagonist and audience, may be an increasingly unsuccessful exercise in the refusal of guilt.

In the BBC *Othello* produced in the early 1980s, "the survival of the lovers' destroyer . . . extends beyond the end of the action," as "Bob Hoskins' mocking laughter continues to echo through the screen credits even after he has been led down a corridor and out of sight" (Clayton, 68). This performance is unusual in degree, but not in kind. As Wine illustrates in abundance, twentieth-century productions have been generally hospitable, not just at the end of the play but throughout, to the commanding presence of Iago which the nineteenth century felt constrained to refuse.[15] This practice certainly constitutes a restoration of the original texts, though whether it amounts also to a return to original performances or to Shakespearean intentions, and whether we even ought to venture after such a quarry — this is much less clear. However (and if ever) these issues may be resolved, I propose simply to focus on the play we've got: what does *Othello* look like, particularly in its final actions, to modern and contemporary eyes, and should we be happy with what we see?

Eliot's credit for inventing the modern *Othello* needs some qualifying detail. His remark about Othello's self-delusion is just an aside, not part of a systematic interpretation of the play, and offered in a very tentative way:

I have always felt that I have never read a more terrible exposure of human weakness — of universal human weakness — than the last great speech of Othello. (I am ignorant whether anyone else has ever adopted this view, and it may appear subjective and fantastic in the extreme.) It is usually taken on its face value, as expressing the greatness in defeat of a noble but erring nature. [Quotes 5.2.336–354, "Soft you . . . smote him, thus."] What Othello seems to me to be doing in making this speech is *cheering himself up*. He is endeavouring to escape reality, he has ceased to think about Desdemona, and is thinking about himself. Humility is the most difficult of all virtues to achieve; nothing dies harder than the desire to think well of oneself. Othello succeeds in turning himself into a pathetic figure, by adopting an *aesthetic* rather than a moral attitude, dramatizing himself against his environment. He takes in the spectator, but the human motive is primarily to take in himself. I do not believe that any writer has ever exposed this *bovarysme*, the human will to see things as they are not, more clearly than Shakespeare. ("Shakespeare and the Stoicism of Seneca," 110–111)

Eliot insists on Othello's self-delusion but also on self-delusion as a "universal" and perhaps definingly "human" characteristic (he packs "human" four times into this passage), so that while he does not back away from his contention that Othello is trying to escape from reality, he suggests that by making the claim he is himself trapped in a similar kind of delusion — as how, since it is universally human, could he not be? Shakespeare alone, at the end of the passage, seems to have transcended this limitation; he sees things as they are, if not uniquely so at least "more clearly" than anyone else. Others abide this question, Shakespeare is free: the bardolatrous implication is odder still in the context of an essay whose overall argument is that Shakespeare suffers from the lack of a systematically Christian belief such as Dante had. Where exactly is Eliot amid these contradictory suggestions? Right from the beginning, the passage calls attention to the pronouncer as much as to the pronouncement. The symmetrical contradiction of "I have always felt that I have never read" is striking. Can a writer of Eliot's self-conscious scrupulousness be so ignorant of the effects of language? Yet being "ignorant" in one sense is part of what the passage is confessing. Eliot is saying something about Othello and *Othello*, but he seems also (and perhaps chiefly) to be dramatizing something about himself — perhaps his own inevitably self-defeating quest for "humility."

For this passage to serve as the rock on which the church of modern *Othello* commentary would be built, Eliot's followers had to turn an equivocal digression about the protagonist's "last great speech" into a securely systematic interpretation of the play as a whole. Othello's final self-absorption is projected back through the play into its beginning and described from a position that is understood with growing confidence

Death without Transfiguration

to be the high ground, superior to the object of its perception. Eliot's conviction that Othello was self-deluded coincided in general with Iago's views inside the play, but this was only a coincidence. As we have seen in chapter 4, however, critical interpretation of *Othello* has increasingly absorbed itself into Iago's unillusioned and self-assured generalizations, to the point where current commentary on the play seems designed as an instrument for Iago's voice, to be performed in the deconsecrating tonality that insists the wine we all drink is made of grapes.

It is hard to figure out what we are getting from our identification with Iago's voice. Even in its purest form, it seems to be qualified with irony. Auden's remark that "given a few more years," Desdemona "might well, one feels, have taken a lover" must mean more than it says. Criticism depends as much as theater does on subtext — "language as gesture" or "symbolic action"; but what is Auden gesturing toward here, what "attitude" is he "dancing"? [16] The same questions might be asked about Calderwood, who has invested most generously in Iago's voice:

> Do we actually take some kind of pleasure in the smothering of the innocent Desdemona? Alas, so it would seem . . . : "How sad but how marvelously right!" As possibility evolves into probability and then into inevitability, a sense of formal completion yields aesthetic pleasure. . . . Thus we too participate in the disinterestedness that borders on motiveless malignity. Not that heartless pleasure is all we feel. Rather, like Othello, we are torn between a soft-hearted pity for Desdemona and a stony-hearted devotion to a "cause" that requires her death to fulfill its destined logic. (126)

The smiling "alas" and the laceration ("we are torn") that heals before it can be registered: this replicates beautifully the charm with which Iago transforms the materials of pain into an achieved insensibility. "Why, there's no remedy, 'tis the curse of service" — but service to what? Calderwood's description of Desdemona's murder sounds almost exactly like Helen Gardner's: "Yet this terrible act has wonderful tragic rightness. Only by it can the tragic situation be finally resolved, and in tragedy it is the peace of finality which we look for" (201). That Gardner's idealism and Calderwood's detachment come to rest in the same chilly formalism suggests again the instinctive affinity between nineteenth- and twentieth-century versions of the play. If the assertion of Othello's transcendent nobility served to deny guilt, then perhaps the denial of any nobility to begin with shares the same plausible motivation. If it's all just insecure ego, the catastrophe was inevitable, always already there, and it makes no sense to feel that anyone ought to be punished — not Iago and certainly not ourselves — for helping to bring it about.

Whatever we are getting out of our embrace of Iago, redemption cannot be part of it. Like Burke, Empson and Bradbrook perceived the ambivalence with which Iago is cast in the role of *katharma* or *pharmakos* — the scapegoat. For Empson, "Iago . . . is so nearly a stage Jew that he talks about his 'tribe' . . . the Jewish side of . . . tainted . . . nature" ("Honest in *Othello*," 236, 238). Bradbrook remarks, of Othello's reference to Iago as "that demi-devil," that "to Iago have been transferred all the qualities normally associated with black men on the English stage" (*Shakespeare*, 177). These comments in effect acknowledge the interchangeability of Iago's and Othello's status: who is really the outsider, who the insider? who is truly black and who white? Both of them are eligible and have been nominated to serve as the *pharmakos*. The exchangeability of opposites doesn't interfere with the economy of ritual sacrifice, quite the reverse, but the problem is that the commodities exchanged are both worthless. Whatever "the cathartic nature of his role" (Burke, "*Othello*," 166), Iago does not fulfill it any more than Othello does, and for the same reason — the inverse relation Girard insists on between the visibility of the scapegoat and his efficacy. All the attention called by Iago himself and others to his diabolical nature makes him less and less the devil; the mythological is naturalized and psychologized, detached from the discourse of sacrificial redemption, which is then *perceived* as mythological discourse — in Othello's phrase, as "a fable." Iago is made into a dramatic character; he functions on our level. This reverse transubstantiation deprives him of sacrificial effect because it deprives us of the enchanted ignorance we need to sustain belief in the sacrificial process.

In "reviling Iago," Burke says, "the audience can forget that his transgressions are theirs" ("*Othello*," 170), but Lodovico's attempt to will such an obliviousness onto us at the very end — "This is *thy* work" — is doomed to failure. The character's offer of catharsis is the play's way of withholding the same offer. Iago simply will not die for our sins; indeed, he won't die at all. His final speech, "From this time forth I never will speak word," is a way of refusing the satisfaction we seek; it suggests his fundamental invulnerability and his unavailability for the assigned cathartic role. (A few years later, Marston's *Dutch Courtesan* reenacts this process of aborted sacrifice in witty detail — perhaps evidence for the claims I am making here.)[17] In this context, "What you know, you know" may be heard as an echo of Pilate's *quod scripsi scripsi*, but Iago is not merely washing his hands of the matter, he is passing it back to us. As Burke says, he provides us our "filthy purgation," which is no purgation at all.[18]

But maybe there is a payoff for our embrace of Iago after all. Though it blocks religious redemption, disenchantment can be argued to provide access to secular liberation. According to Girard, our "growing ability to demystify [scapegoat] effects must coincide, historically, with a decrease in their power to delude" and therefore in a "decreased efficacy" for generating the credulous violence on which cultures have been founded and renewed (218). In the extraordinary *Diacritics* interview from which I am quoting, Girard claims that this "scientific development" (206) has achieved a critical point, the "complete disintegration of sacrificial protections it is our misfortune and privilege to witness" (207), so that we are on the verge of a breakthrough, "a power to demystify persecution that is already effectively within the confines of our culture, at least to a certain extent" (215). Girard's interview dates from 1978, and although he is still committed in his later work to the same interpretive model, he seems to have backed away from the optimism which allowed him to imagine an imminent transformation in human history (the optimism was guarded even then: "misfortune" as well as "benefit," only a "certain extent"). Understandably so. The intervening years have not been particularly rich in confirming evidence, though not extraordinarily unkind either. The project of Enlightenment is always in gradual process and perhaps never achievable.

During the same interim of Girard's retreat, a great throng of commentators have entered onto the field, proclaiming the emancipatory power of skeptical analysis, performed on *Othello* among other literary and theatrical texts and produced by the institutions of literary and theatrical study in general. Hence Ania Loomba tailors her commentary on the play to "our critique of the silencing of women in literature and in the classroom" (40), and Karen Newman produces hers in the service of "a political criticism," the "task" of which is "to expose or demystify the ideological discourses which organize texts" in order to "discover them as partisan, constructed, made rather than given, natural, and inevitable" (157). This argument claims a payoff for enlightened critique that it simply cannot supply — as though the patriarchy would divest itself of its privileges in the face of a revelation that these privileges have been merely constructed through historical processes. It is one thing to argue that theater or literary criticism has consequences in the world, but another to suppose that individual theatrical or critical practitioners understand and control these consequences in their interpretive realization of particular texts. When the particular text is *Othello*, the claim seems generated out of a will to believe in power and freedom inversely related to a literary and theatrical experience of constriction and guilt. Where the nineteenth century puffed the play up, we seem to want to shout it down. Hence Karen Newman's claim that resistant "strategies of reading are particularly necessary in drama because [of] the dramatic immediacy of theatrical representation" (157). Given the immediacy of this particular dramatic representation, resistance, however futile, may be inevitable.

Thomas Clayton, mediating between the "triumphal" interpretations of *Othello*'s ending (he cites Bradbrook and Gardner) and "Brecht's agitprop-oriented perspective," tries to find

> a tenable position neither alienated nor uplifted, dark, perhaps, but no less sympathetic. In tragedies of this kind a balance is characteristically struck between the irreversible loss and the glory of what might have been, which is known as such for what it has been. What was great and potentially greater, once lost, holds good for what it was and memorially remains. (64)

According to Clayton, the play's focus at the end is on Othello and Desdemona's shared love: "both expire on the terminal note of a single heroic couplet, each concerned primarily and affectionately with the other" (61). The same kind of claim is richly developed by Julia Genster:

> In Desdemona's speech, and in its resonances in Othello's, we can recover the "noble Othello of the beginning" who, as John Traugott has it, "is all the more present by his absence at the end"; we can, however fleetingly, reconstitute the union between the Moor and Desdemona. . . . When, in the willow song, [Desdemona] takes Barbary's part, she also — in that act of recalling her mother's maid's name — assimilates Othello's Moorish identity. Her last words are not an act of submission but a challenge: she asks to be commended to her kind lord, but such commendations would be audible only to an Othello who has recovered some part of himself, who has become his own kind again. . . . Othello attempts to find again his own narrative, and rises to Desdemona's challenge though he cannot fully meet it. He does, however, meet her metaphorically: imaging himself as "one whose subdued eyes" (5.2.349) "drop tears as fast as the Ara-

bian trees / Their medicinable gum" (351–52), he circles back to Desdemona's willow song, offering his own exotic version of her weeping willow. He has incorporated her, as she did him, even though he has not heard her, and she has not heard him. But we have heard both. (804–805)

Evidently not all current audiences of *Othello*'s ending have been absorbed wholly into Iago's perspective. Clayton and Genster concede his decisive influence, to be sure. Nothing can compensate for the "irreversible loss" of Desdemona, and only "some part" of Othello's originally perfect soul is restored. Neither Clayton nor Genster would agree with Matthews's claim about Iago's ultimate impotence in the face of "indivisible human dignity." Iago has won; Iago is given his due. But so is the greatness of heart Othello and Desdemona shared with each other at the beginning of the play, and share out again among us even now in living memory at the end.

Clayton and Genster beautifully realize a response that manages to acknowledge the contradictory energies of the play. But although this response corresponds to the "balanced" view I have been looking for from the beginning of this book, it remains something of an abstraction, detached from the action on stage. In performance, *Othello* ends with a dispirited anticlimax, "the most violently abrupted of all Shakespearean endings" (Neill, "Unproper Beds," 383). Some measure of this finality seems to have been represented in Kean's and Olivier's performance of the suicide. Kean "realized that 'death by a *heart* wound is *instantaneous*,' and 'literally dies standing; it is the dead body only of Othello that falls, heavily and at once; there is no *rebound*, which speaks of vitality and of living muscles. It is the dull weight of clay seeking its kindred earth'" (Sprague, *Shakespearian Players*, 85). Olivier "slashes his throat with the hidden stiletto we saw in III.3. And slumps like a falling tower. . . . As he slumped beside her in the sheets, the current stopped. A couple of wigged actors stood awkwardly about. You could only pity them: we had seen history, and it was over" (Tynan, 11; Ronald Bryden, quoted in Tynan, 106). Martin Wine seems to be getting at a similar effect in critical terms, describing the echo in Othello's suicide speech of the Senate speech at the beginning: "It, too, re-enacts in the present a splendid moment from the past but only to give meaning to the present, not to the future. By killing, *in narration*, the 'malignant . . . turbaned Turk' and, *in actual fact*, the Turk that he had become, Othello unifies himself as he destroys himself" (Wine's emphasis, 35). The difference is crucial. Where the earlier speech achieved unity in a capacity for continuity, here integrity is stabilized in the absolute closure of death.

To put it another way, the problem is that the play calls our attention finally not to an image of the dead lovers' embrace but to the fact that they are dead, and to their surviving murderer, the destructive agent in whose malign powers we have participated. This sequence tends to empty the bed of its potential as a memorial reconstruction of beauty and makes it into an object that poisons sight. Wine argues that the "impression of [Othello and Desdemona's] wasted lives should haunt an audience more than the spell of Iago's 'humour' or Machiavellian cleverness" (66). From this perspective, the BBC version was wrong to give Hoskins the last word and the last laugh — a perversity compounded by the controlling medium of television: When "Othello stabs himself and dies 'upon a kiss' [he] simply falls out of the picture, not onto the bed to kiss Desdemona. But, as he falls through the bottom of the frame or screen, the shot reveals Iago, thereby emphasising his dominant role as instigator of this dastardly deed and now as victor in his 'practical joke'" (74). No doubt TV and movies are more coercive than theater in controlling the object of our gaze, but this particular direction seems to derive from the playtext which, after commanding that the curtains on the bed be closed, requires us to focus on "*this* hellish victim" (5.2.366). Wine doesn't want to look Iago in the face at the end of *Othello*, but who does? "Perhaps," as Hankey suggests, "the Victorian instinct to end the play at Othello's death was right" (340).

For Clayton, relentlessly refusing to ignore the textual basis for Bob Hoskins's laugh-over-credits, the

> irony is made almost unbearable. . . . And yet, Desdemona and Othello are at last beyond the reach of envious malice, and theirs is implicitly some version of a peace that passeth all understanding, whether heavenly bliss secured or in prospect, or the nitrogen cycle not yet even dreamt of. So much for the irony. The play's plenitude of Christian reference — more in its own day than in ours — may shed prevenient grace upon the endplay and imply a hope of resurrection and reunion. But even if death is seen as final, there is the sweet oblivious antidote of nothingness, the pain of which is only in the spectacle, the eye of the beholder, the present the dead have passed beyond. (68)

Amen to that, sweet powers! But to what exactly are we assenting? We wish Othello and Desdemona well, but it is hard to fix this desire locally.

Death without Transfiguration

Clayton is surely right to say that the Christian references meant more to Shakespeare's audience than to us, but in the play's final moments as throughout, the references that dominate are to guilt, sin, and hell. We can't say that the lovers have entered into the peace that passes understanding, only that they no longer occupy a world controlled by Iago's understanding. Othello and Desdemona are dead. It's over for them. The "sweet oblivious antidote of nothingness" will have to be enough, because it's all we get. For us, too, the pain of the spectacle ceases, and that's something. Dr. Johnson had it right: *Othello* is not to be endured.

Interpretation as Contamination

After quoting Johnson ("not to be endured") and Halliwell-Phillipps ("rather a painful duty than one of pleasure" — see chapter 6), Furness adds his own corroborating testimony:

> I do not shrink from saying that I wish this Tragedy had never been written. The pleasure, however keen or elevated, which the inexhaustible poetry of the preceding Acts can bestow, cannot possibly, to my temperament, countervail, it does but increase, the unutterable agony of this closing Scene. (300)

Why are such remarks hard to take fully seriously? Conventionality (here comes another iteration of the unendurability topos) and confessionality can't be the main problems: in the present environment, authenticity is a discursive effect, iteration is always reiteration, anecdotes and personal reminiscence have become critical methodology. Perhaps, then, it's Furness's ornate language and mannered syntax, so intricate and ostentatious as to obscure his meaning. This would be a loss. Furness is making a very precise point with real explanatory power about the play's affective economy — the painful quality at the end is directly related to our pleasure earlier, presumably in the protagonist's "elevated" temperament. Furness's point, moreover, like Halliwell-Phillipps's and (*mutatis mutandis*) Dr. Johnson's, may be reinforced rather than obscured by the elaborate displays of complex structure and control. Hence William Winter, who himself gave a memorable performance of the "unendurability" role (see *Shakespeare on the Stage*, 270), writing of the "heartrending and terrible" qualities of *Othello*: the "mind cannot dwell upon it without an effort. No one of Shakespeare's great plays is less stimulative to such reflection as a sensitive mind cares to communicate. You leave a performance of *Othello* with mingled emotions of consternation, disgust, and grief. You feel as if you had seen a murder or attended an execution" (*Life and Art*, 192–193). The wonderfully elaborate periphrasis in the middle ("less stimulative . . . communicate") says exactly what Winter means — namely, that you can't say what you mean, that *Othello* makes you feel things you don't want to communicate directly or even think about. Confronted with this play, you take help wherever you can get it and in whatever form available. It doesn't have to be the truth; it had probably better not be. Winter understood Othello as deluded in his claims about ritual sacrifice, but demanded that these claims be sustained in performance nonetheless — by Booth on the stage, and here by Winter himself in critical reflection. Illusions, even delusions, are necessary if we are to endure the play at all.

Perhaps the chief obstacle to engaging seriously with Johnson and his followers in this line is the moralistic tone and the explicitly moral demands they make on the play. Bradley's anxious intuition that *Othello* might make us want "to accuse its author of untruth or of a desperate pessimism" sounds old-fashioned, a piece of earnest Victorianism with only antiquarian interest. But consider Edward Snow who, taking off from Burke's idea of "filthy purgation," declares that *Othello* is "one of Shakespeare's most cynical plays, taking as it does a certain self-consciously impotent pleasure in demonstrating the moral corruption of its audience and its own form, and confirming in the process the resistance to demystification of the material that is its thematic and psychological core" ("Sexual Anxiety," 387). Critics from Johnson to Bradley should have no trouble understanding the fury in Snow's words; he is describing the play they saw, or couldn't bear looking at. If "cynical" is the right word for *Othello*'s author, then Snow's description in effect makes the accusation against Shakespeare that Bradley worried he couldn't avoid.

The situation might be clearer if we switch over from play or author to audience. Why devote time and energy to a play that constitutes such a sustained assault on the sensibilities? It can be argued that guilt is good for the soul and that suffering builds humanity (*Lear* criticism earlier this century sustained itself with this kind of nourishment), but there doesn't seem to be much evidence to support such claims. It can be argued that the interpretation of *Othello* allows us (with Hazlitt) to substitute "imaginary sympathy for mere selfishness" as a way of attaining "a high and permanent interest, beyond ourselves, in humanity as such," or that it allows us (with Newman) "to expose or demystify the ideological discourses which organize texts." There is not much evidence to support these claims either.

Dr. Johnson and Furness were editing Shakespeare's collected works and so didn't need a higher justification for their work. They had no choice but to engage with the play. It is less clear why I have invested so much time and energy in writing this book or readers who have got this far in reading it. We may be operating under pressures similar to those that constrained Johnson and Furness. *Othello* is an obligation, a professional responsibility — tradition again, inertia: we do what we do because we have been doing what we have been doing. Inertia may be a satisfactory explanation, but it is not a satisfying one. It would be nice to have something more substantial.[1] Our survival, at least professionally speaking, may depend on finding a higher purpose. According to Girard, "if one does not believe that certain texts, at least, can help us, not only esthetically but intellectually and ethically, especially at a time such as ours, which is no ordinary time, then literature is an empty and dying cult" ("An Interview," 225). But as Girard suggests, some texts are more helpful than others, and *Othello* doesn't provide encouragement to a project designed to liberate us from the inherited burden of diseased superstition.

We are back to the position I described at the beginning of this book: that our critical power is just what *Othello* defeats, absorbing any attempts at reflection on the play into a reproduction of the malignancy it seeks to repudiate. If one consequence of this argument is to blur if not totally erase the distinction between *Othello* and its interpretive traditions, then a further consequence — the one I want to develop here finally — is to blur if not totally erase the distinction between good and bad *Othello* criticism, however maintained. Where "wrong" is an impotent predication, how do we distinguish the soldiers of Truth from the armies of Error, or how differentiate between the clergy and laity, between claims made by professional Shakespeareans in books like this and opinions expressed by the "man in the street" — or the person on the information superhighway? In pursuing these matters I am guided, as I have been throughout, by Burke's idea about our "filthy purgation."

In March 1995, conversation on SHAKSPER, the electronic discussion group I described at the beginning of this book, turned to color-blind casting and then meandered into the question of Othello's color. On March 17, a message was posted including the following paragraph:

Ruth Cowlig (I think I've spelled the name correctly) wrote an excellent article on the stage history of the character Othello; apparently, after Shakespeare's own day, it was not until the early 1900's that audiences realized Othello was Black. Even with this realization, many literary critics such as Ripley (infamous editor of The Arden Shakespeare) tried to bleach Othello's Blackness, claiming that the character was not coarse enough to be authentically Black, that the character was a mulatto with only a small fraction of Black blood in him, that the character is best envisioned with a classical profile and an aquiline nose, ad nauseam.[2]

Almost everything in this message is wrong. The names are Cowhig and Ridley. The history is totally botched. Nineteenth-century commentators were very much aware of — and bothered by — Othello's blackness. Ridley's claim was just the opposite of the one attributed to him: he insisted that Othello was indeed conceived by Shakespeare as a black African. Rarely have so many owed so much misinformation to so few words. How can we account for the fact that this contributor, let's call him Tromper, managed to achieve such an appalling concentration of error?

Despite the reference to the "excellent article" by "Cowlig," most of Tromper's details seem to be based on misrememberings of a different and (predictably) unacknowledged piece, Karen Newman's "'And Wash the Ethiop White': Femininity and the Monstrous in *Othello*." The first thing Tromper gets wrong is the title. Newman's piece begins with a nineteenth-century Pears Soap illustration showing "a black baby scrubbed almost white," so perhaps the evocation of modern laundry technology turned "wash" into "bleach" in Tromper's mind. The second thing Tromper gets wrong is Ridley's name. Newman quotes a long passage from Ridley and then discusses it at length at the very beginning of her essay, but how Ridley metamorphosed into "Ripley (infamous editor of the Arden Shakespeare)" is hard to figure. Easy, though, to guess how Tromper came across Newman's essay: it has achieved a richly deserved prominence on the current critical scene. By emphasizing the connections between racist and misogynist feelings, Newman's essay has contributed significantly to the process that has made *Othello* the Shakespearean tragedy of our time — the one speaking most directly and deeply to contemporary interests. As a consequence, it has been republished three times[3] and much referred to in current critical work. (Perhaps Tromper was thumbing through Hendricks and Parker's 1994

Interpretation as Contamination

Routledge anthology, where he would have found more citations of Newman's essay by far than of any other modern work.)[4] This widespread circulation has made the essay particularly subject to misappropriation, and the Internet, as an informal instrument of conversation, has apparently encouraged misrepresentation. Maybe; but let's look a bit more closely.

Here then is Ridley, reproduced in full from Newman, followed by a lengthy excerpt of her opening discussion:

> To a great many people the word "negro" suggests at once the picture of what they would call a "nigger," the woolly hair, thick lips, round skull, blunt features, and burnt-cork blackness of the traditional nigger minstrel. Their subconscious generalization is as silly as that implied in Miss Preston's "the African race" or Coleridge's "veritable negro." There are more races than one in Africa, and that a man is black in colour is no reason why he should, even to European eyes, look subhuman. One of the finest heads I have ever seen on any human being was that of a negro conductor on an American Pullman car. He had lips slightly thicker than an ordinary European's, and he had somewhat curly hair; for the rest he had a long head, a magnificent forehead, a keenly chiselled nose, rather sunken cheeks, and his expression was grave, dignified, and a trifle melancholy. He was coal-black, but he might have sat to a sculptor for a statue of Caesar. (Ridley)
>
>   M. R. Ridley's "they" is troublesome. As scholars and teachers, we use his Arden edition of *Othello* (1958, repr. 1977) and find ourselves implicated in his comfortable assumptions about "a great many people." In answer to the long critical history which sought to refute Othello's blackness, Ridley affirms that Othello was black, but he hastens to add the adversative "but." [Ridley], in the very act of debunking, canonizes the prejudices of Rymer and Coleridge. Can we shrug our shoulders, certain that Ridley's viewpoint represents a long ago past of American Pullman cars and dignified black conductors? Are such prejudices dismantled by the most recent reprint which represents on its cover a "veritable negro" of exactly the physiognomy Ridley assures us "a great many people" are wrong in imagining? (143–144)

Despite all his evident mistakes, Tromper's representation of Newman's representation of Ridley is accurate in one important respect: Ridley emerges as a racist and therefore an infamous figure indeed. Tromper, though apparently not an academic himself, finds himself here in distinguished academic company. Margaret Ferguson refers us to Newman's essay "for an analysis of Ridley's racist remaking of Othello," his "efforts to assure (white) readers . . . that the black hero isn't one of those 'subhuman'-looking Negroes with 'wooly hair' and 'thick lips.'" (26, 46). Ania Loomba refers us to Newman for a discussion of "Ridley's notoriously racist introduction" and of his "notoriously and crudely racist" "efforts to prove Othello's non-negroid racial origins" (62, 42). Oddly enough, though published in distinguished academic presses, both Ferguson and Loomba are themselves not uninfected with the *pseudodoxia epidemica* of Tromper's Internet gab. Loomba also gives Ridley a new name, or at least a new middle initial — he is referred to throughout her book not as M. R. but as M. I. Ridley (as in MI5?). Ferguson misquotes Newman's quotation from Ridley, so that "woolly" comes out as "wooly." But this is splitting hairs. Whatever the details, Tromper, Ferguson, and Loomba all agree with one another in more or less accurately reproducing Newman's view of Ridley as a racist. If there is a problem, it goes back at least as far as this original characterization, not just to the means — electronic, mechanical, textual — by which corruption is spread.

Are Ridley's assumptions "comfortable," as Newman says? In the way his voice slips back and forth between the acknowledgment and the denial of racist feelings, he seems, rather, profoundly ill at ease. The abrupt interjection of an autobiographical anecdote (a much less common rhetorical strategy when Ridley was writing) serves to foreground an intensely personal ambivalence — at once resisting and avowing his share in the "subconscious generalization" that, "even to European eyes" (wonderful neo-Conradian phrase!), offers ocular proof of an embarrassed participation, willy-nilly, in the history of racist sentiment. Ridley's contemptuous dismissal of Miss Preston, the Baltimore woman we encountered in chapter 1 who, as quoted in Furness's *Variorum* (395), declared that "Othello *was a white* man," betrays a similar ambivalence. If Mary Preston is "silly" in her reductio ad absurdum of Coleridge's denial that Othello was "a veritable negro," then Ridley must be a little silly himself, since his overall purpose is to make a similar denial — if not of veritable negritude, then of a common prejudice about black people. It's as if the denial cannot be made except by implicitly affirming what is being denied. Newman herself makes this point. Commenting on Ridley's argument that Othello must be imagined as thick-lipped because "an insult . . . must have some relation to the facts," Newman complains of his "woefully inadequate sense of irony: literary discourse often works by means of negative example" (145). But this is a point that Newman not only makes but embodies. For by eliminating Ridley's discomfort and thereby constructing him as a figure of infamy, she performs the same gesture of repudiation — even exorcism — Ridley had performed upon the silly Miss Preston. By making *them* foolishly blind to their own guilty assumptions, we can by contrast represent *ourselves* as fully self-conscious of our own complicity, expelling the otherwise "troublesome" guilt we purport to declare and accomplishing, thereby, "our filthy purgation."

This discussion may seem to be confusing the issue. Tromper's blatant factual errors are of a different order from Newman's interpretations. Interpretations always admit the possibility of disagreement. But we can clarify the issue by shifting focus to Coleridge. For one thing, Coleridge occupies a position at or near the origin of the debate about Othello's color, as he does in the history of modern literary studies generally. More immediately relevant, Coleridge is the source of Newman's second head quotation, produced as "It would be something monstrous to conceive this beautiful Venetian girl falling in love with a veritable negro," and sandwiched between a Rymer passage (as usual, Rymer occupies the originating position) and the Ridley passage we have seen. Here, from the source cited by Newman (Raysor, 42), is the paragraph in full from which she takes her head quotation:

> It is a common error to mistake the epithets applied by the *dramatis personae* to each other, as truly descriptive of what the audience ought to see or know. No doubt Desdemona saw Othello's visage in his mind; yet, as we are constituted, and most surely as an English audience was disposed in the beginning of the seventeenth century, *it would be something monstrous to conceive this beautiful Venetian girl falling in love with a veritable negro*. It would argue a disproportionateness, a want of balance in Desdemona, which Shakespeare does not appear to have in the least contemplated.

By quoting only the words I have emphasized (and replacing "it" with "It"), Newman has turned the statement into a freestanding and unqualified assertion of belief. But Coleridge is not (or perhaps not only) expressing his disgust at miscegenation; he is defining such disgust as specific to his cultural moment, "as we are constituted." To refer simply, then, to "the prejudices of . . . Coleridge" ignores the way Coleridge detaches himself from these prejudices even as he acknowledges his participation in them.

In this sense, Coleridge anticipates Ridley's and Newman's own performances, both admitting and denying complicity. But unlike Ridley, who projects these conflicts onto a silly Coleridge and sillier Miss Preston, and unlike Newman, who projects them onto an infamous Ridley and racist Coleridge, Coleridge himself does not offer us a scapegoat for our filthy purgation. Elsewhere, and in a context (probably coincidentally) dense with echoes of *Othello*'s language and ideas, he fully acknowledges the guilt of participating in a racist culture:

> My God! it is a melancholy thing
> For such a man, who would full fain preserve
> His soul in calmness, yet perforce must feel
> For all his human brethren . . .
>
>   even now,
> Even now, perchance, and in his native isle:
> Carnage and groans beneath this blessed sun!
> We have offended, Oh! my countrymen!
> We have offended very grievously,
> And been most tyrannous. From east to west
> A groan of accusation pierces Heaven!
> The wretched plead against us; multitudes
> Countless and vehement, the sons of God,
> Our brethren! Like a cloud that travels on,
> Streamed up from Cairo's swamps of pestilence,
> Even so, my countrymen! have we gone forth
> And borne to distant tribes slavery and pangs,
> And, deadlier far, our vices, whose deep taint
> With slow perdition murders the whole man,
> His body and his soul! ("Fears in Solitude," 29–53)

In his comments about *Othello*, however, Coleridge is motivated by a quest for the proper response to poetic drama and heroic tragedy. Hence, shortly before the passage about the monstrosity "of falling in love with a veritable negro," he asks us whether, "even if we supposed [Othello's blackness] an uninterrupted tradition of the theatre, and that Shakespeare himself, from want of scenes and the experience that nothing could be made too *marked* for the nerves of his audience, [sanctioned it,] would this prove aught concerning his intentions as a poet for all ages?" (Raysor, 42). This question assumes that the proper response to *Othello* is independent of any historically verifiable intentions of "Shakespeare himself" or of the play's original reception conditions. It has to do, rather, with "intentions as a poet for all ages," a phrase that confers value and significance on the literary text as an imaginative construct, which in turn allows Coleridge to emphasize his main concern, the strenuous imaginative activity by which we take possession of the literary text.[5] If such activity is inhibited by a black Othello — in our mind's eye and (*a fortiori*) on the physical stage — then a black Othello will not do.

In "a poet for all ages," Coleridge echoes Ben Jonson's famous tribute to Shakespeare as "not of an age, but for all time." We have become very suspicious about such claims for the transcendence of history, dismissing them as silly and infamous in their apparent indifference to the historical contingencies of the social struggle among subjects differentially positioned by the asymmetrical power relations defined by race, class, gender, ethnicity, sexuality, and nationality. But maybe we are too quick to dismiss Coleridge as antihistorical or racist. His refusal of Othello's blackness, though made independently of historical considerations, may have hit by *feliciter audax* on a historically shrewd response. Color in the Renaissance was a category signifying ethical practice and theological belief more than racial identity. For Renaissance audiences, as we have seen, washing an Ethiop white would have represented a genuine (if unliteral) possibility — something which helps to explain Desdemona's claim about seeing Othello's visage in his mind and the Duke's statement that Othello is far more fair than black. Such flexible slippages had become increasingly difficult if not effectively impossible within the scientifically authorized ethnography developing in the nineteenth century ("as we are constituted").[6] Bradley struggled with the same problem at the end of the century, deciding that though "to Shakespeare Othello was a black," he could not "be represented as a black in our theatres now," because "we do not like the real Shakespeare" (*Shakespearean Tragedy*, 165) where the real Shakespeare corresponds to Coleridge's poet for all ages, the idea of an author whose textual embodiment must be encountered above the ground of actual belief as constituted "now" — that is, outside the ideological constructions of late Victorian racial science. Coleridge's tawny Moor was an unhappy solution to an unhappy and probably insoluble problem, in society as well as theatrical production. Whatever his intentions, however, the effect of Coleridge's commentary was to put the concept of race inside inverted commas — the practice of all sophisticated historicist critics like Hendricks and Parker who, as *we* are constituted, understand "race" as the product of specific cultural constructions rather than as a stable and natural signifier. Although Coleridge was not interested in cultural specificity as such, his creation of a transcendent imaginative space for encountering the "poet for all ages" nonetheless allows for the possibility of a defamiliarized text, estranged from contemporary belief, which is arguably a necessary precondition for any authentically historical work.

Again, though, I may seem to be confusing the issue. To claim that Coleridge has been quoted out of context doesn't get us very far; every quotation is perforce decontextualized and in this sense a misquotation.[7] As a consequence, we accept a certain arbitrariness in delimiting the context as consistent with citational accuracy. Whether or not the arbitrariness is excessive here, the fact remains that Coleridge's words are transcribed accurately ("it" and "It" notwithstanding). Turn, though, to R. A. Foakes's authoritative text of Coleridge's literary criticism for the monumental Princeton edition (*Lectures on Literature, 1808–1819*). The offending statement, what Dympna Callaghan characterizes in a recent essay as "Coleridge's infamous phrase" (193), isn't there. The whole paragraph isn't there. Foakes's edition did not appear until the year Newman's essay was first published, but in the edition Newman quotes, Raysor includes a cautionary footnote that "this paragraph is interpolated from *LR*. The authenticity of this passage may be suspected, certainly in part and perhaps even as a whole" (42). By ignoring this disclaimer, Newman winds up quoting Coleridge accurately, but Henry Nelson Coleridge, probably, not STC.

Is this wrong? We might well think so, but consider the other side. There are plausible arguments for attributing the paragraph to STC, even if he never wrote it. For one thing, H. N. Coleridge is himself a reliable commentator; as Terence Hawkes remarks about the paragraph, "insofar as it is successful" as "an attempt to clarify the previous passage," it is worthwhile "to preserve it" (*Coleridge's Writings on Shakespeare*, 169).[8] Much more important, the paragraph has served as an originating point of reference for most of the critics who address the issue of Othello's color — which is to say most *Othello* critics, *tout court*. In attributing the words to Coleridge, Newman follows a tradition that goes back from Ridley to (and beyond) Bradley. Bradley quotes more generously from the paragraph, everything but the first sentence, but only to arrive at much the same position as Newman herself: a patronizing "regret" for the way Coleridge anticipates the "horror of most American critics (Mr. Furness is a bright exception) at the idea of a black

Othello," a response which Bradley takes to be "very amusing" and "highly instructive" (*Shakespearean Tragedy*, 163).[9] The disparaging tone is uncharacteristic; Bradley is normally the sweetest of critics, but even he seems vulnerable to the malign spirit produced by the play. Odder still that Bradley distances himself so carefully from Coleridge and those very amusing Americans, since his own argument is basically a reproduction of theirs from within the same ambivalent sentiments. As we have seen, however, such misrecognition is more of a norm than an anomaly, as in the procedures by which Ridley and Newman labor to reconstruct their own secret sharers into alien creatures. The concept of the alien, indeed, seems to have migrated from the play to the interpretive tradition. Bradley's transatlantic resonances, those "very amusing" Americans, figure (much as they do in Ridley) as part of the process by which contamination is quarantined in the stranger. Graham Bradshaw picks up on these resonances, referring ironically to Johannesburg or "cities in the American South" where references to Othello's "sooty bosom" would constitute a problem, in contrast to "more hygiene zones" (184).[10] The same feeling underwrites Dympna Callaghan's contemptuous allusion in the essay I mentioned just earlier to "one Miss Preston, writing in the notoriously racist pre–Civil Rights South" (193–194): *one Miss Preston, a Southerner . . . one Michael Cassio, a Florentine.* Iago's xenophobic resentment seems to have slipped into Callaghan's speech, like the wine and song by which Iago transforms Cassio from courtly gentility into murderous rage.

This tradition flourishes still. Starting with the year of Newman's essay, the same decontextualized and inauthentic statement has been quoted as Coleridge by Joel Altman (152), Martin Orkin (182), Michael Neill ("Unproper Beds," 405), Graham Bradshaw (307), Jyotsna Singh (287), Stanley Wells (246), and Mythili Kaul ("Background," 7). In terms of prestige and of geographic and critical range, these might constitute the board of directors of International Shakespeare Inc.[11] In 1991, John Salway published an essay titled "Veritable Negroes and Circumcised Dogs." By putting Coleridge's "infamous phrase" into apposition with Othello's last speech, Salway promotes it to the ultimate canonical status, equivalent in authority to the Shakespearean text itself.

Michael Neill is a case apart. Much, to be sure, is predictable: Ridley's Pullman porter anecdote is dismissed as "ludicrous" and "most disgraceful"; Coleridge is misread to "assert that Othello was never intended to be black," and his "application of critical skin-lightener" said to begin "a tradition of sterile and seemingly endless debate" continuing "until well into the present century." Entirely unpredictable, however, is Neill's sudden acknowledgment that he is himself still trapped in the same guilty anxieties when, after complaining about "those liberal critiques" that treat "Othello's color simply as a convenient badge of his estrangement from Venetian society," he feels moved to repudiate an earlier essay of his own: "I ought to have noticed more clearly the way in which racial identity is constructed as one of the most fiercely contested 'places' in the play" ("Unproper Beds," 391, 392, and 394). O, he has taken too little care of this; he was wrong. Such mea culpas are extremely rare in *Othello* commentary, but ubiquitous as a subtextual presence (so I have been arguing), felt along the blood if not registered in consciousness, the unuttered guilt that generates and gives meaning to our response. Neill brings it to the surface here, and even if he relegates it to a footnote about an earlier self, the effect is movingly impressive.

Like "Deformed" in *Much Ado* — a lighter play about misprision, jealousy, pain, and deceiving men — "Coleridge" is a word that turns into a thing in whose concrete existence we have come to believe. The "Coleridge" of interpretive tradition, the creature who declared it "something monstrous to conceive this beautiful Venetian girl falling in love with a veritable negro," is a monster in our thoughts, a dangerous conceit, like poison. What then? Beware the monster. We can take our stand with Ananias in Jonson's *Alchemist*: "I hate traditions: / I do not trust 'em" (3.2.106–107). This would be an understandable response to a play that spits out "abhor," "hate," and "despise" in its opening exchanges and has by the end lodged a grievous load of guilt on us as the consequence of our inability to escape from the accumulated weight of historical prejudice. But trying to extirpate the errors of tradition is quixotic in its endeavor to retrieve an original purity and authenticity at all costs; like the Oxford editors' reversion to Oldcastle, it makes us grieve to have a soulless image on the eye which had usurped upon a living thought.[12]

Besides, Ananias's admirably proto-Enlightenment position is simply impractical. Denial doesn't work. If it did, the interpretive traditions of our response to the play would be much less painful than the record indicates. It would not feature the persistent denial and continual rage and pain we have seen in such abundance, going back to Rymer and to Henry Jackson's description of an audience "moved to . . . tears" at the Oxford performance of 1610. And it would not include the "surprising . . . *personal* acrimony" and "peculiar viciousness" of current *Othello* interpreters, qualities Peter Davison thinks "may stem from what in *Othello* subconsciously disturbs them" (10 and 13, Davison's emphasis).

In sharing my disturbances with you in this book, dear readers, I may seem animated by a peculiar viciousness. Some of you may be reminded of Pandarus, bequeathing his diseases to the audience at the end of *Troilus and Cressida*. Do not believe it. I deny it. You would be wrong. I've just been trying to put in a good word for my predecessors among *Othello* interpreters, who have been much maligned of late. For M. R. Ridley and Samuel Coleridge and the others, certainly; but for Karen Newman and Dympna Callaghan and the others as well, who have been much maligned still more recently — even now, now, very now. And here's a good word for that silly woman scribbling down in Maryland in 1869. Mary Preston said a notorious thing, but she lived in a notorious place and time. What she knew, she knew. Working on *Othello* means inhabiting a contaminated site; you want to say the right thing, but it comes out sounding terribly wrong. We need to show forbearance to our forebears; we are they and they are we and we are all together. "The time has come for us to forgive one another" (Girard, *The Scapegoat*, 212). So, here's to the *Othello* interpreters. God bless them, every one. Not least the infamous Ripley, believe it or not, *mon semblable, mon frère!*

APPENDIX

"Character Endures"

At the beginning of *I Want to Tell You*, the book produced during his murder trial, O. J. Simpson provides a kind of prefatory headnote:

> Fame is a vapor;
>   popularity an accident
>   And money takes wing;
>   And those who cheer today
>   will curse tomorrow.
>   The only thing that
>   endures — is character.

There are two related appeals here, one to "character" as an inner truth that sustains itself against the transient appearances of the material world, the other, implied in the decision to print the statement as verse, to the idea of poetry as the appropriate discursive category for making such transcendent claims. Perhaps these appeals were successful to some of *I Want to Tell You*'s target audience (a pretty substantial one, I assume: in my local Chapters I found the book in the true crime section, which takes up more space than the poetry and theater sections combined); but the readers of the present book will probably dismiss such claims as self-evidently banal clichés. Nonetheless, I want to argue here that "O. J." (to quote the signature to which these "words that I've / tried to live by" are attached) had it right in significant respects, though for reasons he (or more likely his ghost writer) probably never dreamed of.

The story of Shakespeare studies' gradual abandonment of "Bradley" and "character analysis" should be a familiar one, conventionally beginning in 1933, when L. C. Knights's "How Many Children Had Lady Macbeth?" repudiated the notion of treating dramatic characters as the authors and origins of their own histories, autonomous agents with lives outside the dramatic action. Knights's essay coincided with a redirection of Shakespeare studies from character to language, from Bradley's "whole nature" of the protagonist to the coherent artifice of the play itself. Wilson Knight's "spatial hermeneutics" figures notably in this shift, as part of a "modernist paradigm";[1] psychological integrity is fragmented into linguistic patterns that reachieve wholeness in a self-reflexive rather than representational text. If a play begins to resemble *Les Demoiselles d'Avignon*, it makes more sense to speak of the structural relation of geometric forms — image patterns contributing to symbolic coherence in a dramatic poem — than about which if any of the characters has a noble nature.

More recently, these antihumanist tendencies have become systematized. In Richard Rorty's view, there is no such "thing as 'human nature' or the 'deepest level of the self.' . . . Socialization, and thus historical circumstance, goes all the way down" (xiii). Rorty wants to collapse the distinctions between depth and surface, inner and outer (or, more precisely, to displace them from the status of ontological categories, where they inscribe a foundational difference between Reality and Appearance, and put them into service for a rough-and-ready pragmatist use, specific to a particular context). If modernists reconceived representation, renouncing the mirror of nature for an abstract and self-referring esthetic text, a view like Rorty's seems to abandon the concept of representation altogether, denying that there is any stable substance out there (or in here) to be imitated, or that the esthetic text itself exists with any authority beyond that given by a contingent historical process.

From another angle, however, current critics have not abandoned representation but universalized it. If everything is a text, then nature (including Bradley's "whole nature" of Othello's "character") and art (including *Othello*) are just different cultural constructs or discursive practices — of many, two. As a consequence, we can exchange the question of Othello's jealousy for an enquiry into the sex/gender system; and this newly negotiated interest in *Othello* leads us away from Shakespeare or heroic tragedy, authors or theatrical genres, and over to the literary system and its contribution to the production and reproduction of cultural value. Hence Valerie Traub declares that

> I am less interested in the ways works of art are empowered than in the ways characters are represented as negotiating and struggling *for* power, the extent to which they are granted or denied agency — in

"Character Endures"

short, the ways their subjectivity is constructed through representational means [and] the "processes whereby sexual desires are constructed, mass-produced, and distributed." (4)

Traub isn't concerned particularly with *Othello* in this passage, but the
interests and assumptions she articulates are clearly the ones which
have produced the culture- rather than character-centered interpretation with which we now take possession of the play.

But an understanding of *Othello* in our time as the product of an
ongoing movement away from Bradley and the nineteenth century cannot be the whole truth. Whatever the real explanatory power of such a
story, it cannot account for the remarkable persistence of those interpretive strategies and assumptions from which we have supposedly detached ourselves. As W. B. Worthen points out, the typical "actorly
reading" of Shakespeare remains, in contrast to academic criticism, "notably trained on questions of 'character' [as] integrated, self-present,
internalized, psychologically motivated" (127). As with acting, so with
teaching Shakespeare: drop into most Shakespeare classes and you will
hear Bradley-speak. Since academic criticism is a different mode of understanding from teaching or theatrical performance, we should not
expect an identity of interests and assumptions. At the same time, the
remoteness of academic discourse from two such influential ways of representing Shakespeare as pedagogy and theater is remarkable.

Even more remarkable are the residues of Bradley surviving in academic criticism itself, especially in earlier twentieth-century criticism.
Margaret Mikesell points out that the "renewed criticism of Bradleyan
traditions in the early 1950s" often rested in the very methods that were
being repudiated, treating "Othello and Iago as characters [with] the
personalities of real people" (xvii). G. M. Matthews unpacks the assumptions that underlie this surprising continuity:

> The classic dilemma of *Othello* criticism has been that if the hero is
> as noble as he seems, a villain of superhuman intelligence would be
> needed to break him down. There are therefore critics who make Iago
> superhuman: a symbol or embodiment of Evil. Alternatively, if Iago
> is as ignoble as he proves, the hero must be a very poor type to be
> taken in by him. This (broadly speaking) is the line followed by critics
> from F. R. Leavis to Laurence Lerner. Both views depend ultimately
> on the Aristotle-Bradley doctrine of the "tragic flaw" — a doctrine
> that has obscured the true nature of Shakespearian tragedy far more
> than any over-emphasis on "character." Indeed, it is only when a

man's "character" is pictured as a sort of hard, fixed core somewhere inside him (rather as the essential particles of matter were once pictured as miniature billiard-balls) that looking for "flaws" in it makes any sense. The idea is that if a dramatic character changes into something different from what he was, he must really have been like that all along. (137)

What Matthews sees is that modernist critics from Leavis onward, despite their anti-Bradleyan pronouncements, are in practice as locked as critics from Bradley backward into an idea of character as a stable, autonomous, and coherent entity. Claims about nobility seduced by an irresistible force or about egoism eventually collapsing into its own nature are made from the opposite edges of what remains a common ground.

Most remarkable of all is the persistence of a character-based commentary on *Othello* even now, and even among those critics most passionately wed to the theoretical claims by which such commentary has been explicitly disavowed. According to Mitchell Greenberg, when Stephen Greenblatt says of Othello that "he comes dangerously close to recognizing his status as a text," he offers "an analysis that is, in essence, a 'psychological' description of character," a "full subject" capable of standing self-consciously above his own situation. By pointing "to the 'text' Othello speaks as if it originated in the person 'Othello' and thus reveals to us something of his states of mind," Greenblatt contradicts what (according to Greenberg) "we know" to be the case — namely, "that there is no 'person' there and therefore no (individual psychology)" but only "a particular linguistic situation that through its opposition to the other rhetorical 'knots' in the play (the other 'characters') constructs Othello" (11–12). Within a few pages, however, Greenberg is describing Othello in a way that flatly contradicts his principles: although "Othello, perhaps like all colonized people, believes, must believe, that he has become a part of" the dominant society, he comes "dimly and gradually" to "perceive" that "his role is from the beginning of the play already undermined" (20–21). This is a scenario for the growth of the protagonist's mind, a regression from the truth it is asserted "we know" of "Othello" as a linguistic situation back to an illusory Othello, the "full subject" we were supposed to have abandoned. Ania Loomba is another case in point. "It is important, of course," Loomba declares, "to guard against reading dramatic characters as real, three-dimensional people"; but these words follow the description of an

Othello who, though "seemingly well entrenched in and accepted by Venetian society" at "the beginning of the play," is nonetheless rendered anxious by the "insecurity" of his alien status ("he appears confident," she says, but like Greenberg Loomba knows that this is only because "Othello needs to believe" he is accepted by "the white world"), which he tries to exchange for a "conception of his own worth" that "slowly comes to centre in" and then depart from Desdemona (52–58) — a description that could be assimilated without difficulty to Kirsch's argument ("Othello eventually internalizes . . .") or for that matter to the pages of *Shakespearean Tragedy*.

The simplest way to explain the survival of character is inertia. Tradition is powerful, especially for practice. Whatever we think we are doing or ought to be doing, we tend to go on doing what we have been doing. As Richard Halpern says, "High modernism not only dominated the cultural and critical reception of Shakespeare during the first half of our century, but continues to exert a powerful influence that is often unacknowledged or disavowed" (2).[2] Or go back a step, to the modernist reaction against Bradley. A. D. Nuttall, pointing to the discrepancy between the frequently outrageous claims of Knights's attack and the general acceptance of his claims as self-evidently true, remarks that "the whole debate may be complicated by the presence of unacknowledged historical factors," a "pre-rational historical reaction" against "the overheated Victorian age" ("The Argument about Shakespeare's Characters," 109). This shrewd suggestion allows us to understand Bradley-bashing as an overdetermined gesture by which Shakespeareans tried to proclaim their authentic modernity as wholly liberated from the naivetes of eminent Victorianism, but in an anxiously assertive way that betrays residual doubts: they protest too much.

Further still, these "unacknowledged historical factors" may extend deeper than Victorian sentiment. Consider Michael Bristol who, after proposing recently that audiences should "efface their response to . . . Othello, Desdemona, and Iago as individual subjects endowed with personalities and with some mode of autonomous interiorized life," has to admit the difficulty of such an effacement, "not least because the experience of individual subjectivity as we have come to know it *is* objectively operative in the text" (184, Bristol's emphasis). Bristol is one of many recent critics who have remarked that "inwardness" or "interiority" — the character effect — is not an anachronistic concept we impose on Shakespeare's plays but something for which the plays themselves may claim substantial responsibility.[3] As Michael Neill puts it, "our own deeply ingrained way of thinking about the self as something contained *within* the body was very much an artefact of the early modern period in Europe" (*Issues of Death*, 157). From this perspective, an interest in Othello's character is not merely a hangover from Bradley or nineteenth-century novels, some recently acquired detritus to be jettisoned, but part of a continuing engagement going back to the origins, as best we can determine them, of our interest in the Shakespearean text.

But how far back does this really go? The material conditions of Shakespeare's theater justify Peter Thomson's claim "that it was by no means the priority of working playwrights to create a gathering of subjectivities — what later criticism would call 'characters'" (324–325). There are many good reasons to believe that Burbage wouldn't have based his performance on an answer to the question "What's my motivation?" But even if Elizabethan performance was as rhetorically conventional and stylized as is sometimes claimed, acting by the numbers, this doesn't decide the issue. As Bernard Beckerman argued years ago, the question framing the debate about Renaissance acting styles — natural or artificial? — is the wrong question, because it confuses means and effects. Betterton may have chanted — that is, have sounded like chanting to us if we were able to travel back in time to the Theatre Royal in the late seventeenth century (Sprague, *Shakespearian Players*, 9–20); but to his audience, tuned to a different frequency, his performance might have seemed like life itself.

The histrionic system was certainly different in the Renaissance, and if it's the system that interests us, then the exceptions need to be ignored or underplayed. "Outstanding individuals do not . . . best represent the predominant acting styles of an age. They are more often esteemed in retrospect because they herald the shift in style that will become the norm of the subsequent age" (Thomson, 325). Beckerman saw it the other way around:

> Perhaps in other acting companies the actors relied on conventional expressions of emotions. But Shakespeare gave his actors too rich a variety of emotions of too fine a subtlety to permit them to rely upon a stock rendition of outworn conventions. Although the actor did not have to search for the emotion, as actors do now, he had to discriminate among the various emotions and individualize each of them in order to project an effective character. (155–156)

Which is the better way to see it? The answer depends on whether we are chiefly interested in cultural history or in theatrical power, and this is not a question that can be decided, right or wrong, on the basis of historical accuracy.

Wherever character originates, what exactly makes the concept so enduring? What are we hanging onto? The term "character" is overloaded. Worthen's description includes "integration, self-presence, internalization, and psychological motivation" as though these are all necessary constituents of a single unified package. From this angle, he laments "the persistence — despite the supposed inroads of deconstruction, multiculturalism, and other demons of the New Right — of the unified subject (and its various avatars/epigones/guises, the author, the individual, character) as a paradigm for cultural analysis and interpretation" (91). But there is no necessary connection between character and what Alan Sinfield calls "essentialist humanism" — that is, "an ideology of a transhistorical human nature and an autonomous subjectivity, the second being an instantiation of the first; in short, a metaphysics of identity [that] occludes historical and social process." Sinfield himself remains attached to a "redefined concept of character" involving "an impression of subjectivity, interiority, or consciousness" without the metaphysical baggage (61, 62). In this respect, he carries on in a *materialist* tradition going back to Empson and G. M. Matthews who, without investing in the idealizing abstraction of an autonomous psychological integrity, are nonetheless committed to understanding the actions performed in Shakespeare's plays in terms of the values, desires, and even particular histories of the agents that perform them.[4]

Their commitment, I think, derives from a sense of the impoverished alternatives. Without it, characters tend to be conceptualized as the mouthpieces for the author's ideas, or the ideas of the time, or as allegorical representatives of ethical or ideological or psychological concepts (this is the Bodkin-Stewart line of *Othello* criticism, in which Othello and Iago's agon is understood as a psychomachia within a single collective consciousness), or of linguistic or epistemological situations ("'Othello' is a product of displacements and condensations, put into a chain of constant oppositions to other rhetorical structures" [Greenberg, 12]).[5] Even in its more sophisticated versions, such functionalism leaves out something crucial, as witness Kenneth Burke's argument against Bradley:

> Shakespeare is making a play, not people. And as a dramatist he must know that the illusion of a well-rounded character is produced, not by piling on traits of character, until all the scruples of an academic

scholar are taken care of, but by *so building a character-recipe in accord with the demands of the action that every trait the character does have is saliently expressed in action or through action*. . . . The stress upon character as an intrinsic property, rather than as an illusion arising functionally from the context, leads towards a non-dramatic explanation. (*"Othello,"* 187; Burke's emphasis)

Burke is right to say that character has no existence apart from dramatic action, and Bradley himself said much the same thing.[6] But we should add one crucial point to the claim that character is a functional illusion — namely, that the function won't be achieved *unless the illusion succeeds*. If we cannot suspend disbelief that Othello acts as though he is the author of his actions, then the sacrificial ritual Burke understands to be enacted by *Othello* will fail to be theatrically interesting. It will be the idea of a sacrificial ritual rather than its dramatic enactment, something we could read about in the pages of *The Golden Bough* or the *Journal of Anthropological Studies*. "The risk in 'portraiture' of the Bradleyan sort," according to Burke, is that, "as Jimmy Durante has so relevantly said, 'Everybody wants to get into the act'" (188). Burke's point is funnier than it is true; we *do* want to get into the act. Why go to a Shakespearean tragedy if not (among other things) to engage affectively with the values and desires of the agents who perform the actions?[7]

Character in this sense of a basis for affective engagement with the dramatic action is an essential part of theatrical and, *mutatis mutandis*, literary interest as generally understood. The rejection of character in so much recent work testifies to the fact of a diminished interest in theatrical and literary study. The esthetic has lost market share to a variety of disciplinary alternatives grouped under the designation of "cultural studies."[8] Plenty of reasons are offered for this shift of disciplinary interest, but they remain logically unconvincing because they are produced from inside one or another of the new intellectual commitments they claim to be justifying. When Greenberg tries to trump Othello with "Othello," he scores only within his own disciplinary context. That "'Othello' is a textual situation" is something "we know" only if we are doing a kind of epistemological theory; but if we are doing theatrical or literary studies Greenberg's pronouncement is, if not wrong, minimally relevant or useful. It is as though he responds to Aristotle's idea about the probable impossible — "a likely impossibility is preferable to an unconvincing possibility" (1460^a) — by saying "but it really *is* impossible," or purports to refute Coleridge's idea about a willing suspension of disbelief with a mere Bartleby-like refusal, "I prefer not." Greenberg evidently believes that the knowledge produced by his preferred mode of scrutiny is somehow higher than the knowledge available through literary or theatrical study; but what passes for a justification of this belief is no more than a repetition of it.

The circularity of such arguments does not make them any less persuasive and may make them more so; circular arguments reinforce established belief.[9] Cultural studies — by which I mean any and all of the various forms of analysis defined essentially and probably exclusively by their shared refusal of the esthetic — has evidently established itself as the interpretive practice of choice, and its establishment may signal a crucial transition in the long and gradual process by which we transcend any felt interest in the esthetic as a cultural value. It's hard, though, to see the future in the instant, and in the meantime there is the past and the inertia sustained by its continuing influence. Poetics is a powerful body of thought with roots going back as far as we can see, and as the scandalously substantial residues of character in contemporary commentary suggest, it continues in fundamental ways to drive critical and theatrical practice.

NOTES

Introduction: *Othello* and Interpretive Traditions

1. To subscribe to SHAKSPER, send the following one-line message, "SUB SHAKSPER Firstname Lastname," to LISTSERV@ws.BowieState.edu. Logbooks of all the material quoted here are available for examination.

2. The topics of this restless kind of cultural studies tend to have a short shelf life. The summer 1997 *Critical Inquiry* has the white Bronco on its cover and a long piece, smart and thoughtful, about the Simpson trial and *The Kreutzer Sonata*; but by the time most subscribers would have got to it, the "trial of the century" had been supplanted by the "funeral of the century," and an abundance of commentary, sometimes smart and thoughtful, about the meaning of it all for British society at the putative end of the monarchy, the English-speaking world at the end of colonialism, and the whole world at the end of the millennium. A year later, approaching the anniversary of the Paris car accident, the *Guardian* refers to the diminished interest as "Diana fatigue" (29 August 1998, 2).

3. For the idea that dirty talk or hate speech inevitably repeats itself, see Pechter ("Of Ants," 90 ff.) and Judith Butler: "The proposals to regulate hate speech invariably end up citing such speech at length, offering lengthy lists of examples, codifying such speech for regulatory purposes, or rehearsing in a pedagogical mode the injuries that have been delivered through such speech. It seems that the repetition is inevitable. . . . No matter how vehement the opposition to such speech is, its recirculation inevitably reproduces trauma as well. There is no way to invoke examples of racist speech, for instance, in a classroom without invoking the sensibility of racism, the trauma and, for some, the excitement. . . . The liberal capacity to refer to such terms as if one were merely mentioning them, not making use of them, can support the structure of disavowal that permits for their hurtful circulation. The words are uttered and disavowed at the moment of the utterance, and the critical discourse on them becomes precisely the instrument of their perpetration" (37–38). Butler sees this uncontrollability as a general characteristic of all speech (it's a version of Derrida's idea that writing is inevitably orphaned) with potentially benign as well as malign consequences. In *Othello*, the situation seems to be peculiarly painful and the consequences exclusively malign — even more so than in most tragedies.

1. *Othello* in Theatrical and Critical History

1. The Pepys entry is dated 11 October 1660. I am quoting from the Warington edition. In the Latham-Matthews edition, "called out" is rendered somewhat ambiguously as "cried" (1.264). The Forrest comment is quoted in Rosenberg, 93.

2. See Rosenberg, 67–69, and Hankey, 60–61. For a fully detailed (and melodramatically moving) account, see Furness, 402–404.

3. Hankey gives some additional instances at the beginning of her introduction (1–2), and Vaughan passes along a wonderful anecdote about over-the-top responses to Spranger Barry's performance in the eighteenth century (120).

4. Compare Harry Levin: "Rymer attacked [the play] because it seems to have been the most popular tragedy on the English stage" (15).

5. Hankey, 317, who reproduces a drawing on 323.

6. Compare Gardner's concluding declaration that "the significance of *Othello* is not to be found in the hero's nobility alone, . . . in his vision of the world. . . . It lies also in the fact that the vision was true" (205).

7. Consider Othello's famous self-description at the end as "one that loved not wisely but too well" (5.2.342), and Iago's sneering references to Othello's uxoriousness in his descriptions of Desdemona as "our general's wife [who] is now the general" (2.3.310), and of Othello himself just afterward:

His soul is so enfettered to her love
That she may make, unmake, do what she list,
Even as her appetite shall play the god
With his weak function. (1.3.340–343)

Cassio's description of Desdemona as "our great captain's captain" (2.1.74) is wholly idealized, but as Honigmann points out, the same phrase occurs in a judgmental context in *Antony and Cleopatra*, 3.1.22 (and see chapter 2, note 21). A nervous suspicion of the emasculating effects of female sexuality seems to have been commonplace in the Renaissance; hence Milton's description of the fallen Adam as "fondly overcome with Female charm" (John Milton, *Paradise Lost*, 9. 999 in Hughes).

8. See Whallon, Nathan, and Nelson and Haines, and the generously annotated discussion in Adelman, 271–273. For a particularly revealing current example, consider Bradshaw's argument (148–168), with its confessional detail, investment in the authority of personal experience, and rage directed against an influential critic of opposing views (in this case not Bradley or Leavis but Stephen Greenblatt).

9. See Greenblatt (*Shakespearean Negotiations*, especially 114–128; more recently, "What Is the History of Literature?," especially 469–470; and the general introduction to the *Norton Shakespeare*, 1–2); and Bristol.

10. The description and analysis of these developments has been the endeavor of a vast amount of recent commentary, including, for the invention of modern ideas about racial identity, Young, especially 90–117; for sexual identity, Foucault and Laqueur; for individual inner selfhood, Foucault again, almost anywhere, and with particular reference to Renaissance drama, Catherine Belsey (*The Subject of Tragedy*); and, for the invention of modern Shakespearean commentary, de Grazia.

11. For instance, in Jameson (who popularized "Always historicize"): "The task of cultural and social analysis thus construed within this final horizon will then clearly be the rewriting of its materials in such a way that this perpetual cultural revolution can be apprehended and read as the deeper and more permanent constitutive structure in which the empirical textual objects know intelligibility" (97).

12. Just how diverse is still a hotly debated topic. In *Shakespeare's Audience* and to a lesser extent *Shakespeare and the Rival Traditions*, Alfred Harbage argued for a very broad-ranged audience. These claims have been strongly contested by Ann Jennalie Cook (*The Privileged Playgoers*). Most recently Cook's own claims have been contested and Harbage's partly vindicated. See Martin Butler and Gurr. The question is not resolved and, considering the malleability of the evidence and how much is at stake in its interpretation, probably never will be. Nonetheless, that the public theater audience was more broadly diverse than subsequent audiences, including our own, seems indisputable.

13. "It will hold you, it will move you, it will affect you," said the reviewer of a French adaptation, pointing to qualities that are limited to the book's early reception conditions and limited even then, for as the reviewer immediately adds, the "dreadful strokes" are "tempered by the soft colors of the most tender & faithful love" (Behn, 154). In John Whaley's "On a Young Lady's Weeping at *Oroonoko*," the tears shed are the refined expression of sensibility. "When the Prince strikes who envies not the Deed? / To be so Wept, who would not wish to Bleed?" (Behn, 152). Any relation to the audience moved to tears in Henry Jackson's description of *Othello*'s besieged audience seems remote. For the afterlife of *Oroonoko*, see Lipking (under Behn in the bibliography), who includes selections from Thomas Southerne's theatrical adaptation estimated as "the most commonly produced of all the post-Shakespearean tragedies" for a forty-year period (125); and Roach. For a different take on the fact that Behn "virtually disappeared from view for over two hundred years," see Owens and Goodman (v).

14. For the statistics, see Russ McDonald (219–220).

15. At least nowhere else among Bradley's "major four." *Romeo and Juliet, Richard II, Julius Caesar*, and *Antony and Cleopatra* resemble *Othello* in this respect but, local differences aside, all are much cooler plays than *Othello*; they carefully distance us from their action, offering us the protection which *Othello* so notably withholds.

16. From a commendatory poem prefixed to the 1640 edition of Shakespeare's *Poems* (quoted Evans, 1972), though for reasons suggested by Honigmann (*Shakespeare's Impact*, 38–40), likely written for the 1623 Folio.

17. According to William Winter, "Macready seems neither to have satisfied himself . . . , nor deeply moved his auditors, in the acting of *Othello*, but he particularly excelled as *Iago*"; whereas "Kean, according to some, if not all, contemporary testimony, was as fine in *Iago* as in *Othello*. Hazlitt declared Kean's *Iago* to have been the most thoroughly sustained of all his performances" (*Shakespeare*, 260, 313–314).

18. Cf. Winter's comment: "Not that Booth's *Iago* was universally thought to excel that of Irving, but that Irving's *Othello*, compared with that of Booth, was ineffective and decidedly inferior" (*Shakespeare*, 275).

19. Ego certainly explains Macready's practice. When he alternated the roles with his second man, George Vandenhoff, he choreographed the action so that Vandenhoff delivered his lines with his back to the audience, allowing Macready to shine whichever part he was playing (Hankey, 64).

20. The other four productions are Margaret Webster's, 1943–44, on Broadway, with Paul Robeson, Jose Ferrer, and Uta Hagen; John Barton's, 1971–72, RSC, Stratford and London, Brewster Mason, Emrys James, and Lisa Harrow; Peter Coe's, 1981–82, American Shakespeare Theatre, New York, James Earl Jones, Christopher Plummer, and various Desdemonas; Jonathan Miller's, 1981, BBC, Anthony Hopkins, Bob Hoskins, and Penelope Wilton.

21. Hence Stanley Kauffmann complains about the "shrinking" of the protagonist ("lacks size," "begins to dwindle," etc. [31]); and Terence Rafferty objects to a "thoroughly, helplessly Iagocentric" production: "Fishburne looks lost, and Branagh walks off with the movie. . . . Lacking a strong hero, the movie just drifts aimlessly from scene to scene; it's 'Othello' unmoored" (126, 127). Compare Olivier's comment (chapter 4, note 41) about the way twentieth-century Othellos have all wound up "look[ing] a credulous idiot."

22. See *Shakespearean Tragedy*, 190–191. I quote and discuss the passage in chapter 6.

23. Wilson Knight, for instance, is troubled by the protagonist's atypical remoteness. "One watches the figure of Othello [but] we do not watch Lear: 'We are Lear.'" He declares, however, that the same remoteness defines the play as a whole, with Iago just a relatively inconsequential exception: "*Othello* is essentially outside us, beautiful with a lustrous, planetary beauty. Yet the Iago-conception is of a different kind from the rest of the play" ("The *Othello* Music," 100, 118–119). This definition allows Knight to maintain Othello's domination, but if we define the protagonist as the affective center of the action, not merely the object of our attention but the vocal embodiment of our desires, then Knight's entire discussion may be directed to a contrary conclusion: it is Iago, not Othello, who dominates the play.

The Bradleyan tradition achieved its (presumably) final and purest expression in Gardner's "Noble Moor," a wonderfully moving and intelligent essay, which actually succeeds in doing what Bradley is often accused of doing: limiting the focus so thoroughly to the nominal protagonist that all other aspects of the play — including Iago, most notably — simply disappear.

24. See Bayley, 129–130; Kirsch, 31. For a more recent example, consider Martin Wine: "Ironically, just because he needs 'little music,' or even lacks it, Iago seems 'well tuned now' to the prevailing anti-heroic outlook of our time. His 'alehouse' idiom, as Desdemona calls it, often sounds to the modern ear more 'honest' than Othello's 'music.' Which is, of course, what Iago would have his listeners believe!" (36).

2. Disconfirmation

1. See Webster's *White Devil*, 1.2.239, a play saturated with *Othello* echoes, for what the editor, Christina Luckyj, calls "the obvious pun" on ewe/you. See also Neill ("Changing Places," 122).

2. The standard account emphasizes the dislocation of social and economic life in sixteenth-century England, when an agrarian society, characterized by relatively stable and familiar relationships, began to give way to a more urban market economy inhabited by strangers bound tenuously to each other by money.

3. Much has been made of an increasingly appalled fascination with the favoritism of the Jacobean court, but this connection shouldn't be pushed. For one thing, *Othello* may be an Elizabethan play. Though it is usually dated 1603–4, Honigmann offers strong arguments for 1601 (344–350), and in any case a sense of arbitrariness in James's court took some time to develop. Besides, the Malcontent's role was substantially formed in Elizabethan drama. The designation is taken from the title of Marston's play of 1599 (though there are Malcontents taking shape before this), which seemed to inspire a renewed interest in revenge plays and therefore probably contributed to the production of *Hamlet*, which in turn led to the productions of *The Revenger's Tragedy* (probably by Middleton, around 1607) and Webster's *White Devil* and *Duchess of Malfi* (around 1612), with the grandest and most resonant of the Malcontents, Vindice, Flamineo, and Bosola.

4. According to George Best's more or less standard sixteenth-century account, "all these blacke Moores which are in Africa" trace their origin to the time of the great flood. Entering the ark, Noah "strictly commaunded his sonnes and their wives, that they . . . should use continencie, and abstaine from carnall copulation with their wives," but his "wicked sonne Cham disobeyed," tempted (like Adam earlier) by "our great and continuall enemie the wicked Sprite," and convinced that he would sire "the first childe borne after the flood" who would therefore "by right and Lawe of nature . . . inherite and possesse all the dominions of the earth." As a punishment, God made this child (Chus) and all his posterity "so blacke and lothsome, that it might remaine a spectacle of disobedience to all the worlde." Best was writing about his travels in a book published in 1578 and reprinted in Hakluyt's enormously popular compendium of such writing in 1600. For details and more of Best, see Newman, "And Wash," from whom the quotation is taken (146–147).

5. Any attempt to recapture the play's experience for the original audiences is bound to be speculative and should allow for the counterintuitive. Lupton offers an interesting and plausible argument that Othello's Moorishness would be felt as more threatening than his black identity, the reverse of nineteenth-century and later sentiment; her basic claim is that the Moslem *refusal* of the New Law, like the Jewish, "might actually challenge more deeply the integrity of the Christian paradigms set up in the play as the measure of humanity" than the image of the black Othello as barbarian, unexposed as yet to the revelation of Christ (74). Bak demonstrates that color signified differently in different discursive and rhetorical contexts and sees the drama as taking advantage of these differences for its own purposes.

The topic of race is of course very controversial in current criticism, and not everyone would agree with my emphasis on the distinctly "pre-racialist" quality of Renaissance belief (I take the word as well as the basic analysis from Appiah). For claims that Renaissance audiences had a more fully developed and generally dispersed sense of racial categories, see Hall, especially 254–268, and Shapiro, especially his critique of Hunter, 83–85. Perhaps they are right. In distinguishing Renaissance pre-racialism, nineteenth-century racialism, and current post-racialist belief (as it might be called), I do not mean to deny clear elements of continuity, still less to suggest that we have liberated ourselves from the prejudices of a benighted tradition. Although biologists now tell us that racial differences are too trivial to count as scientifically significant, race obviously remains a category with immense social significance. In a stunning recent book, Walter Benn Michaels argues that contemporary critics arguing for multiculturalism and ethnicity in specific opposition to racial agendas in fact radically depend on and therefore effectively sustain the idea of race they wish to eradicate. According to Young, "if there is one constant characteristic of the history of the use of the word 'race,' it is that however many new meanings may be constructed for it, the old meanings refuse to die. They rather accumulate in clusters of ever-increasing power, resonance and persuasion" (83). Whether we emphasize continuity between us and the Renaissance (like Hall and Shapiro) or discontinuity (like Hunter and Appiah) depends on critical purpose. For an astute analysis of what is at stake for our own politics as well as for the peculiarities of *Othello* for its original audiences, see Chaudhuri.

6. For this material, see Vaughan, 13–34, and D'Amico, 7–40.

7. For the wealth of the Levant trade, which far exceeded trade in the Americas, see Davis. According to Brenner, the real forces driving English economic expansion were the "new-merchants," essentially freebooters who tended to undermine the authority of the aristocratic and officially sanctioned merchant companies, and who therefore had the effect, comparable to the Barbary pirates evoked in *Othello* and elsewhere in Shakespeare (as by Hal to Francis in *1 Henry IV*, 2.4), of threatening established order. This blurring of distinctions might lead to a version of Portia's question in the Trial Scene of *The Merchant*: who is the Merchant here, and who the pirate?

8. See Lacey Baldwin Smith, who is chiefly concerned with child-rearing practices, the sorts of things that led Lawrence Stone to conclude that Tudor England was a "low-affect society" (*The Family, Sex, and Marriage*). As Maus argues, however, the peculiarly intense level of anxiety and suspicion reflected in Elizabethan and Jacobean textual, cultural, and political practice must have been "overdetermined" by a vast number of "mutually interacting social and ideological factors," and she too is inclined to emphasize the influential consequences of religious differences (*Inwardness and Theater*, 14 ff.). Patricia Parker similarly points to "the context of this paranoid atmosphere" generated out of religious differences in late Elizabethan and early Jacobean England ("*Othello* and *Hamlet*," 62). In "Torture and Truth," Elizabeth Hanson brilliantly analyzes the jurisprudential consequences of this uniquely threatened situation in late Tudor and early Jacobean England: the only period when torture was systematically and institutionally legitimated.

9. For a fascinating argument claiming that Shakespeare's geography is consistently and fundamentally symbolic, see Gillies.

10. For the Renaissance context, see Greenberg (6 ff.), Jones, David McPherson, and Vaughan (13–34). For later, see Tanner.

11. This idea is brilliantly developed by Neill with special reference primarily to

the protagonist's story ("Changing Places") and by Genster with special reference to the audience's unstable position.

12. I quote the maxim from Jonson's *Volpone* (2.1.1) where, unfortunately for my purposes, it is spoken by Sir Politic Wouldbe. For the history and authority of the idea, see Kerrigan and Braden (18–19).

13. I am particularly indebted here to Newman's argument that the "play is structured around a cultural aporia, miscegenation" (145).

14. In declaring that his services will out-tongue Brabantio's complaints, Othello imagines his actions speaking for him, as if he existed in an objective form. A moment later he uses a similar formula to describe not his actions but his inner qualities: "My parts, my title, and my perfect soul / Shall manifest me truly." Like private self and public order, subjective and objective existence seem to merge into an integrated consciousness. The breathtaking wholeness with which Othello experiences his life gives a nontheological way of understanding Othello's "perfect soul." (See 5.c and 5.d in the revised *OED*. Cf. Hamlet's more ambiguous "perfect conscience" [5.2.67]. Cf. Calderwood: "By 'my perfect soul' Othello probably means completeness of self, perfect in the sense in which Macbeth uses the term" 3.4.20 [13]). Ulysses' address to Achilles as "thou great and complete man" (*Troilus and Cressida*, 3.3.181) is ironic, for Achilles' sense of self-worth depends on the unstable and arbitrary fashions of public reputation; but Othello is the thing itself.

15. For an interesting discussion of Dickens's opening, see Nuttall (*Openings*, 172 ff.).

16. Honigmann points out that "Say it, Othello" at the beginning of the speech is part of a short line. In his edition, he speculates about missing words, but in his book on the text, he speculates about short lines as contributing to emphatic effects (*The Texts of "Othello,"* 103–26).

17. According to Hunter, these "complicating factors" include "Renaissance primitivism." See his discussion, 47 ff.

18. Romantic comedy, Shakespearean and otherwise, typically writes us into sympathy with the undutifully desiring daughter against the oppressive father (think of Hermia and Egeus in *A Midsummer Night's Dream*), but *Othello* has evoked darker feelings. Although Brabantio resembles the blocking father of Shakespearean comedy, his grief ("And what's to come of my despised time / Is nought but bitterness" [1.1.159–160]) and loving concern ("O unhappy girl!" [161]) endow him with authority well beyond the insufferably self-absorbed Egeus or even Leanato in *Much Ado*. The news of his death at the end, "pure grief / Shore his old thread in twain" (5.2.203–204), should seem shocking but not surprising.

19. "(Roderigo stumbles, speaking hastily): he means 'your daughter *has been* transported . . . *than* with a knave'": Honigmann's clarifying note.

20. "Transported" regularly means passionately carried away in Shakespeare (see Spevack). In Webster's *Duchess of Malfi*, a play that frequently echoes *Othello*, Ferdinand's imagining of "some strong-thigh'd bargeman" (2.5.43) as one of his sister's succession of lovers may owe something to the gondolier here.

21. The standard Renaissance story — dominating if not wholly constituting the category of gender — represented women as weaker vessels, less able to mas-

ter passionate feelings and more highly sexed than men, therefore requiring super-vision ("guardage," as Brabantio says), the enclosure of their wandering appe-tites both for their own good and for the good of the men they might tempt into unmanly sexual interest (see Stallybrass and Ziegler). By the time of the Victori-ans, these views would be transposed — women are naturally demure and under-sexed compared with men. To the extent that we are still enthralled by residual nineteenth-century thought, it may take some work to be able to acknowledge the emotional power of Iago's views in the play. Brabantio's anxiety may inspire coarse and sadistic laughter ("O heaven, how got she out? O treason of the blood!" [1.1.167]), like so many of Iago's productions, but for Shakespeare's audience, the old man's horror at Desdemona's escape from within evokes a fearful threat to the foundations of legitimate order no less serious than Othello's assault from outside.

Renaissance models of manliness are also likely to seem bizarre. The Lothario or Don Juan figure, heroic in sexual conquest, another Victorian (or perhaps eighteenth-century) residuum for us, would have probably been rendered as per-verse in the Renaissance, when sexual conquest was typically understood as the reverse of manly — a conquest *by* the sexual appetite, always gendered female, over the rational self-command of true masculinity. Hence the two images of Hercules in *Much Ado About Nothing*, one in which Omphale has made him do women's work in women's clothes and "cleft his club," the other as "the shaven Hercules [whose] codpiece seems as massy as his club" (2.1.254 and 3.3.136–138), are not contradictory but emphatic: both of them, the massy as well as the cleft club, are images of emasculation.

22. Desdemona's behavior may have evoked echoes (with the gender changed) of Genesis 2:24, "Therefore shall a man leave his father and his mother, and shall cleave unto his wife; and they shall be both one flesh," and Paul in Ephesians 5:31, "For this cause shall a man leave his father and mother, and shall be joined unto his wife, and they two shall be one flesh."

23. I have used Q1 here, departing from Honigmann, who follows F's "Nor would I there reside."

24. In sum: many sixteenth-century Protestants vigorously contested the older view, associated with Saint Paul's "better to marry than burn," which they regarded as part of the monastic ideal of medieval Catholicism. Seeking to legitimate the active life and to redeem the natural sphere, they reconceptualized marriage as a positively virtuous relationship in its own right. Without abandoning the idea of parental consent, they emphasized the value of marriage partners freely choosing each other. Still committed to the supremacy of husbandly authority, they none-theless recentered marital relations in terms of companionship, a mutual affection, including sexual intimacy, sustained over a lifetime between two equally (though differently) contributing partners. This new concept achieves its climactically tri-umphant expression in *Paradise Lost*, a poem heavily invested in marriage as a sanctified relationship ("Hail, wedded Love," [4, 736]) conspicuously including a mutual sexual delight (see 4, 492–501).

The inaugurating modern research on these topics was performed by Mande-ville and William Haller. For an excellent recent exposition of these ideas and their literary and dramatic implications, see Rose. Companionate marriage generated an enormous amount of critical excitement in historical criticism during the 1980s but is now either ignored or relegated to the trivial, as in Diana Henderson's remark that "for all the post-Reformation talk of companionate marriage, household management was modeled not upon collaborative equality but upon monarchy" (175). This may be true, but it seems odd for literary scholars to dismiss so much discourse ("all the . . . talk") as inconsequential. Over- and then under-investment in the discursive is coming to feel like the business cycles of academic life under late capitalism.

25. Coleridge anticipates John Holloway, who (as we saw in the previous chapter) presumes to possess the "simple facts" of "everyone's familiar knowledge about love, marriage, and affection between men and women." Both of them are anticipated by Othello himself, who adopts the generalizing tone of the canny insider at the very moment he abandons his love for Desdemona in order to credit Iago: "O curse of marriage / That we can call these delicate creatures ours / And not their appetites!" (3.3.272–274). All three make ridiculous spectacles of themselves, and this may suggest some practical advice along the lines of one of the three "very instructive" morals Rymer found in the play: "a lesson to Husbands, that before their Jealousie be Tragical, the proofs may be Mathematical" (132). The problem is that mathematical proofs in the sense of a totally disinterested (unprejudiced) perception of an external reality is impossible. "Generalizations are bad" may be a good thing to say, but it's a paradox which cannot provide a basis for behavior. Shakespearean tragedy is not very good at furnishing role models.

26. Kirsch is talking about "theological" or "psychological" criticism, but these terms pretty well cover the field in general. The Dexter-Olivier *Othello*, to which I shall want to return, is an interesting anomaly. It self-consciously goes with the flow of academic criticism out of Leavis but with surprisingly stunning results.

27. "Unproper Beds," 395–397, Neill's emphasis. I am deeply indebted to Neill's brilliant essay as to the Burke essay Neill acknowledges.

28. Honigmann suggests that the Duke's words may explicitly constitute "an appeal against racial prejudice." "Superstition" is Edwin Booth's word, commenting in his promptbook that "the dream is convincing proof" only "to the superstitious Italian" and that witchcraft, similarly, is generated out of "the superstition that pervades" such a mind (Furness, 24, 27). There is something self-contradictory about Booth's dependence on ethnic prejudice as a way of distinguishing himself from superstition. "Reflections like these," he adds, "help the actor to *feel* the character he assumes"; but why does he have to feel his way into an assumed role? — in a sense he's already there.

29. That Brabantio's case collapses with Desdemona's testimony seems oddly literal. Desdemona was not of course actually drugged, but Othello certainly charmed her in a metaphorical sense, and his sexual charisma could fairly be described as magical in its ability to transform her nature into a passionate arousal quite beyond the culturally constructed norms of dutiful daughterhood.

30. The play apparently wants to keep Iago's suggestion available. Consider the bathetic drop from the Duke's unqualified assurance early in the scene that Brabantio will get full satisfaction "though my proper son / Stood in your action" (69–70) to the response after Brabantio identifies Othello as the offending party:

"We are very sorry for't" (74). A much more noncommittal response, this, and its attribution to "ALL" makes the reduction in commitment more emphatic. "ALL" is not uncommon as a speech prefix in Shakespeare, and there are divergent hypotheses about its implications for performance. See Honigmann, "Re-enter the Stage Direction," and Parker's edition of *Coriolanus*, 93–94.

31. For Altman, the Duke's judgment is "driven by the unspoken need to believe that the Turks behave like the Venetians" (136), but "fearful" allows us to be more specific about the feeling generating the behavior. According to Altman, "that the Duke's composition turns out to correspond, in large part, to the shape of external events does not lessen its fictive status; it merely suggests that probabilities are more reliable in public matters than in private" (153). Brabantio's domestic anxieties also turn out to be justified — Desdemona *has* eloped. Even paranoids have enemies; even people with enemies may be paranoid. As Neill remarks, "It is difficult to say whether" these "anxieties are ones that the play discovers or implants in an audience" ("Unproper Beds," 395).

3. Iago

1. Furness gives examples of the dumb shows. For the acting stage business, see Sprague: "Here Fechter's [1861] production became very modern indeed. 'The furniture was so disposed that it was available to histrionic purposes'; and John Ryder, the Iago, actually sat on the council table and coolly swung his leg" (*Shakespeare and the Actors*, 189).

2. In Stanislavski's 1929 notes for a Moscow Art Theatre production, Iago, having escorted Othello and Desdemona to their exits, "sits down on seat 7 to wait for papers and instructions from Othello. Secretaries collect the papers from the tables.

The chief secretary and his assistant take their seats at the senators' table. They begin their night's work.

Weapons are carried by, behind the lattice window and across the stage. Sacks are dragged along, probably with money.

Iago sits with his back to the lattice window, deep in thought. His face is bestial, it is his real face, the mask removed. (72)

A pause indeed! It should be noted that Stanislavski was very eager to avoid the scene-changing intervals of earlier theatrical practice, which he thought interrupted the momentum of the action; hence the focus on Iago's expression keeps us engaged psychologically — something for which there are antecedents going back to the Fechter example cited in the previous note, or even Kean.

3. As Wine points out, though F *Othello* divides the play into five acts, Q1 doesn't. Such haphazard practice is typical of the early texts which, even when they indicate act divisions, do so independently of Shakespeare and in a way that can be misleading in terms of original performances. (Most modern productions of *Hamlet*, no doubt guided by currently available printed texts, provide an intermission after the "closet scene" with Hamlet and Gertrude at the end of act 3; but Gertrude may well remain on stage as Claudius enters, meaning that 4.1 isn't technically even a new scene, let alone a new act.) It is often noted that act divisions

weren't systematically introduced until Rowe's edition of 1709, where they catered to the new French neoclassical taste. For Rymer, the unexplained shift to Cyprus was one of many "absurdities" in *Othello*: "The Audience must be there too; And yet our Bays had it never in his head to make any provision of Transport Ships for them. In the days that the *Old Testament* was Acted in *Clerkenwell*, by the *Parish Clerks* of *London*, the Israelites might pass through the *Red sea*; but alass, at this time, we have no *Moses* to bid the Waters *make way*, and to Usher us along. Well, the absurdities of this kind break no Bones. They may make Fools of us; but do not hurt our Morals" (142). As often, Rymer is very funny in his depiction of Shakespearean practice as a barbaric phenomenon of an unenlightened and super-stitious age. But few people take him seriously: we're more interested in the specu-lative reconstruction of early theatrical experience than in self-congratulation for own progress. Nonetheless, the act divisions have been adopted by almost all post-Rowe editions into the present, so we're still stuck with the vestiges of Rymer's taste. Such unwanted but apparently inescapable burdens from the past are what this book (and *Othello* as I understand it) are about.

4. First we see him manipulating Roderigo, then in a soliloquy he begins to work out a strategy to "poison" Othello's "delight" (to recall the phrase we can now understand from the beginning). Iago is offstage until line 83 of the next scene but takes control of the action almost immediately, displacing Cassio as the center of interest and dominating the tone with his witty "praise of women." With Othello's triumphant entry the focus shifts to the ecstatic reunion of the lovers, but the stage is quickly vacated, leaving us again with Iago and Roderigo. Iago continues to work on Roderigo, then gets him offstage in order to deliver another soliloquy, developing his strategy in yet more detail. He is then offstage for two brief fillips of action. In 2.2, the Herald reads Othello's proclamation. Scene 2.3 begins with Othello, Cassio, and Desdemona for eleven lines. With the departure of Othello and Desdemona, Iago enters to Cassio and begins to choreograph the plot that results in Cassio's cashiering. Having accomplished his goal, he convinces Cassio to ask for Desdemona's intercession and is then left alone for another so-liloquy. He is interrupted by Roderigo, who is immediately manipulated again into the ongoing strategy, before Iago returns to soliloquy, eagerly anticipating the swift enactment of the plot he has put into place.

5. "When Othello asked Iago for the 'proof,' Iago, the stud beach boy, proudly displayed the bulge of the handkerchief in his crotch. And during the 'pr'ythee, unpin me' scene, Emilia, dressed as a vamp with designer sunglasses, completely undressed Desdemona and during the speech on 'husbands' faults' pulled the 'innocent' naked Desdemona on to her lap and vividly rubbed her breasts and 'flipped' her nipples. Perhaps no other Zadek production polarized the critics and public opinion as much, especially the brutal 'sex murder' of Desdemona. De-mented, he hugged the dead body and flung her over the curtain guide-line with her bottom towards the audience. On display like a 'slaughtered steer,' he threw a kiss at her naked posterior. Othello's berserk state of mind evoked laughter and shouts from the audience to which Othello responded by shouting back" (Engle, 101).

The spirit of bitter carnival emanating from Iago has taken over the whole production here, absorbing the protagonist and Desdemona into its own delighted self-disgust. The tone aside, the rowdy atmosphere of this production may be closer in some ways than "straight" productions to performances in Renaissance public playhouses, where there's some evidence — Iago's "what's he then that says I play the villain?" and the grocer and his wife who intrude on the action in Beaumont's *Knight of the Burning Pestle* (1607), for examples — to suggest that audiences were invited to and sometimes actually did talk back to the actors.

6. *Critique of Cynical Reason*, quoted in Halpern (105–106). I am indebted to Halpern's discussion, 92–113.

7. Apart from Iago himself, Edmund's wonderfully insouciant naturalism in *King Lear* constitutes evidence, as does the opinion attributed to Marlowe that "the first beginning of Religioun was only to keep men in awe." See *King Lear*, 1.2.1–22 and 118–133; see MacLure (37).

8. It's easy for us to see that the foundation of religious faith was being undermined, but we can't attribute our retrospective understanding to Renaissance consciousness. As Empson understood, to be fully absorbed into the assumptions of Iago's naturalism would mean "to disbelieve the Fall of Man" ("Honest in *Othello*," 219); although some among the original audiences might have been willing to deny the meaning of the Fall, none of them could have disbelieved it in our sense, as a concept present to the mind only as a metaphorical curiosity recaptured by the historical imagination. For Renaissance audiences, the Fall was simply part of the air they breathed. It may be that the materialist domination of criticism during the last quarter-century has underrepresented religion in the Renaissance. See McEachern and Shuger, and Shuger for recent work that tries to restore a sense of its importance.

9. Disenchantment with social privilege is variously inflected: the silly irrelevance of the romance plot to the real middle-class center of feeling in Heywood's *Woman Killed with Kindness*; the petty resentment of Roger Otley in Dekker's *Shoemakers' Holiday*; the much grander contempt of the Malcontents later in Webster. The demystification of the aristocracy is no doubt connected with an actual erosion of aristocratic power and prestige (Stone, *The Crisis of the Aristocracy*).

10. Bradley (174), Empson (219), and Carlisle (230) all note the play's refusal to be specific about Iago's social position.

11. Cf. *Merchant*, 4.1.66–69:

Bassanio. Do all men kill the things they do not love?
Shylock. Hates any man the thing he would not kill?
Bassanio. Every offense is not a hate at first.
Shylock. What, wouldst thou have a serpent sting thee twice?

12. Quoted in Honigmann. Heilman goes through the play scrutinizing Iago's behavior along the lines of Coleridge's "motiveless malignity," in a way that I am following here (25–44).

13. For instance: "Moors are changeable in their wills," and "The Moor . . . / Is of a constant, loving, noble nature" (1.3.347 and 2.1.286–287). "We work by wit and not by witchcraft, / And wit depends on dilatory time," and "Dull not device by coldness and delay!" (2.3.367–368 and 383). "It is thought abroad that 'twixt my sheets, / He's done my office. I know not if't be true, / But I for mere suspicion in

that kind / Will do as if for surety," and "Reputation is an idle and most false imposition, oft got without merit and lost without deserving. You have lost no reputation at all, unless you repute yourself such a loser" (1.3.386–389 and 2.3.264–267). You can approach this problem by trying to identify what Iago *really* believes, as opposed to the front he puts on to the world, but the distinction is impossible to sustain, and the impressions of radical contradiction will remain.

14. The claim for Iago's normative authority has been a commonplace among materialist critics going back to G. M. Matthews: "Iago's view of Othello is not — except in pathological intensity — a unique aberration, but an attitude held by the Venetian ruling class" (131). Peter Stallybrass's view, that Iago's "voice is the voice of 'common sense,' the ceaseless repetition of the always-already 'known,' the culturally 'given'" (139) is quoted with approval by both Loomba (61) and Traub (35). Compare Karen Newman's claim that "the white male sexual norm [is] represented in the play most emphatically by Iago," who "does not oppose cultural norms so much as hyperbolize them" ("And Wash," 151). But the same point is made by critics operating in very different traditions. Hence Arthur Kirsch argues that Iago "exists as part of the unconscious life of all men," and that "within the world that Shakespeare creates in the play honest Iago is a spokesman for what everyone else, save Desdemona, feels or believes or represents" (36). According to Jane Adamson, "Iago serves as a crucial *limit case* in the play, a man whose life and being vividly demonstrate, in extreme form, certain habits of feeling, certain ways of viewing and responding to the world, that the drama gradually makes us recognize as to some extent characteristic of everyone in it (and of us watching it), each in his own particular (and definitive) form and degree" (65).

15. Greenblatt doesn't wholly ignore this line but relegates it to an afterthought in an endnote: "The vertigo intensifies if we add the sly preceding line" (298). But it works the other way around; it's the second line that's added to the first, and the first line says it all.

16. Freud is quoting much of this material from Karl Abel and later Alexander Bain; I have elided the quotation marks and notes by which Freud acknowledges his indebtedness.

17. And again in *The Christian Doctrine*: "It was called the tree of knowledge of good and evil from the event; for since Adam tasted it, we not only know evil, but we know good only by means of evil" (Merritt Hughes, 993).

18. In the note to his edition, Sanders informs us that nettles/lettuce and hyssop/thyme "were considered horticultural opposites, having the complementary qualities of dryness and wetness," used by "good Gardeiners," according to John Lyly, "as ayders the one to the growth of the others" (81). But Iago doesn't see it this way; characteristically, he assumes that different qualities are mutually threatening and require separation: nettles *or* lettuce, and if you *set* hyssop you have to *weed up* thyme. I take it that supplying it with one gender is preferable to distracting it with many. "Distract" can be neutral, "divide among," but it is usually negative in Shakespeare, as in "this distracted globe" in *Hamlet* (1.5.97), and "supply" is positive, as in "perfume and suppliance of a minute" from the same play (1.3.9). In a context endorsing segregation, the secondary meaning of "distract" seems unlikely, at least as an expression of Iago's *intentions*. The speech culminates in the

alternative of "either to have it sterile with idleness or manured with industry," a phrase I can fit into this interpretation, but I'm unsure about it. In any case, the main point remains that the Renaissance norm seems to have been for a cosmopolitan variety, at least in horticulture, and that Iago's protectionist homogeneity would have presumably seemed anomalous.

19. "Comfort" fits the play's subject of married or domestic sexuality. It's a vast emotional distance away from seduction and romantic love, the theatrical intensity of *A Midsummer Night's Dream, Romeo and Juliet, Troilus and Cressida*, or *Antony and Cleopatra*. On the other side is what Edmund wittily describes as the "dull, stale, tired bed" of marriage where "a whole tribe of fops" are "got 'tween asleep and wake" (*King Lear*, 1.2.13–15).

20. See *Paradise Lost*, 1, 107, and *Othello*, 4.2.132. Honigmann's note refers us to "th'eternal devil" in *Julius Caesar*, 1.2.159–160 and, though acknowledging "eternal" as an intensive, comments that "*eternal villain* almost = a devil."

21. Marienstras tries to connect *Othello* with the question of English as distinct from Scottish identity, following on James's accession (99–125). Honigmann's early date makes this a less immediate plausibility, though as early as *1 Henry IV*, in 1597, Shakespeare is treating seriously the idea that the nation is made by acts of exclusion.

22. Consider the citizens of Oceania, summoned to the telescreen for their daily "Two Minutes Hate" in *1984*; it's Big Brother's way of securing their loyalty to the state (Orwell, 15). Lenny Bruce had a bit where, as a standup comic playing to an increasingly hostile audience at the London Palladium, he appealed as a last resort to their hatred of the Irish: "Screw the Irish, right? Waddaya say?"

23. See W. A. Adamson for a wide-ranging sample of the complicated and often anxious responses Desdemona has evoked, and for an astute discussion to which I am indebted here.

24. Think of Henny Youngman's signature line: "Take my wife — please!" This kind of shtick is, of course, not limited to nightclubs ("alehouses") or military barracks. Wherever the Battle of the Sexes is joined, then wander forth the sons of Iago, and some of their voices are a lot nastier than Henny Youngman's. Rent a stalker movie, or put Niggaz Wit' Attitude on the CD player and crank up the volume. Or settle back with a good read — *In the Beauty of the Lilies*, for instance, a recent Updike where you'll meet Jared, Teddy's hard-boiled platitudinous older brother. "If there's one thing this war taught me, it's that money is more important than pussy. Money makes the man, Ted, and pussy unmakes him. Money gives, and pussy takes" (119). This last sentence, like "put money in thy purse" in the play, recurs as a kind of litany throughout the book; Iago couldn't have put it better himself.

25. Hence Henny Youngman can do "take my wife — please!" and its many variants night after night and meanwhile (so I am told and do in part believe) sustain a happy marriage over a lifetime. (Updike's Teddy also does so, almost uxoriously, despite Jared's voice echoing in his ears.)

26. The *locus classicus* in Milton is Adam's explanation to Eve that "evil into the mind of God or Man / May come and go, so unapprov'd, and leave / No spot or blame behind" (*Paradise Lost*, 5. 117–119), but it's a recurrent idea.

27. Two ambiguous examples: Sacvan Bercovitch, illustrating the concept of ideology in a lecture at Concordia, described the results of a poll given to inner-city (read "black") women in, I think, Philadelphia. Two of the true/false questions were (1) *In America, anyone can grow up to be President*, overwhelmingly declared true; and (2) *My son can grow up to be President*, overwhelmingly declared false. The second anecdote dates from when I first moved to Montréal. I had become casually friendly with my downstairs neighbor, Mme. Lacombe, who one day came up clutching her copy of the rent-increase notice we had just received from the Royal Bank of Canada, complaining about "the Jew owner." When I felt constrained to identify myself ("Mais Mme. Lacombe, je suis moi-même un juif"), she was less embarrassed than irritated with me for missing the point: "Je ne parle pas de toi, je parle du juif propriétaire": "I'm not talking about you, I'm talking about the Jew owner."

4. The Fall of Othello

1. "*Othello* comprises an astounding total of some five-hundred shots, of which only the long-tracking shot of Othello and Iago walking along the fortress wall is distinctly sustained" (Davies, 101).

2. For this material, see Furness, 163 ff.; Hankey, 217 ff.; Sprague (*Shakespeare and the Actors*, 194); and Alan Hughes, 143.

3. For earlier versions, see Dover Wilson's introduction and G. M. Matthews. (It is noteworthy that two such different critics should come to the same basic conclusion.) For more recent versions, see Berry; and Bevington's introduction.

4. The *Othello* subtext in Rushdie is clearly intentional (see Cantor) and is similarly explicit in Caryl Phillips's extraordinary recent novel, *The Nature of Blood*:

> My reputation. Some among these people, both high and low, were teaching
> me to think of myself as a man less worthy than the person I knew myself to
> be. My own people, although degraded and without the sophistication and
> manners of these Venetians, at least regarded me with respect and dignity,
> and among them I had many friends, and some few enemies, all of whom
> were easily identifiable. Among the Venetians, all was confusion as I attempted
> to distinguish those who beheld my person with scorn and contempt, from
> those who simply looked upon me with the curiosity that one would associate
> with a child. (118)

My thanks to Mary Jacobus for calling my attention to this book.

5. Compare Iago's "after some time" and the temporal process suggested by "already changes . . . at the first" (1.3.394 and 3.3.328, 330). Like Rushdie, Phillips goes out of his way to internalize the passage of time: "Spring gave way to summer, and summer, in turn, to a strangely melancholic autumn, and many times I wondered if I had not chosen gold and self-advancement above the more important consideration of my own happiness" (116).

6. See Ridley's introduction, lxvii–lxx, for the basic data. Furness's appendix, "Duration of the Action," goes into greater detail, 358–372.

7. Harley Granville-Barker tries to demonstrate that double time solves a

problem of audience belief, but since it is Shakespeare who creates the problem, Granville-Barker's argument goes around in circles (141–147). Graham Bradshaw has tried to explain away the problem, but his claims, which depend on inventing a predramatic career for a Venetian Bianca, are implausible (148–168). In "'Preposterous Conclusions,'" Altman argues persuasively that double time is part of the coherent strategy of the play. For versions of the distinctions at work in the double time of *Othello*, see Paul Valéry's discussion of the way "our poetic pendulum travels from our sensation toward some idea or some sentiment, and returns toward some memory of the sensation and toward the potential act which could reproduce the sensation" (7.72); and Kenneth Burke's distinction between plots driven by lyrical associationism and by rational extension (*The Philosophy of Literary Form*, 30–32).

8. For the uncertainty, which we pick up from the characters, consider Brabantio's "Are they married, think you?" (1.1.165), echoed by Iago in the next scene, "But I pray you, sir, / Are you fast married?" (10–11), which are in the first instance likely and in the second almost certain to evoke sexual images. For the erotic passages, recall Cassio's description of Othello and Desdemona's lovemaking in 2.1.77 ff., echoed in the lovers' ecstatic reunion later on (180–196), richly resonant with sexual pleasures experienced on distinct male and female registers.

For critics (many of them following in Cavell's wake, as I am) who claim that *Othello* "refers us to a hidden scene of desire that . . . is a focus of compulsive fascination for audience and characters alike," see (in alphabetical order) Adelman; Boose, "'Let it be hid,'" and "Othello's Handkerchief"; Calderwood, 125 and 154; Greenberg, 27; Little; Maus, "Horns of Dilemma," and "Proof and Consequences"; Neill, "Changing Places," "'Hidden Malady'" (from which the quotation about the "hidden scene of desire" at the beginning of this paragraph is taken [98]), and "Unproper Beds"; Patricia Parker, "Dilation," "Fantasies," and "Shakespeare and Rhetoric"; and Rudnytsky.

9. Laura Mulvey, who established the idea of "the gaze" ("Visual Pleasure"), twice subsequently cautioned against applying it to all movies ("Afterthoughts" and "Changes"; all this material is now conveniently available in *Visual and Other Pleasures*). We should be even more skeptical about transferring "the gaze" to theater, and even more skeptical yet again when the theater was produced in such a remote period. Notions of ocular proof associated with experimental science were developing in the Renaissance, as were notions of true perspective in painting and a single privileged vantage point in the masque. These ideas, however, had not achieved anything like their subsequent authority. They competed with other ideas about perception and different epistemological theories. Renaissance ideas about poetry and theater, moreover, often repudiated the primacy of the visual, an integrated objective stage *gestalt*, and a single controlling point of view. In support of these claims, see Desmet, 112–133; Freedman; Hawkes, *Shakespeare's Talking Animals*, 43 and 130; Siemon, *Shakespearean Iconoclasm*; Sypher, 116–120; Tuve; and Weimann. There have been others, apart from Mulvey herself, who have warned against overinvesting in the idea of the gaze (see Snow, "Theorizing the Male Gaze," and Greenblatt, *Learning to Curse*, 175–181); nonetheless, critics carry on

with the gaze sometimes in full knowledge of Mulvey's disclaimers. Its power seems to be irresistible.

10. Wentesdorf richly illustrates this association with textual and pictorial ex-amples (369–371).

11. Performance cannot resolve the crux any more than textual study. No actor can deliver the line in a way that effectively limits the word to one meaning or the other. (This is a version of Booth's point about the free-floating "no more" in modern editions of *Hamlet*'s "to be or not to be" [165].) Shakespeare famously plays with the ay/I homonym, or has his protagonist do so, in the Deposition Scene of *Richard II*. Here, though, it is impossible to be sure who is responsible for the equivocation — another way of saying that the effect is produced by Iago.

12. For discussion and illustrations of the iconography of hellmouth, see Shein-gorn. Wickham, who reproduces several illustrations, points out "that the concept of *teatrum mundi* which had informed the stage-conventions of liturgical music-drama in Christian basilicas of the tenth and eleventh centuries was carried for-ward in unbroken tradition into the vernacular religious drama of the fifteenth and sixteenth centuries. . . . Since the stage was still expected to represent the whole of God's creation, and not simply the mortal world, the invisible worlds of heaven and hell had to be accommodated not only in physical and tangible terms, but in their proper relationship to the visible world of daily experience" (89). The toad-like creatures from the Winchester Psalter may help to contextualize Othello's bi-zarre references: they are conventional in a way that must have been familiar or at least accessible to some of Shakespeare's audience. Adelman describes a sixteenth-century German painting reproduced in Wentesdorf "in which a toad crouches at a naked woman's genitals" (274). Even closer to my purposes, Wentesdorf includes a 1595 emblem "in which a weasel . . . is being swallowed by a toad" (363) and quotes a 1658 emblem book's statement that toads "were believed by some to per-form carnal copulation . . . by the mouth" (370).

13. Greenblatt locates Iago's enterprise in the context of what he argues to be mainstream Christian belief (if not necessarily doctrine) that sexual pleasure, even in marriage, is sinful and guilt-inducing.

14. William Worthen simply dismisses performability as an inappropriate cri-terion: "There is no way to translate between different modes of producing the text; acting practice and critical practice remain in dialogue because they are in-commensurable" (150). But Worthen is arguing for performance as an autonomous mode, and since I am working rather out of a conception of performance and text as reciprocally dependent, I'm reluctant to finesse the question in this way.

15. John Barton directed his Othello "to pull Desdemona down on the ground and at 'there' . . . to grab her 'muffin.'" Hankey, quoting the promptbook for Barton's 1972 production, adds, "Perhaps the idea had come from the production at the Mermaid (shortly before Barton's 1972 Aldwych season)" in which, accord-ing to Robert Cushman, "Othello delivers the speech beginning 'Had it pleased heaven / To try me with afflictions' looking Desdemona straight in the crotch, which makes unusual sense of the lines 'the fountain from the which my current runs' and particularly of the instruction 'Turn thy complexion there'. No other

Othello I've seen has shown much interest in where *there* might be" (quoted Hankey, 283). Either or both of these productions may have influenced David Harewood's Othello to "put his hand on her crotch on *'there*, where I have garnered up my heart'" in Sam Mendes's 1997 production at the National's Cottesloe Theatre (Liston, 23; Liston's emphasis).

16. Booth's exit from the Temptation Scene was accompanied with "a rapid clutch of the fingers, as though squeezing his very heart (Othello's face is buried in his hands)" (Furness, 188), a gesture which seems to connect the physical pressure of Iago's hands on themselves with Othello's hands on his face, and which further embodies emotional pressure (the grief Othello feels) in a corporeal experience (his "very heart"). Sprague, commenting on Roderigo's unexpected entries, notes that at one point "Booth has them 'run against each other,'" and that when "Iago offers to shake hands with him, Roderigo has often 'turned away,' or 'sulkily declined' at first. . . . But 'Iago wheedles, and gets his hand laughingly' (Booth), or retains it '*in spite of him*' (Fechter)" (*Shakespeare and the Actors*, 206).

17. Christopher Plummer was "a sexless Iago who playfully kisses men and women alike because he has no use for either." Frank Finlay's "Iago cannot tolerate Emilia's hands on him, although he often takes Roderigo's hand in his" (Wine, 64, 61). Virginia Vaughan remarks "how often [Trevor Nunn's 1989] promptbook calls for [Ian McKellen's] Iago to touch, caress, or 'cuddle' his fellows," adding, though, that he "does not touch Othello . . . until the end of the temptation scene" and by the time of the fit "goes so far as to 'brush him . . . down' and 'brush hair with his handky'" (224, 221).

18. Carlisle quotes Clara Morris, a late nineteenth-century American performer, "the foremost emotional actress of her day" (469), first on the Cyprus greeting, then on the Collaring Scene. In the first instance, Morris was reminded of "a tiger's spring upon a lamb" when Salvini's Othello "fiercely swept into his swarthy arms the pale loveliness of Desdemona. . . . Passion choked, his gloating eyes burned with the mere lust of the 'sooty Moor' for that white creature of Venice. It was revolting, and with a shiver I exclaimed aloud, 'Ugh, you splendid brute!'" (203). In the second instance, describing the "marvellous effect" that Salvini produced "when he seized Iago by the throat and threw him down as if to trample the life out of him: then suddenly remembering himself, he gave him his hand and helped him to his feet," Morris was reminded of "the perfect animal man, in his splendid prime, . . . in a very frenzy of conscious strength" (205). As Carlisle says, picking up on the resonant similarities in both descriptions, "Even Clara Morris remembered with admiration — though no doubt with another shiver — the picture presented in that climactic moment" of the Collaring Scene (205).

19. Olivier's Othello chooses "to focus upon the sensational element in the love [and] insists upon a potent sexuality . . . deliberately meant to be shocking" (Carlisle, 197). His performance has an "almost aggressive" bodily presence, "hairless shins, drooping eye-lids, the stipulated 'thick lips' of the text and a loose hip-rolling walk," producing a "strong physical aura" and "an atmosphere of the most potent sensuality" (Bamber Gascoigne, quoted in Tynan, 107).

20. For the omission of the trance and for speculation about the very rare ex-

ceptions, see Carlisle, 178–179; Hankey, 265; Matteo, 128–129; Odell, 34; Sprague, *Shakespeare and the Actors*, 203; and Winter, *Shakespeare on the Stage*, 245 and 270.

21. Consider, for example, the way the "'gasping struggles' of Iago 'heightened the effect' of McCullough's fury" (Sprague, *Shakespeare and the Actors*, 200). Similar embodiments of perverse contact and/or of sudden shifts of feeling were available in the scene of Iago's promotion and "marriage" to Othello, the slapping scene, the brothel scene, as well as the ending. See Sprague, *Shakespeare and the Actors*, 201–205, for examples from Booth, Fechter, and Salvini productions, among others. For more recent productions, see Wine's description of Ferrer in the Collaring Scene: "He starts to run away in fright from the threatening Othello . . . but then runs back and embraces his general" (59); and Tynan's of Finlay at the end, "brought back unharmed, turning to the vengeful Moor and opening his arms with a simple, virile gesture seeming to say 'OK, do it'" (19).

22. In 3.4.9 and in his next speech: "I know not where he lodges, and for me to devise a lodging and say he lies here, or he lies there, were to lie in mine own throat." "Lodge" is a resonant word in the play (the early texts disagree in the famous crux about the tragic loading or lodging of the bed at the end), and it connects with Othello's "there . . . / Where I must either live or bear no life" in the bordello scene.

23. "In Freudian terms, Iago is alienating Othello from the sexual act by making him participate in it from the place of superego. (Shakespeare's 'supervisor,' in fact, neatly condenses the watching, controlling, and judging functions that Freud defines as the superego's three attributes.)" ("Sexual Anxiety," 396).

24. From within Brabantio's position, Othello's trembling enacts the *ne plus ultra* of vindictive rage. Delaying confession until after death, he imagines himself damning Cassio's soul — like Hamlet, sending Rosencrantz and Guildenstern to it "not shriving time allowed" (5.2.47). But the trembling also betrays a fearful acknowledgment of his own unexpiable guilt and punishment (to *be* hanged, not to hang. Cf. *Much Ado* [4.1.4 ff.]: "*Friar*: You come hither, my lord, to marry this lady. *Claudio*: No. *Leonato*: To be married to her. Friar, you come to marry her."). The belated and therefore inefficacious ritual marks how far Othello has come from his own innocence at the beginning, when he could "confess the vices of my blood" with absolute confidence of redemption. The "preposterous" reversal of confession and punishment is one of the most striking instances of *hysteron proteron* in the play, the figure in which "that that is done afterwards, is set in speaking in the former place" (Altman, 133, quoting Richard Sherry). As Altman claims, Iago is "the presiding minister of *hysteron proteron*" (147), and the location of Othello's speech inside Iago's language adds another identity to the repertoire.

25. The pun, central to the play, is made explicit by Desdemona: "I cannot say whore? / It does abhor me now I speak the word" (4.2.163–164).

26. "Representation and Its Discontents," 148, Bersani's emphasis. For Bersani's later development of this material, see *The Freudian Body*, esp. 31–40.

27. Various stage traditions seem to be picking up on these contradictions, in particular Othello's 5.2 entry with a sword, quickly put aside, and his finishing off the revived Desdemona with a dagger. The sword and the dagger have uncertain and inexplicable origins somewhere in the eighteenth century, and carry on into

current productions, though Hankey remarks about the dagger that "modern Othellos have tended to respect Othello's intention of not scarring her, and have strangled her at 'So, so'" (319). In this context, Carlisle discusses in great detail a 1773 letter written to Garrick by George Swan, focusing on these ambiguous details in the murder scene in an extraordinarily rich and overdetermined way that helps to identify the play's own powerfully ambivalent and intense emotional effects about blood, flesh, guilt, scarring, etc. (254–261).

28. Snow develops this idea in a richly suggestive discussion ("Sexual Anxiety," 391–392). Bradshaw's "the mind now floods" is responding to the same kinds of suggestions in the play ("*flooded* seems the right word," he adds, until "the images smash against *dries up*, and reform into the wrenchingly gross, unhinging image of 'it' — 'it!' — as a foul *cistern*" [179]). Danson talks about the "fluid metaphors . . . suggested by Othello's figuring Desdemona as either 'fountain from which [his] current runs' or 'cistern for foul toads to knot and gender in.' In *Cymbeline* the idea of the wife as a watery site is complexly joined with the idea of the wife as property — the one idea, as we would expect, confounding the other, since you can't *keep* things that flow like a fountain or breed like a cistern" (75). All such discussions, including my own, seem to me indebted to Lynda Boose's brilliant suggestions associating the handkerchief, "spotted with strawberries" (3.3.438), with the virginal, menstrual, and guilty blood of the wedding sheets ("Othello's Handkerchief").

29. For matter as pus, cf. Thersites in *Troilus and Cressida* (2.1.1–9): "Agamemnon, how if he had biles — full, all over, generally? . . . And those biles did run — say so — did not the general run then? Were not that a botchy core? . . . Then would come some matter from him; I see none now." See also the discussion in Hillman, especially 296 and 305, including citations. For remarks on the powerful sense of sexual disgust in Othello's "appalling line," see Empson, "Honest in *Othello*," 226–227, and Snow, "Sexual Anxiety," 388. Othello appropriately locates the sentiment in Iago's honesty: "An honest man he is, and hates the slime / That sticks on filthy deeds." The slime allows for a return appearance of the toads which "even in their origins . . . seemed repulsive, since they were believed to be engendered in slimy mud" (Wentesdorf, 370, citing *Metamorphoses*, 15.375). For the toads as part of a network of suggestions evoking smell and touch rather than sight in the play, see Pechter, "'Have you not read of some such thing?'" 209–212.

30. This is Iago, talking of Cassio's analogous fall (2.3.180–181); and although he is lying (for he is himself the origin), he is also telling the truth (for he is himself also without origin, motiveless malignity). As in *Paradise Lost*, the initial manifestation of evil is inexplicable in the sense that any explanation we might generate seems itself to require an explanation, precipitating an endless regression in quest of an absent origin. "Say first," the poem begins, after its invocation, "what . . . Moved our grand parents . . . to fall off," but once the answer is given, "Th'infernal Serpent; he it was," we need to understand Satan's fall. In narrative terms Satan's fall is rendered as a response to the begetting of the Son, which Satan takes as an incursion into his power, but since the Son was there "from the beginning" (and was in fact the necessary agency for the creation of Satan), this narrative makes no

sense. The real question is how and why Satan came to understand his identity in terms of distinction from God — questions that are never answered conceptually, though perhaps they are imagistically in the myth in book 2 of the poem when, in the words of a personified Sin, "All on a sudden . . . Out of thy head I sprung" (752–758).

31. Although there were dissenting voices — Gardner, Arthos, Bayley, Everett and, more recently, Kirsch and Bulman — they were distinctly in the minority. Complaints about Othello's latent insecurity, immaturity, and self-absorption proliferated during this period, becoming something of a routine, almost — like claims for the undissociated sensibility of the Metaphysicals — a mantra. See Scott for substantial excerpts of this material, and Bulman, who provides a richly annotated and highly critical discussion of this Eliot-Leavis line on the play.

32. Hence according to G. R. Elliott, commenting on Othello's response to Brabantio at the beginning ("She has deceived her father . . . My life upon her faith"): "If Othello's part is properly acted the audience perceives that he has a suppressed anxiety" (quoted Scott, 473). From this perspective, the overt anxiety of the Temptation Scene in response to the same assault ("She did deceive her father. . . . And so she did") merely confirms a prior suggestion and thus reinforces a sense of continuity in the protagonist. In the same way, Derek Traversi argues that the voices inside the play attesting to Othello's shocking alteration lack authority. Reflecting on the Lodovico-Iago exchange in 4.1 ("Is this the noble Moor . . . He is much changed"), Traversi claims that "in spite of Iago's reply," Othello's later behavior simply accentuates the "egoistic basis" of the early Othello: as "his ruin proceeds, the egoism which had always been a part of the character comes more and more to the fore" (quoted Scott, 499).

33. Heilman goes on at length to talk of "a deficiency in adult self-awareness . . . his self-protectiveness, and even some pompousness in his portrait of himself as the undeflectable commander . . . his unredeemed egotism" (171–174). According to Calderwood, "warriors like Othello are particularly anxious to set women and sex at a safe remove from their military activities," "recoiling almost in disgust from the notion that he might want to take Desdemona to Cyprus for sexual reasons" and making "vehement denials of erotic desire before the Senate" (30, 62, 125). Calderwood sees the fault in terms of patriarchal interpellation, the "collective masculine unconscious into which men's anxieties about women's whorishness have been driven" (31); but the shift from Othello's idiosyncrasy to the general condition is without significant practical consequence. In a similar way, Greenblatt and Belsey shift — inconsequentially — from the particular to the general. According to Greenblatt, "If it were now to die" generates a pathos derived "not only from our awareness that Othello's premonition is tragically accurate, but from a rent, a moving ambivalence, in his experience of the ecstatic moment itself" (*Renaissance Self-Fashioning*, 243). Belsey, commenting on the premonitory "when" in the address to the Senate, acknowledges that "Othello is not making a declaration of intent" but claims nonetheless that "the utterance permits us to glimpse as reality what the speech rejects," thereby "betray[ing] the trace of antipathy which inhabits desire itself" (97). Despite their emphasis on the general

condition (ecstasy "itself," "desire itself"), Belsey and Greenblatt continue to operate within the same interpretive economy as Heilman et al., folding the protagonist's ignorance of his situation into the audience's superior knowledge.

34. Of "if it were now to die," Booth said, "To be uttered in low, foreboding tones"; of "when I love thee not," with "joyousness, yet there should be an undertone of sadness — as at their first embrace in Cyprus" (quoted Furness, 113 and 166). This tone is a theatrical possibility in Othello's speech going back to the very beginning of the play, as in Elliott's claim that "my life upon her faith" should reveal "a suppressed anxiety" if "properly acted." When Othello supports Desdemona's request to the Senate, we may hear Calderwood's "vehement" (see note 33) or Snow's "strenuous" disavowals ("Sexual Anxiety," 399); or we may hear confident self-possession. What constitutes "proper" acting?

35. Hence Lodovico's choric-sounding anguish at the end: "O thou Othello, that wert once so good, / Fallen in the practice of a cursed slave, / What shall be said to thee?" (5.2.288–290). Not *of* thee, but *to* thee: Lodovico feels the need to offer consolation, cheer Othello up, not to account for his situation. Good people fall, these things happen all the time. (An exchange about the birds' attack in the Hitchcock movie: "But there's no reason . . ." "It's happening, isn't that a reason?")

36. Note the tone of normative certainty I emphasize in the following passages from Calderwood (keyed to the order of the four versions of contemporary criticism as I described them above: (1) The alien's abject dependency and Iago's inevitable triumph: "But *after all what should we have expected*? The Moor is a stranger" (68); (2) The impossible condition of male desire: "This masculine appropriation of women in Venice helps explain why Othello's faith in Desdemona succumbs with such surprising ease to Iago's beguilements. He loses faith in part because he never really had any. Though he endows his wife with heavenly qualities, deep down he suspects, *like any other husband*, the sorry truth" (31); (3) Lacan: "To see yourself in another, as he does — *as we all do* in our psychological extensions of Lacan's mirror stage — is to divide as well as unify the here/thereness of the body/self" (105); (4) The submission to narrativity: "*Normally* the speaking subject is enormously in excess of the grammatical subject; we *are* [Calderwood's emphasis] far more than we can say" (58).

37. Dramatic power is a contestable category; for some it is not diminished but apparently constituted by predictability: we are "enabled by Shakespeare in the first two acts to perceive that inward force and danger of Othello's love" so that "the great temptation scene . . . does not surprise us" but is rather something we "enjoy dramatically" (Elliott, quoted Scott, 472). "The egoistic nature of Othello's love must not only be defined; we must watch it crumble, through its own blindness, into helplessness and incoherence. The process must be strictly dramatic" (Traversi, quoted Scott, 495). This sense of dramatic power seems to me appropriate, if at all, to comedy. See Bersani's polemic against what he calls a "mortuary esthetic" in which "the reader is encouraged *to read without suspense* — or, in other terms, to invent a motive for reading unsustained by a promise of epistemological gain. Everything is present from the start" ("Death and Literary Authority," 14–15; Bersani's emphasis).

38. The "tawny Moor" is usually said to originate with Coleridge — a matter I

shall be discussing at some length in the afterword. The *locus classicus* of claims for the superiority of reading to theatrical spectatorship is Lamb: Desdemona "sees Othello's colour in his mind. But upon the stage, when the imagination is no longer the ruling faculty, but we are left to our poor unassisted senses, I appeal to every one that has seen Othello played, whether he did not, on the contrary, sink Othello's mind in his colour" (108). Bradley's version at the end of the century is substantially similar, granting that Shakespeare's Othello was black but claiming that Othello should not "be represented as a black in our theatres now," for "as Lamb observes, to imagine is one thing and to see is another. Perhaps if we saw Othello coal-black with the bodily eye, the aversion of our blood, an aversion which comes as near to being merely physical as anything human can, would over-power our imagination and sink us below not Shakespeare only but the audiences of the seventeenth and eighteenth centuries" (165).

39. Cf. Hodgdon's strong cultural critique: "Fetishizing his blackened body, Olivier erases distinctions between self and other, claiming the character ('he belongs to me') as though he were colonial property. . . . Olivier's Othello confirms an absolute fidelity to white stereotypes of blackness and to the fantasies, cultural as well as theatrical, that such stereotypes engender. . . . The 'real' black body, and the histories it carries, can be elided, displaced into and contained by theatricality, which embraces a long tradition of whites blacking up, primarily, as in minstrelsy, for comic effect. Such impersonation . . . deflects analysis by aligning racist ideology with theatrical pleasure. . . . Most importantly, a made-up Othello ensures that both blackness and whiteness remain separate, unsullied. Putting race matters succinctly, blacking up is whiting out" (26–27).

But this very smart analysis doesn't seem to correspond to what happened. To be sure, Robert Kee's response to Olivier's Othello offers some supporting evidence for this claim. Though Kee saw it as "exploiting a modern audience's sensitised and partially confused state of mind on the subject of colour," he added that it "manages by use of some ordinary Negro tricks of behaviour both to illuminate Othello's extreme simplicity of character and at the same time to give a colour-less universality" (quoted Tynan, 106). But Kee's response was not typical. Most of the witnesses testify rather to a self-conscious and often anxious sense of racial matters as part of the theatrical excitement, not as a reassuring absorption into theatrical pleasure. They felt the minstrel tradition as a shameful residue from the past, alluded to but not occluded by Olivier's impersonation. See Carlisle ("risked laughter," "grotesquerie," "more caricature than idealization" [198]); Tynan ("not . . . a sentimental reading . . . nor one that white liberals will necessarily applaud" [5]); and Bamber Gascoigne ("he walks like a Negro, talks like a Negro . . . which I thought at first might prove a caricature" [quoted Tynan, 107]).

40. Anxiety and a guilty conscience about race are likely to cut across all constituencies of the current theatrical audience, and although anxiety and guilt are entirely appropriate responses to the play (to say nothing of the enduring history of racialist belief), the problem is the context of liberal sensitivity within which these emotions are expressed. Theatrical audiences can't be expected (and are thus not asked) to make the leap of historical imagination by which they can enter into the overt contempt of Iago at the beginning. The magnitude of Othello's own pow-

erful presence may depend on this identification and its surprising subsequent disconfirmation, but a diminished Othello seems a better fit with contemporary taste. In academic terms, it avoids an illicit "orientalist" exoticism; more generally, an abject Othello becomes the basis for solidarity with the marginalized and dispossessed. This is Cowhig's claim, a "humiliated and degraded" protagonist: "However great Othello's confidence, his colour makes his vulnerability plain" (9). We can become one with the victim, black like him — a reversal and repetition of Mary Preston's notorious claim that he was white like her ("Othello *was* a *white* man!").

41. This is hypothetical, but the fact that there are and have been for a considerable period no heroic Othellos onstage tells us something. There have been successful productions which play Othello sympathetically, but typically in a small frame (Clayton cites Trevor Nunn's 1989 *studio* production originally mounted at The Other Place [68], and the 1997 David Harewood–Simon Russell Beale version designed originally for the National's Cottesloe is apparently another). The one bravura modern success in the role was Olivier's at the National in 1964, a performance which even its detractors remember as shattering, without question the premier Othello of the modern stage. But it refused the heroic (lots of Leavis excerpts in the playbill — though probably fewer, to be sure, in the performance itself) and depended on getting a non-show-stealing Iago: "It took careful wooing to talk him into Othello, the only major role in Shakespearean tragedy that he had not played. He pointed out that no English actor in this century had succeeded in the part. The play, he said, belonged to Iago, who could always make the Moor look a credulous idiot — and he spoke with authority, since he had played Iago to Ralph Richardson's Othello in 1938 [in an "unrepentant scene-stealing spirit," according to Hankey (339)]. 'If I take it on,' he said, 'I don't want a witty, Machiavellian Iago. I want a solid, honest-to-God N.C.O.' The director, John Dexter, fully agreed with this approach" (Tynan, 2) — as how could he not?

5. The "Pity" Act

1. See Honigmann's discussions (346–348 and *The Texts of "Othello,"* 39–40).

2. For information and discussion of these cuts as well as occasional restorations, see Carlisle, 180–182; Alan Hughes, 144; Odell, 33–35; Sprague, *Shakespeare and the Actors*, 203 ff.; and Winter, *Shakespeare on the Stage*, 270.

3. Elsewhere Orgel marshals evidence to conclude that Renaissance drama is not "generically pure. . . . Even the purest of Renaissance tragedies would have appeared *to an audience* to belong to a mixed genre because in performance it would have included *intermezzi* between the acts, or in England, jigs at the end. . . . The genres constituted not an idea about the necessary structure of plays, but an idea about the potentialities of theaters to realize the classic forms. And what the models then offered . . . was just the opposite of that rigid consistency we find in them: a very fluid set of possibilities" ("Shakespeare Imagines a Theater," 46; Orgel's emphasis). Orgel develops a similar claim in "Shakespeare and the Kinds of Drama." The *locus classicus* remains Johnson's *Preface to Shakespeare*, where it is

offered with mixed feelings — at once the transcendence and transgression of generic norms.

4. Quoted Hankey, 321, who gives three other instances of Emilia's domination in twentieth-century productions.

5. Burke's in good company making this argument about Emilia's function, including Bradley ("the only person who utters for us the violent common emotions which we feel, together with those more tragic emotions which she does not comprehend" [197]); Empson ("the mouthpiece of all the feelings in us which are simply angry with Othello, but this judgement of him is not meant to keep its prominence for long" ["Honest in *Othello*," 227]); Siemon ("a particularly telling displacement of energy from the idealized feminine victim onto a domestic 'virago' double" ["Nay," 45]); and McAlindon ("fearless and ferocious condemnation . . . calculated both to vent and to dispose of our feelings of moral outrage" [144]). The basic claim is a version of Empson's tremendous idea about *Hamlet*, imagined as Shakespeare's reflection: "He thought: 'The only way to shut this hole is to make it big. I shall make Hamlet walk up to the audience and tell them, again and again, "I don't know why I'm delaying any more than you do; the motivation of this play is just as blank to me as it is to you; but I can't help it." What is more, I shall make it impossible for them to blame him. And *then* they daren't laugh'" ("*Hamlet*," 84; Empson's emphasis).

6. Brutus is the substantial instance in Shakespeare. Honigmann cites a very close analogue to Emilia's speech from *Henry VIII*, 3.2.387 ff., but the speaker is Wolsey. "To suffer, as to do, / Our strength is equal" (*Paradise Lost*, 2.199–200) is another good analogue which, according to Merritt Hughes's note, echoes Mucius Scaevola thrusting his hand into the fire, but the speaker is Belial.

7. Swan played Othello at the Theatre Royal, Dublin, in 1742, but it "is not clear whether his notes reflect the business that he himself had used or whether they were the result of his ruminations after his retirement from the stage." In either event, "the typical stage Desdemona in the eighteenth century probably did not put up the vigorous struggle Swan imagined for her. Nor did she in the nineteenth century." Perhaps George Skillan's advice much later in the French's Acting Edition, that anyone of Desdemona's "'quality and strong spirit' naturally reacts with abhorrence to the sudden threat of violent death and fights for self-preservation," was also relegated to the realm of unrealized potential. For this material, see Carlisle, 258–261.

8. Adamson herself, working in an attenuated Leavis tradition, claimed no systematic grounding for her response, though such claims were being made, particularly in America, by critics subsequently designated "first-wave feminists." According to W. D. Adamson, writing the same year "*Othello*" *as Tragedy* was published (and perhaps exaggerating), "many of today's younger critics find it hard to write 'innocence' without writing 'life-denying' in front of it. [They] often see [Desdemona's] innocence as a neurotic defense mechanism, or even at one extreme a 'life-destroying' characteristic, the epitome of 'the sexual unreality the race longs for'" (179).

9. The Renaissance stage at this time was rich in examples of the performance

of passivity, faithful wives who were astoundingly acquiescent to bizarre husbandly assaults on the model of the protagonist of *Patient Grissil*, a joint venture by Dekker, Haughton, and Chettle produced in 1600, which was evidently quite popular and generated a series of spinoffs and imitations. The passivity of Annabel in *The Fair Maid of Bristow* and Luce in *The London Prodigal*, both in the King's Men's repertoire at the same time as *Othello*, is especially worth noting (see Pechter, *Patient Grissil*; and Knutson, 115 ff.).

10. The question itself may be declared illegitimate if we assume with Burke that Desdemona has no existence apart from her function in the sacrificial plot or, in the current version, that "there is no 'person' there," only "a particular linguistic situation" (Greenberg, 12); or that "Desdemona has no character of her own; she is a convenience in the story of Othello, Iago, and Venice . . . written into a script that is organized through the perceptions and needs of male dominance in heterosexuality and patriarchal ideology" (Sinfield, 54). Loomba cites an earlier version of Sinfield's claim that Desdemona is "less a developing consciousness than a series of positions that women are conventionally supposed to occupy . . . in patriarchal ideology . . . scripted by men" (58). More of this in the appendix.

11. According to Wine, " 'my kind lord' is the Othello whose 'visage' she saw 'in his mind'; her 'nobody' could be only the 'false,' stereotypical Moor as Othello is now. The effect of these words is to remind Othello of what he knew when he addressed the Senate" (34). Calderwood pursues a similar line: "She announces in effect that her acceptance of his authority has derived not from his institutional status as her husband, not from his masculine capacity to do her harm, but from consent freely given, from nothing more forceful than the 'downright violence' of her own love as she declared it before the Senate" (36).

12. Honigmann (340) reproduces from Furness (277) the version derived from Percy's *Reliques* (1765), cautioning that we "should not assume, however, that Percy's version gives the ballad verbatim as Shakespeare found it" (339).

13. Compare Maggie Smith's reaction to the slap: it "is not the usual collapse into sobs; it is one of deep shame and embarrassment, for Othello's sake as well as her own. She is outraged, but tries out of loyalty not to show it. . . . 'I have not deserved this' is not an appeal for sympathy, but a protest quietly and firmly lodged by an extremely spunky girl" (Tynan, 10). The sentiment described here is similar to Faucit's, explaining why Desdemona struggles against the murderous Othello: "I felt for *him* as well as myself, and therefore I threw into my remonstrances all the power of passionate appeal I could command. . . . I thought of all his aftersuffering, when he should come to know how he had mistaken me! The agony for him which filled my heart, as well as the mortal agony of death which I felt in imagination, made my cries and struggles no doubt very vehement and very real" (quoted Carlisle, 260).

In both these passages, Desdemona's feeling for herself is represented as inextricably bound up with her feeling for Othello. It may be, though, that the performance is being thought through as much in terms of theatrical dynamics as character. Faucit's Brabantio said that her strength "restored the balance of the play by giving [Desdemona's] character its due weight in the action," and Faucit herself reports that Macready liked her strength: "I added intensity to the last act by 'being so difficult to kill'" (quoted Carlisle, 249). This sounds like Tynan's point (quoted in chapter 5) about the greater theatrical interest and excitement in a "less one-sided" struggle.

Fanny Kemble's explanation of the desirability of struggle is superficially similar but really going in the opposite direction: it emphasizes Othello's "inefficient clumsiness . . . his half smothering, his half stabbing her," which in turn reflects on "Othello's agony" in the deed: "*That* man not to be able to kill *that* woman outright . . . how tortured he must have been" (quoted Carlisle, 259). Here the effect is to draw the attention away from Desdemona and over to the protagonist's internal struggle — of which much more in the next chapter. This is closer to the self-erasing false consciousness which contemporary criticism tends to find in the play.

14. Role models don't work well with tragedy, where no prudent course of action is available and where every path leads to catastrophe; but current critics are just doing what Coleridge was doing, and Rymer, and (more generally) Sidney and Heywood and other apologists for poetry around the time *Othello* was written: claiming some influential connection between the actions performed on the stage and the beliefs of the spectators. There are always connections between fictional plots and ideological agendas, though we tend to sound foolish when we make them. Empson says that "you ought to be able to appreciate in literature beliefs you don't agree with" but immediately adds that "when these rather subtle points are broadened into a confident dogma they lead I think to bad criticism" ("Honest in *Othello*," 242).

15. "I also liked the way Kate Skinner played Bianca: a sexy woman for Cassio but no strumpet. I believed her when she said — and this is important for our sense of women in the play — 'I am no strumpet, but of life as honest / As you that thus abuse me.' . . . Iago's word, of course . . . I don't think I'd ever really heard or thought about Emilia's reply before — 'As I?'" (Swander, 13).

16. Margaret Mikesell has described this view as "part of a significant group of studies which . . . broadly scrutinize the role of masculine (and feminine) codes of behavior, misogyny, and gender differences in *Othello*." From this perspective, "the play's ideals . . . appear not so much in Desdemona alone . . . but in the actions of all the women. Often Emilia or Bianca is cited as the true iconoclast in a society strangled by its gender codes and particularly by male notions of vengeance and women — stereotypes consistently belied by the actual behavior of the female characters" (xx).

17. Though writing an exemplary text in the currently powerful critical mode Mikesell describes (see previous note), Grennan nonetheless seems to assume about Bianca what his whole critical agenda should be calling into question: "Bianca's is the smallest of the three women's roles in *Othello*. Small as it is, however, it is nonetheless an indispensable element in the dramatic design. As a prostitute . . . " (282). The exceptions include Evelyn Gajowski (who, however, is able to exonerate Bianca only by apparently making the implausible claim that she is "completely lacking in sensuality" [106]); Kay Stanton (in an unpublished SAA paper she has kindly let me see called "Iago, the Whore of Venice"); Singh (who generously sent me an essay making a number of the claims about Bianca similar

to the ones I am making here); and Vanita (who writes interestingly about the guilt attributable to men in the play who fail to intervene to protect slandered women. She is chiefly concerned with Desdemona, but comments in passing about Bianca's vulnerability to Iago's slander that "none of the men present intervenes to save her, even Emilia self-righteously joining in the condemnation" [354]).

18. Both original texts have "huswife." Honigmann modernizes, like most editors, but adds that "perhaps we should read hussy (a woman of light character, or prostitute)." Ridley in the New Arden was also uncertain: "The word has not usually in Shakespeare the 'pejorative' sense of 'courtesan' or 'hussy' . . . but there can be no doubt that that is what Iago here means and it represents the fact. But there is also little doubt that Bianca is also a housewife in the normal sense, a citizen of Cyprus, with her own house, and not a mere camp-follower" (141). By attaching first "no doubt" and then "little doubt" to apparently contradictory propositions on either side of "but," Ridley succeeds in communicating much doubt indeed — which is arguably the appropriate response, preferable to the practice of most editors who, by simply glossing the term as "hussy," thereby assure us that any uncertainty we may have registered should be ignored. Still more problematically, the Oxford editors make a preemptive strike against even any initial registry of uncertainty by actually printing "hussy." They record this modernization, consistently with their policy of noting "modernizations . . . when it seems desirable to draw attention to ambiguity in the control-text, or in conspicuous departures from standard practice" (Wells and Taylor, *Textual Companion*, 155). Why, though, modernize to begin with, when it has the effect not of calling attention to but of concealing the original ambiguity?

19. It must have been obsolete by the time of Dr. Johnson's gloss, "a common woman, one that invites custom" (quoted Furness, 243), or Johnson would not have felt the need for an explanatory note. The modern meaning of "buyer" was already current and looks to have been standard in the Renaissance. In addition to the *OED* examples, consider the use of "customer" in Marston's *Dutch Courtesan* (5.3.112): although the context is full of sexual innuendo, the economic meaning of purchaser is clearly primary, and the sexual meaning of prostitute need not even be inferred. As for the possible regional rather than standard (London) usage of "customer" as seller: "Wise in his *Glossary* . . . gives this word as in use in this sense among the peasantry of Warwickshire at this day" (Furness, 243). If Wise is reliable, this may help to explain why the *only* Renaissance examples of "customer" as seller in the *OED* are from Shakespeare (this one and *All's Well That Ends Well*, 5.3.286, where the meaning seems unambiguously to be prostitute).

20. Grennan comments on "the curiously pliable speech of Cassio, whom circumstances can alter from Petrarchan idealist to sexual cynic" (276). Both Catherine M. Shaw (312–315) and Graham Bradshaw perceive the contrast between Iago's unsuccessful and later successful attempts to evoke a sneeringly homosocial response from Cassio. As Bradshaw puts it, "The moral comedy in that exchange [2.3.11 ff.] is all the more welcome and enjoyable because it momentarily defeats the vulgarly reductive Iago — but only for a while; in 4.1, when Bianca rather than Desdemona is the subject of the conversation between Iago and Cassio, we see

the sniggering, vain, and rutting young buck, whom Iago can easily lead by the nose" (157).

21. According to Barbara Mowat, "the list's description of Bianca as a "curtezan" has . . . had an impact on attitudes taken toward Bianca" (321). As Singh puts it: "Critical and editorial traditions are complicit with assigning sexual roles to female characters in ways that replicate the ideologies of the male characters within the plays" (50).

22. For Crane generally, see Howard-Hill, *Ralph Crane and Some Shakespeare First Folio Comedies*. For Crane's influence on the preparation of the Folio, see Howard-Hill, "Shakespeare's Earliest Editor, Ralph Crane." For Crane's influence on F *Othello*, see Honigmann, *The Texts of "Othello,"* esp. 59–76. Honigmann pointed out years earlier that dramatis personae lists were theatrically useful (*The Stability of Shakespeare's Text*, 44–46). While this may be true, Crane's aggressively interventionist scribal work seems to be based on his particular attention to readers' needs.

23. Despite Ridley's implied equation in "the 'pejorative' sense of 'courtesan' or 'hussy,'" the terms are not identical. The *OED* describes "courtesan" as "a somewhat euphemistic appellation," thereby begging the question (how euphemistic is it? what's the tone?). Shakespeare's tone, to judge from the evidence in the Spevack Concordance, was generally winking and nudging: a "high-class whore," so to speak. On the other hand, as Traub suggests, some more substantial distinction may be available. (She refers us to Jones; Rosenthal is relevant as well.) What Shakespeare knew of contemporary continental sociosexual categories is unclear. Obviously he had read in and around *Gli Hecatommithi*, though Cinthio's term is not "*una cortigiana*" but "*una meretrice*," and it is possible that Shakespeare read Cinthio in a French translation (Bullough, 249). The author of *The Comedy of Errors* certainly knew something about dramatic types from ancient New Comedy, and Imogen's reference in *Cymbeline* to "some Roman courtesan" (3.4.123) in a context highly reminiscent of *Othello* — jealousy and misprision; Pisanio uses "honest" and "abused" in the preceding speech — is interestingly suggestive. So is Marston's *Dutch Courtesan*, which generally represents Franceschina as a whore *tout court*, but which also gives Freevil a speech at the beginning that performs a witty deconstruction *avant la lettre* on the distinction between a whore and a wife — the distinction declared to be the play's whole matter. Crane's knowledge and understanding of these matters is anybody's guess.

24. In the case of this play, anyway, Cloud's representation of the editorial tradition as a mindless reproduction of error or opinion is a caricature. Although it is true that the 1623 identification of Bianca is reproduced in one or another version by virtually every modern editor (for some eighteenth- and nineteenth-century examples, see Singh, 49), many of these editors call attention to what Ross, to take one example, calls its "questionable authority" and frequently provide alternatives or elaborations that reflect upon the problem even as they reflect it. "Courtesan" in various spellings is reproduced (with or without some consideration of its authority) in Brown, Evans, Harbage, Ridley, and Ross. Bianca is described as "mistress to" or "of" Cassio in Muir, Walker, and Sisson. Honigmann

and Sanders give us both, "a courtesan [and Cassio's mistress]" and "'a courtesan,' mistress of Cassio" (Honigmann's square brackets and Sanders's inverted commas indicate derivation from F, with explanations in both cases). Ridley keeps "courtesan," adding that "I have retained F's description of Bianca, since the usual '*Mistress to Cassio*' implies a more permanent relationship than is anywhere implied in the text, except (possibly) in one disputed line" (presumably the "housewife" line, about which I have quoted his comment). Alexander gives us Bianca as "a courtezan, in love with Cassio," and Wells and Taylor follow suit (*William Shakespeare: The Complete Works*), thereby reproducing the apparent contradiction in Iago's description, but without explaining it (as Iago claimed to do) or noting that it might need an explanation.

"Mistress to Cassio" is worth some consideration in view of "The Cardinals Mrs" (that is, "The Cardinal's Mistress"), which is the designation, very probably Crane's, for Julia, the Bianca character in Webster's *Duchess*. I speculate that Crane balked at describing Bianca as Cassio's mistress because of her greater economic and sexual autonomy. Julia is married and much more dependent upon her man (or indeed men, three of them, counting Bosola) than Bianca, however "circumstanced." (In passing, I note that the 1681 Quarto based on a Theatre Royal performance calls Bianca "Cassio's wench" [see Shakespeare].)

25. See Teague, and see Dessen's discussion of lighting imagery (*Elizabethan Stage Conventions*, 80–83).

26. I take it as self-evident that Bianca's denial cannot be processed as disinterested evidence, but for some interesting contextual detail on the matter, see Jardine,"'Why Should He Call Her Whore?'"

27. Apart from the different dramatis personae designations (note 24), we have already seen some of the contradictory inferences drawn about Bianca: Neill's "jealous camp-follower," Ridley's "citizen of Cyprus, with her own house, and not a mere camp-follower" (note 18). Catherine Shaw refers to Cassio as "quartering a doxy" and "keeping a whore" (314) and seems to believe that Bianca (like Desdemona) has followed her man to Cyprus, a belief sometimes explicitly assumed, as most recently by Graham Bradshaw.

6. Death without Transfiguration

1. Rudnytsky comments that Othello's opening speech in 5.2 "is difficult to construe because the word 'it' has no antecedent, and thus the 'cause' in fact remains unspecified. . . . This impersonal construction, however, perfectly conveys the way that Othello's jealousy is itself without a 'cause,' except insofar as it is a 'monster' incestuously arising out of his own mind. The word 'cause,' derived etymologically from the Latin *causa*, is cognate with the French *chose*, and thus returns us to that Freudian 'thing,' the absent yet indispensable phallus Othello refuses even to 'name'" (186). To be sure, the French *chose*, like Alysoun's "*belle chose*" in Chaucer, is more likely in the context of this play's language to evoke some other "thing," but who's to say?

2. Responding to Johnson-Haddad's remark that the "whole performance emphasized particularly the sense of smell," Stewart says, "Mind you, Othello has

said, in the brothel scene, 'O thou weed, / Who art so lovely fair, and smell'st so sweet / That the sense aches at thee. . . . ' I can't quite remember why, but I do know that the first two times he leans down in 5.2, I was convinced that smelling, breathing in, was what he was doing, and the third time kissing her" (Johnson-Haddad, "Patrick Stewart on Playing Othello," 12). The passage Stewart quotes coincides with the moment in the Olivier production when "desire almost overcomes disgust" (Tynan, 11; quoted in chapter 4).

3. He avows his debt to Hegel early on in *Shakespearean Tragedy*, "certainly the most important theory since Aristotle's" (10), and develops Hegel's ideas in his first lecture, "The Substance of Shakespearean Tragedy."

4. At the end of his first lecture, Bradley adds a note stating that he has "abstained from treating fully here" the effects of "reconciliation and sometimes even exultation" in order "not to anticipate later passages" (29). This not wholly satisfactory explanation leads to exhortations to the reader to look at the entries for "reconciliation" in the index and to consult his essay "Hegel's Theory of Tragedy" — which is itself full of qualifications. At the end of the passage quoted at the beginning of this chapter about the way "there is almost nothing" in the murder scene "to diminish our admiration and love" for Othello, Bradley refers us to an appendix ("Note O") where he explains the qualification "almost." He acknowledges himself to be "shocked by the moral blindness" in Othello's response to Desdemona's dying words. "Here alone," he says, "sympathy with Othello quite disappears. Did Shakespeare mean us to feel thus . . . ? I suppose so." He then tries to explain away the passage as the consequence of "a touch of personal animus" on the part of an author "intentionally striking at conventionally 'religious' ideas"; but he is aware that this runs completely contrary to his foundational assumption of an ideologically disengaged Shakespeare, and these contradictions are left conspicuously unresolved in the appendix's concluding words: "I admit that this fancy seems un-Shakespearean, and yet it comes back on me whenever I read this passage. [The words 'I suppose so' . . . gave my conclusion; but I wish to withdraw the whole Note]" (*Shakespearean Tragedy*, 374).

5. Such insistence is rare in Shakespeare and in Renaissance tragedy in general. The old Duke's murder in *The Revenger's Tragedy* is a notable exception, but it's played for grotesque laughter. Antony's death is a notably exceptional Shakespearean example of the effort required to surmount the body's resistance to its own extinction. But here too the effect is largely comic, even with the pain and embarrassment, apparently as a way to set up Cleopatra's easeful death in act 5 into which the play's contradictory feelings are absorbed. *Othello* seems to be striving after an effect similar to that of the unbearably protracted strangulation scene in Hitchcock's otherwise undistinguished *Torn Curtain*.

6. Cf. Gauntlett (quoting Neill): "Like the pictorial tradition of epitomizing the play in the representation of the murder scene, . . . and, ironically, like the nineteenth-century theatre's effacement of the bed as the scene of the action, Bradley's reconstruction serves in the end 'to foreground not merely the perverse eroticism of the scene but its aspect of forbidden disclosure'" (79).

7. It is actually his penultimate speech. "Discussion of Othello's 'last speech' has not seldom been bedevilled by ambiguity, though 'Othello's last *great* speech'

is obviously enough 'Soft you, a word or two'. It is *not* his 'final lines', however, although at least one recent critic apparently believes they are, because that is what he called them" (Clayton, 63, citing Calderwood, 109).

8. The nineteenth-century practice of costuming Othello in a conspicuously new way for 5.2 is continued in the twentieth century, in productions featuring Robeson, Scofield, and Olivier (Hankey, 309), though it seems clear enough that any idea of the protagonist's final transcendence is explicitly refused (at least in the Scofield and Olivier performances). Perhaps such a practice has been emptied out of its original significance and left to produce merely a formalist effect of closure by itself. We (or at least I) don't have a clear idea of a systematically coherent modern theatrical *Othello* equivalent to the nineteenth-century tradition, maybe because we haven't achieved the reductive clarification of retrospection, maybe because there isn't one.

9. Compare Girard, 218: "The only 'real' scapegoats are those we are unable to acknowledge as such"; and "Violence and Representation," 192: "The 'best' scapegoats, the only 'good' scapegoats, really, are the scapegoats who are not recognized as such."

10. I am aligning myself here with Greenblatt's brilliant argument about the theater's "emptying out" of religious belief, developed at the end of his essay "Shakespeare and the Exorcists" (*Shakespearean Negotiations*, 114–128). To put this another way, I am somewhat skeptical of Liebler's (also brilliant) argument about the residual efficacy of ritual foundations in Shakespearean tragedy.

11. Uniquely at least among Bradley's "major four." Some of the Roman plays, especially *Julius Caesar*, also heavily advertise their own status as ritual ceremony, as a consequence withholding or diluting any potential cleansing power. They do so, however, to very different effect; the Roman plays consistently emphasize the historical distance of their setting as a way of helping to establish a persistently ironic detachment from the audience's own beliefs — the reverse of *Othello*'s strategy.

12. Honigmann points out that the stage direction here, "*The Moore runnes at* Iago. Iago *kils his wife*," is "the only centred SD in Q, and it is unusually specific."

13. Siemon's explanation, that "audiences demanded the final scene" as written ("Nay," 39), is advanced without much evidence. *Lear* has a broader range of characters and action, uses an old plot whose happy ending would have been familiar to at least some of the original audiences, and (most important) strongly encourages expectations throughout its own action for a happy ending.

14. It would be helpful, for instance, to have a more developed and clearer idea of Coleridge's point behind the notes for his 9 November 1813 Bristol lecture (part of the series including the passage with which I began — his point that Shakespeare "never walked in twilight" was from a lecture less than two weeks earlier): "Othello's *belief* not jealousy; forced upon him by Iago — and such any man would and must feel who had believed of Iago as Othello. His great mistake that WE know Iago for a villain from the first moment" (Foakes, *Coleridge's Criticism*, 111). Whose great mistake, Shakespeare's or Othello's, and why exactly?

15. Hankey provides many other interesting examples (339–340), including

some residual nineteenth-century sentiment in Gordon Crosse's and Robert Speaight's objections to recent Iago-centered endings.

16. "Gesture" is Blackmur's term, which he illustrates with Desdemona's "I understand a fury in your words / Not the words" (4.2.32–33): "a fair example of the situation in which language gains the force of gesture" (4). "Symbolic action" is Burke's phrase, though I am making use here not of his book with that title, but of his capsule discussion in *The Philosophy of Literary Form* (8 ff.) from which I have borrowed the phrase "dancing of an attitude" (9). Perhaps Auden (like Eliot) is motivated by a poetic agenda, trying to purify the language of the tribe of its used-up sentimentality. Auden then isn't so much talking about Desdemona or *Othello* but of a way to secure territory for poetic possession: "Lay your sleeping head, my love, / Human on my faithless arm" (*Collected Shorter Poems*, 238).

17. Franceschina, foreigner and whore, is referred to as the "monstrous . . . devil" (5.2.100), and Freevil tells us at the end that "only what you can think / Has been extremely ill is only hers" (5.3.53–54). Like Iago, who is condemned to the worst tortures imaginable (5.2.331–333), Franceschina is sent off to the "severest prison" and "the extremest whip and jail" (5.3.55, 59), but like Iago, she remains untouchable: "Ick vill not speak. Torture, torture, your fill" (57). Marston plays the whole thing for cynical laughter, but *The Dutch Courtesan* is a stylized city comedy performed by boys in a private theater, different in all respects from *Othello*, and cynical laughter may be a suitable exit strategy for his play. Even so, Marston in fact provides something a lot more "festive" at the very end in the hilarious Cockledemoy.

18. There are times when Burke seems to suggest that *Othello* is providing a real purgation to its audience, as though the filthiness belongs only to a retrospective critical consciousness, but in *Othello* this consciousness is written into the theatrical experience. Audiences are made up of individuals diversely informed by analytical intelligence, and it is possible to argue that *Othello* is working on different levels — scapegoating for the groundlings, enlightened skepticism for the better sort. This is Girard's claim about *The Merchant* and other plays ("'To Entrap the Wisest'"), but even if we were to accept the argument in general terms, I cannot imagine any spectator leaving *Othello* feeling cleansed.

Afterword: Interpretation as Contamination

1. This desire may help to explain the proliferation of recent work motivated apparently by the desire to install us in a position from which we can claim greater control over history, all the interest in the "making" or "reinventing" of Shakespeare and in the recovery of original production and reception conditions, as though we can get out from under the weight of history by analyzing the processes by which tradition has established and developed its authority. This is arguably a healthy and reasonable endeavor — though a highly speculative one, most obviously in the case of recovering original conditions. What conclusions does Henry Jackson's report really justify? We know that *Othello* was one of twenty King's Men plays chosen to be performed at court between Christmas and the end of May,

1612–1613, "in connection with festivities celebrating the betrothal and marriage of Princess Elizabeth" (Kernan, 208, who lists the plays; see also Bradbrook, *The Living Monument*, 160); but there is no way to determine the meaning or effects of this particular choice. The evidence we have allows only for plausible generalizations about "the repertory *system*" of the King's Men (Knutson, 168; my emphasis): its admixture of conventional materials, spinoffs, new plays and revivals, etc.; and only for generalizations about Shakespeare's popularity in furnishing the repertory (he "supplied the kinds of plays that audiences liked, with stories that they liked, in dramatic formulas that they liked" [Knutson, ibid.]). Gurr demonstrates that there was a considerable crossover of repertory and clientele among the various theatrical milieus where the King's Men performed (Globe, Blackfriars, court), so claims about cultural work specific to the interests of one or another constituency in one or another of the milieus ("serving the Leviathan State," "interrogating the hegemonic") are at best interestingly suggestive.

2. I reproduce some of the SHAKSPER discussion generated by Tromper's contribution in "*Othello*" (141–142), but readers who want more detail should consult the SHAKSPER archives, accessible by following the directions provided in note 1 to the introduction.

3. Tromper might have come across the essay in any of four currently available publications. After the first publication in the edition listed in the bibliography (from which all my quotations are taken), the essay was reprinted as a chapter in Newman's *Fashioning Femininity and English Renaissance Drama*; in Barthelemy, 124–143; and in Wain, 209–223 (which, however, did not include the discussion of Ridley).

4. There are thirteen citations of Newman's essay. The only modern critic with more is Ann Rosalind Jones with nineteen, but these are divided among three separate works and include two personal acknowledgments.

5. For Coleridge's primacy of interest in "inward illusion" (that willing suspension of disbelief which constitutes poetic faith) rather than textual properties as such, see Foakes, "*Hamlet*" *versus* "*Lear*," 125–137.

6. This argument parallels claims about the early modern meaning of "sodomy" before the nineteenth-century invention of homosexuality or sexual identity. Such major conceptual shifts are very gradual. Some historians argue plausibly that something like our notions of sexual or racial identity were already in place in Shakespeare's time, but, as earlier, I am more inclined to emphasize the differences (see the discussion in chapter 2, including note 5).

7. The beginning of *Hamlet*'s final scene thrusts this problem on us, when the protagonist requires Horatio to "Remember all the circumstance." Whether Horatio can do so (his response, "Remember it, my lord," is punctuated differently in the three original texts, with a question mark, a period, and an exclamation point), the audience certainly cannot. We have no way to delimit contextual relevance and must therefore assume that *everything* needs to be remembered that can be, a paralyzing impossibility that prevents us from asserting rights of memory in the kingdom of the play.

8. Perhaps the only true begetter of the argument attributed to Coleridge is William Kenrick, whose lecture of 16 February 1774 is reported to argue that

"though none of Shakespeare's Commentators ever doubted but that Othello was of a real *black* complexion, and though every performer of that character has followed the same opinion and put on *absolute negro face*, yet . . . he was *not a black*, and at worst only of a *tawny* colour," an assertion supported by three arguments, of which the first is "that a young Lady of Desdemona's delicacy of sentiment could never have fallen in love with a Negro; and more particularly, if we suppose him 'ill-favoured and old,' as Shakespeare calls him, we must conceive a greater idea of Desdemona's indelicacy; whereas supposing him *tawny* there is nothing very unnatural in it" (Vickers, 6.116). Such sentiments were widespread through the nineteenth century. Whether or not either Henry Nelson or Samuel Taylor Coleridge read Kenrick, it is not implausible to believe that they both might have believed what he was saying.

9. See chapter 4, note 38, for a lengthier excerpt from Bradley.

10. Winter is another example. Compare his almost obsessively sustained denigration (*Shakespeare on the Stage*, 270–306) of Fechter, Salvini, and the other Italians for the "polyglot representations with which the American stage has been disfigured" (270), an attack filled with uncharacteristically aggressive language ("completely wrong," "deformity," "radically wrong and supremely repulsive" [296, 297]), and of which the following may be considered representative:

> What relation does a street-suicide committed by an Italian barber who cuts his throat with a razor bear to the tragedy of "Othello"? . . . Foreign actors, in particular, visiting America, show themselves to signal disadvantage, often creating a harmful impression of ill-breeding. . . . There are persons, indeed, considerable in number, who admire all foreign forms of art only because they are foreign, and who accept with meek and humble provincial gratitude the patronizing precepts of foreign performers; but the American community, as a whole, naturally regards as an impertinence the top-lofty attitude of foreign visitors to the American Stage who assume to dispense instruction as to the function of dramatic art and the meaning of English dramatic literature. . . . Some of the views promulgated by foreign actors and some of the performances exhibited by them would speedily exile any English-speaking actor to the obscurity of the backwoods. (305–306)

As an American protecting the purity of English dramatic literature against foreign contamination, Winter's position is indeed "very amusing" and "highly instructive."

11. All but Singh and Orkin quote from Raysor's edition. Of these, only Bradshaw cites Raysor's warning about authenticity, which he then ignores. Like Newman, Singh uses the statement as a head quotation, without any attribution but with the scrupulous uses of introductory ellipses and a lower-case first letter: ". . . it." Orkin quotes from Hawkes's edition, ignoring Hawkes's warning and printing the text as: "[I]t would be . . ." Kaul cites the wrong pages in Raysor and deletes the phrase "as we are constituted" without ellipses: "No doubt Desdemona saw Othello's visage in his mind; yet it would be something monstrous . . ."

12. The analogy is far from perfect. Foakes was editing Coleridge for the Collected Coleridge. In terms of that project, the paragraph probably doesn't belong, though it arguably ought to remain at least in any Coleridge-on-Shakespeare

project, and Foakes does not include it in his selection for *Coleridge's Criticism of Shakespeare*. This is an area in which it's easier to criticize than to act.

Appendix: "Character Endures"

1. The phrases are taken from Grady, esp. chapter 2.

2. James Bulman makes the point more specific to *Othello* criticism: "The apparent ease with which Iago is able to exchange Othello for a goat has prompted an ever-increasing group of critics to find, deep within Othello's being, an element responsive to Iago's cynicism" (109). Bulman represents commentary on the play as a unified discourse, going back to its origins in Eliot/Leavis (indeed, he traces it back to Lewes in the nineteenth century), and continuing to our own day (or at least until 1985, when Bulman was writing).

3. This is Honigmann's point (*Shakespeare: Seven Tragedies*, 4–15): the plays invite us to wonder about the predramatic histories of some of the characters as a way of trying to make sense of their desires and actions. Alan Sinfield makes the same point in his claim that "when critics believe they find a continuous consciousness" in Shakespeare's characters, "they are responding to cues planted in the text for the initial audiences" (63). For a powerful argument that Shakespeare not only sustains but originates modern notions of subjectivity, see Fineman (*Shakespeare's Perjured Eye*). For "inwardness," see Maus; for "interiority," see Yachnin (93–128).

4. According to Empson, rejecting objections to Bradley by "some recent critics" (presumably Knights and Knight), "it is clearly wrong to talk as if coherence of character is not needed in poetic drama, only coherence of metaphor and so on," but he immediately adds that coherence of character is historically specific and later detaches himself from ideas of integrity and self-presence as either esthetic or social facts: "Perhaps I am a bad judge of inconsistency, because it seems to me that few writers have dared to make people as eccentric as they really are" ("Honest in *Othello*," 231, 244). A similar distinction underlies Matthews, whose materialist credentials may be illustrated in the claim that "in all Shakespeare's tragedies except, perhaps, *Macbeth*, the determining 'flaw' is in society rather than in the hero" (138). For Matthews the problem is not character as such but its conception as a closed and coherent system in "the Aristotle-Bradley doctrine of the 'tragic flaw.'" (If *hamartia* means error rather than flaw, this may not be an Aristotelian doctrine at all, but a relocation of Aristotle inside of an enclosed psychological space. The Greeks in antiquity, Aristotle included, distinguished between *ethos* and *physis*, the conduct of a person's behavior and his unchanging inner nature, endowing the former with great significance [see Pechter, *Dryden*, 74 ff.]).

5. For a development of this argument, see S. L. Goldberg (36–67).

6. "The centre of the tragedy, therefore, may be said with equal truth to lie in action issuing from character, or in character issuing in action. Shakespeare's main interest lay there. To say that it lay in *mere* character, or was a psychological interest, would be a great mistake, for he was dramatic to the tips of his fingers" (*Shakespearean Tragedy*, 7). To be sure, Bradley more than occasionally writes in a way not wholly consistent with this claim.

7. Compare Dawson's insistence on "participation," a word resonant with Renaissance ideas about Eucharistic ritual. Burke himself would probably not disagree with this point, to judge from his discussion of "Identification" in *A Rhetoric of Motives* (55–65).

8. The connection between character and the literary is made explicit in Jonathan Culler's 1994 review of the previous twenty-five years of *New Literary History*: "Even a cursory comparison" of the 1973 and 1993 volumes "yields an evident tale. In the early years we see a focus on literature: not on literary history . . . but on poetics, with special issues on 'What Is Literature?' and 'Changing Views of Character' (character *in literature* is taken for granted — would this be true today?), whereas in 1993 there is much less coherence, both within single issues, whose topics are broader and less focused." In 1993, "twenty-one out of forty-nine articles . . . do not deal with literature at all. Given what has happened to literary and cultural theory, this is not a startling result — people teaching in literature departments and writing for literary and theoretical journals may be working on film and popular culture, on the construction of women's bodies in the nineteenth century, on political discourses of the seventeenth century, without referring to literary works at all" (873).

9. Hence Barbara Herrnstein Smith's argument that since recent demonstrations in the "re-grounding of transcendental rationalism" depend for their force "on the prior acceptance of just the system of ideas, claims, and definitions at issue, the supposed re-grounding is thoroughly circular"; but that they "are evidently powerful and persuasive for many people, largely, it seems, *because* they are circular; that is, because they appeal to established ideas" (118; Smith's emphasis).

WORKS CITED

Adamson, Jane. *"Othello" as Tragedy: Some Problems of Judgment and Feeling.* Cambridge: Cambridge University Press, 1980.

Adamson, W. A. "Unpinned or Undone? Desdemona's Critics and the Problem of Sexual Innocence." *Shakespeare Studies* 13 (1980): 169–186.

Adelman, Janet. *Suffocating Mothers: Fantasies of Maternal Origin in Shakespeare's Plays, "Hamlet" to "The Tempest."* New York and London: Routledge, 1992.

Alexander, Peter, ed. *Complete Works of Shakespeare.* London and Glasgow: Collins, 1951.

Altman, Joel B. "'Preposterous Conclusions': Eros, *Enargeia*, and the Composition of *Othello.*" *Representations* 18 (1987): 129–157.

Anderson, Perry. *In the Tracks of Historical Materialism.* Chicago: University of Chicago Press, 1984.

Appiah, Kwame Anthony. "Race." In *Critical Terms for Literary Study*, ed. Frank Lentricchia and Thomas McLaughlin, 274–287. Chicago: University of Chicago Press, 1990.

Aristotle. *Poetics.* Trans. John Warrington. London: Dent, 1963.

Arthos, John. "The Fall of Othello." *Shakespeare Quarterly* 9 (1958): 93–104.

Auden, W. H. *Collected Shorter Poems, 1930–1944.* London: Faber, 1947.

———. "The Joker in the Pack." In *The Dyer's Hand and Other Essays*, 246–272. New York: Random House, 1962.

Bak, Greg. "Different Differences: Locating Moorishness in Early Modern Culture." *Dalhousie Review* 76 (1996): 197–216.

Banville, John. "An Interview with Salman Rushdie." *New York Review of Books* (4 March 1993): 34–36.

Barthelemy, Anthony Gerard, ed. *Critical Essays on Shakespeare's "Othello."* New York: G. K. Hall, 1994.

Bate, Jonathan, ed. *The Romantics on Shakespeare.* Harmondsworth: Penguin, 1992.

Bayley, John. *The Characters of Love: A Study in the Literature of Personality.* London: Constable, 1960.

Beckerman, Bernard. *Shakespeare at the Globe, 1599–1609.* New York: Macmillan, 1962.

Behn, Aphra. *Oroonoko: An Authoritative Text, Historical Backgrounds, Criticism*, ed. Joanna Lipking. New York: Norton, 1997.

Belsey, Catherine. *Desire: Love Stories in Western Culture.* Oxford: Blackwell, 1994.

———. "Desire's Excess and the English Renaissance Theatre: *Edward II*, *Troilus and Cressida*, and *Othello*." In *Erotic Politics: Desire on the Renaissance Stage*, ed. Susan Zimmerman, 84–102. London and New York: Routledge, 1992.

———. *The Subject of Tragedy: Identity and Difference in Renaissance Drama*. London: Methuen, 1985.

Bentley, Eric. *A Century of Hero Worship: A Study of the Idea of Heroism in Carlyle and Nietzsche, with Notes on Other Hero-worshippers of Modern Times*. Philadelphia: Lippincott, 1944.

Berry, Edward. "Othello's Alienation." *Studies in English Literature* 30 (1990): 315–334.

Bersani, Leo. "Death and Literary Authority: Marcel Proust and Melanie Klein." In *The Culture of Redemption*, 7–28. Cambridge and London: Harvard University Press, 1990.

———. *The Freudian Body: Psychoanalysis and Art*. New York: Columbia University Press, 1986.

———. "Representation and Its Discontents." In *Allegory and Representation: Selected Papers from the English Institution, 1979–80*, ed. Stephen J. Greenblatt, 145–162. Baltimore and London: Johns Hopkins University Press, 1981.

Bevington, David. Introduction to *Othello*, ed. Bevington. 1980; rpt. Toronto and New York: Bantam, 1988.

Blackmur, R. P. *Language as Gesture: Essays in Poetry*. New York: Harcourt, Brace and Co., 1952.

Bland, Sheila Rose. "How I Would Direct *Othello*." In Kaul, ed., "*Othello*," 29–44.

Bodkin, Maud. "The Images of the Devil, of the Hero, and of God." In *Archetypal Patterns in Poetry: Psychological Studies of Imagination*, 217–270. Oxford: Oxford University Press, 1934.

Boose, Lynda E. "Grossly Gaping Viewers and Jonathan Miller's *Othello*." In *Shakespeare, the Movie: Popularizing the Plays on Film, TV, and Video*, ed. Lynda E. Boose and Richard Burt, 186–197. London and New York: Routledge, 1997.

———. "'Let it be hid': Renaissance Pornography, Iago, and Audience Response." In *Autour d' "Othello*," ed. Richard Marienstras and Dominique Guy-Blanquet, 135–143. Paris: C.E.R.L.A., à l'Institut Charles V, 1987.

———. "Othello's Handkerchief, 'The Recognizance and Pledge of Love.'" *English Literary Renaissance* 5 (1975): 360–374.

Booth, Stephen. "On the Value of *Hamlet*." In *Reinterpretations of Elizabethan Drama: Selected Papers from the English Institute*, ed. Norman Rabkin, 137–177. New York: Columbia University Press, 1969.

Bradley, A. C. "Hegel's Theory of Tragedy." In *Oxford Lectures on Poetry*, 69–98. 1909; rpt. Bloomington: Indiana University Press, 1961.

———. *Shakespearean Tragedy: Lectures on "Hamlet," "Othello," "King Lear," "Macbeth*." 1904; rpt. London: Macmillan, 1964.

Bradbrook, M. C. *The Living Monument: Shakespeare and the Theatre of His Time*. Cambridge: Cambridge University Press, 1976.

————. *Shakespeare: The Poet in His World*. London: Weidenfeld and Nicolson, 1978.

Bradshaw, Graham. *Misrepresentations: Shakespeare and the Materialists*. Ithaca: Cornell University Press, 1993.

Brenner, Robert. *Merchants and Revolution: Commercial Change, Political Conflict, and London's Overseas Traders, 1550–1653*. Princeton: Princeton University Press, 1993.

Bristol, Michael D. *Big-time Shakespeare*. London and New York: Routledge, 1996.

Brown, John Russell, ed. *Othello*. In *Shakespeare in Performance: An Introduction through Six Major Plays*. New York: Harcourt Brace Jovanovich, 1973.

Browne, Sir Thomas. *Religio Medici and Other Works*. Ed. L. C. Martin. Oxford: Clarendon, 1964.

Bruster, Douglas. *Drama and the Market in the Age of Shakespeare*. Cambridge: Cambridge University Press, 1992.

Bullough, Geoffrey. *Narrative and Dramatic Sources of Shakespeare*, vol. 7. London: Routledge, 1973.

Bulman, James C. *The Heroic Idiom of Shakespearean Tragedy*. Newark: University of Delaware Press, 1985.

Burke, Kenneth. *Language as Symbolic Action: Essays on Life, Literature, and Method*. Berkeley and Los Angeles: University of California Press, 1966.

————. "*Othello*: An Essay to Illustrate a Method." *Hudson Review* 4 (1951): 165–203.

————. *The Philosophy of Literary Form*. 1941; rpt. Berkeley and Los Angeles: University of California Press, 1973.

————. *A Rhetoric of Motives*. New York: Prentice-Hall, 1952.

Butler, Judith. *Excitable Speech: A Politics of the Performative*. New York and London: Routledge, 1997.

Butler, Martin. "Shakespeare's Unprivileged Playgoers 1576–1642." In *Theatre and Crisis 1632–1642*, 293–306. Cambridge: Cambridge University Press, 1984.

Calderwood, James. *The Properties of "Othello."* Amherst: University of Massachusetts Press, 1989.

Callaghan, Dympna. "'Othello Was a White Man': Properties of Race on Shakespeare's Stage." In *Alternative Shakespeares*, vol. 2, ed. Terence Hawkes, 192–215. London and New York: Routledge, 1996.

Cantor, Paul A. "*Othello*: The Erring Barbarian among the Supersubtle Venetians." *Southwest Review* 75 (1990): 296–319.

Carlisle, Carol Jones. *Shakespeare from the Greenroom: Actors' Criticisms of Four Major Tragedies*. Chapel Hill: University of North Carolina Press, 1969.

Carlson, Marvin. "*Othello* in Vienna, 1991." *Shakespeare Quarterly* 44 (1993): 228–230.

Cavell, Stanley. *Disowning Knowledge in Six Plays of Shakespeare*. Cambridge: Cambridge University Press, 1987.

Charney, Maurice. *All of Shakespeare*. New York: Columbia University Press, 1993.

Chaudhuri, Sukanta. "Shakespeare and the Ethnic Question." In *Shakespeare and Cultural Traditions: The Selected Proceedings of the International Shakespeare*

Association World Congress, Tokyo, 1991, ed. Tetsuo Kishi, Roger Pringle, and Stanley Wells, 174–187. London and Toronto: Associated University Presses, 1994.

Clarke, Mary Cowden. *The Girlhood of Shakespeare's Heroines.* 1850–55; rpt. New York: AMS, 1974.

Clayton, Thomas. "'That's She That Was Myself': Not-so-famous Last Words and Some Ends of *Othello.*" *Shakespeare Survey 46,* 61–68. Cambridge: Cambridge University Press, 1994.

Cloud, Random. "'The Very Names of the Persons': Editing and the Invention of Dramatic Character." In *Staging the Renaissance,* ed. David Scott Kastan and Peter Stallybrass, 88–96. London and New York: Routledge, 1991.

Coleridge, Samuel Tayler. "Fears in Solitude: Written in April, 1798, During the Alarm of an Invasion." In *Coleridge: Poetical Works,* ed. Ernest Hartley Coleridge, 256–263. 1912; rpt. London: Oxford University Press, 1967.

Cook, Ann Jennalie. "The Design of Desdemona: Doubt Raised and Resolved." *Shakespeare Studies* 13 (1980): 187–196.

———. *The Privileged Playgoers of Shakespeare's Theatre, 1576–1642.* Princeton: Princeton University Press, 1981.

Cowhig, Ruth, "Blacks in English Renaissance Drama and the Role of Shakespeare's *Othello.*" In *The Black Presence in English Literature,* ed. David Dabydeen, 1–25. Manchester: Manchester University Press, 1985.

Culler, Jonathan. "*New Literary History* and European Theory." *New Literary History* 25 (1994): 869–879.

D'Amico, Jack. *The Moor in English Renaissance Drama.* Tampa: University of South Florida Press, 1991.

Danson, Lawrence. "'The Catastrophe Is a Nuptial': The Space of Masculine Desire in *Othello, Cymbeline,* and *The Winter's Tale.*" *Shakespeare Survey 46,* 69–79. Cambridge: Cambridge University Press, 1994.

Davies, Anthony. "Orson Welles's *Othello.*" In *Filming Shakespeare's Plays: The Adaptations of Laurence Olivier, Orson Welles, Peter Brook and Akira Kurosawa,* 100–118. Cambridge: Cambridge University Press, 1988.

Davis, Ralph. "England and the Mediterranean, 1570–1670." In *Essays in the Economic and Social History of Tudor and Stuart England, in Honour of R. H. Tawney,* ed. F. J. Fisher, 117–137. Cambridge: Cambridge University Press, 1961.

Davison, Peter. *Othello.* The Critics Debate Series. Atlantic Highlands, NJ: Humanities Press International, 1988.

Dawson, Anthony B. "Performance and Participation: Desdemona, Foucault, and the Actor's Body." In *Shakespeare, Theory, and Performance,* ed. James C. Bulman, 29–45. London and New York: Routledge, 1996.

de Grazia, Margreta. *Shakespeare Verbatim: The Reproduction of Authenticity and the 1790 Apparatus.* Oxford: Clarendon Press, 1991.

Derrida, Jacques. *The Margins of Philosophy.* Trans. with additional notes by Alan Bass. Chicago: University of Chicago Press, 1982.

Desmet, Christy. *Reading Shakespeare's Characters: Rhetoric, Ethics, and Identity.* Amherst: University of Massachusetts Press, 1992.

Dessen, Alan C. *Elizabethan Stage Conventions and Modern Interpreters.*
Cambridge: Cambridge University Press, 1984.

———. "Postcards and Snapshots: Shakespeare (and Others) Onstage in 1997."
Shakespeare Bulletin 16 (1998): 5–8.

Dimock, Wai Chee. "A Theory of Resonance." *PMLA* 112 (1997): 1060–1071.

Eliot, T. S. "Four Elizabethan Dramatists." In *Selected Essays*, 91–97.

———. "Hamlet." In *Selected Essays*, 121–126.

———. *Selected Essays.* New ed. 1927; rpt. New York: Harcourt Brace, 1950.

———. "Shakespeare and the Stoicism of Seneca." In *Selected Essays*, 107–120.

Empson, William. "*Hamlet.*" In *Essays on Shakespeare*, ed. David B. Pirie, 79–136.
Cambridge: Cambridge University Press, 1986.

———. "Honest in *Othello.*" In *The Structure of Complex Words*, 218–249.
London: Chatto and Windus, 1951.

———. *Milton's God.* London: Chatto and Windus, 1961.

Engell, James, and W. Jackson Bate, eds. *Biographia Litteraria or Biographical
Sketches of My Literary Life and Opinions.* In *The Collected Works of Samuel
Taylor Coleridge*, vol. 7, part 2. Princeton: Princeton University Press, 1983.

Engle, Ron. "Audience, Style, and Language in the Shakespeare of Peter Zadek."
In *Foreign Shakespeare: Contemporary Performance*, ed. Dennis Kennedy, 93–
105. Cambridge: Cambridge University Press, 1993.

Evans, G. B., et al., eds. *The Riverside Shakespeare.* Boston: Houghton Mifflin, 1997.

Everett, Barbara. "Reflections on the Sentimentalist's Othello." *Critical Quarterly*
3 (1961): 127–138.

Faucit, Helena. *On Some of Shakespeare's Female Characters.* 1885; rpt. New York:
AMS, 1970.

Ferguson, Margaret. "Transmuting Othello: Aphra Behn's *Oroonoko.*" In *Cross-
Cultural Performances: Differences in Women's Revisions of Shakespeare*, ed.
Marianne Novy, 15–49. Urbana: University of Illinois Press, 1993.

Fineman, Joel. *Shakespeare's Perjured Eye: The Invention of Poetic Subjectivity in
the Sonnets.* Berkeley and Los Angeles: University of California Press, 1986.

———. "The Sound of O in *Othello*: The Real of the Tragedy of Desire." *October*
45 (1988): 77–96.

Fish, Stanley E. *Surprised by Sin: The Reader in "Paradise Lost."* Berkeley and Los
Angeles: University of California Press, 1967.

Foakes, R. A. "The Descent of Iago: Satire, Ben Jonson, and Shakespeare's
Othello." In *Shakespeare and His Contemporaries: Essays in Comparison*, ed.
E. A. J. Honigmann, 16–30. Manchester: Manchester University Press, 1986.

———. "*Hamlet*" Versus "*Lear*": *Cultural Politics and Shakespeare's Art.*
Cambridge: Cambridge University Press, 1993.

———, ed. *Coleridge's Criticism of Shakespeare: A Selection.* London: Athlone,
1989.

———, ed. *Samuel Taylor Coleridge: Lectures on Literature 1808–1819.* 2 vols.
Vol. 5 of *The Collected Works of Samuel Taylor Coleridge.* Princeton: Princeton
University Press, 1987.

Foucault, Michel. *The History of Sexuality. Volume 1: An Introduction.* Trans.
Robert Hurley. New York: Pantheon, 1978.

Freedman, Barbara. *Staging the Gaze: Postmodernism, Psychoanalysis, and Shakespearean Comedy*. Ithaca: Cornell University Press, 1991.

Fultz, Lucille P. "Devouring Discourses: Desire and Seduction in *Othello*." In Kaul, ed., *"Othello,"* 189–204.

Furness, Horace Howard. *A New Variorum Edition of Othello*. 7th ed.; Philadelphia: Lippincott, 1886.

Gajowski, Evelyn. "The Female Perspective in *Othello*." In *"Othello": New Perspectives*, ed. Virginia Mason Vaughan and Kent Cartwright, 97–114. London and Toronto: Associated University Presses, 1991.

Gardner, Helen. "The Noble Moor." *Proceedings of the British Academy* 41 (1955): 189–205.

Gauntlett, Mark. "The Perishable Body of the Unpoetic: A. C. Bradley Performs *Othello*." *Shakespeare Survey* 47, 71–80. Cambridge: Cambridge University Press, 1994.

Genster, Julia. "Lieutenancy, Standing In, and *Othello*." *English Literary History* 57 (1990): 785–809.

Gillies, John. *Shakespeare and the Geography of Difference*. Cambridge: Cambridge University Press, 1994.

Girard, René. "An Interview with René Girard." In *"To Double Business Bound": Essays on Literature, Mimesis, and Anthropology*, 199–229. Baltimore and London: Johns Hopkins University Press, 1978.

———. *The Scapegoat*. Trans. Yvonne Freccero. Baltimore and London: Johns Hopkins University Press, 1986.

———. *A Theater of Envy: William Shakespeare*. New York: Oxford University Press, 1991.

———. "'To Entrap the Wisest': A Reading of *The Merchant of Venice*." In *Literature and Society*, ed. Edward Said, 100–119. Baltimore and London: Johns Hopkins University Press, 1980.

———. "Violence and Representation in the Mythical Text." In *"To Double Business Bound": Essays on Literature, Mimesis, and Anthropology*, 178–198. Baltimore and London: Johns Hopkins University Press, 1978.

Goldberg, S. L. *An Essay on "King Lear."* Cambridge: Cambridge University Press, 1975.

Grady, Hugh. *The Modernist Shakespeare: Critical Texts in a Material World*. Oxford: Oxford University Press, 1991.

Granville-Barker, Harley. "*Othello*." In *Prefaces to Shakespeare*, vol. 4, 120–266. Princeton: Princeton University Press, 1965.

Greenberg, Mitchell. "Shakespeare's *Othello* and the 'Problem' of Anxiety." In *Canonical States, Canonical Stages: Oedipus, Othering, and Seventeenth-Century Drama*, 1–32. Minneapolis and London: University of Minnesota Press, 1994.

Greenblatt, Stephen J. *Learning to Curse: Essays in Early Modern Culture*. New York and London: Routledge, 1990.

———. *Renaissance Self-Fashioning from More to Shakespeare*. Chicago: University of Chicago Press, 1980.

———. *Shakespearean Negotiations: The Circulation of Social Energy in Renaissance England*. Berkeley and Los Angeles: University of California Press, 1988.

———. "What Is the History of Literature?" *Critical Inquiry* 23 (1997): 460–481.

———, et al., eds. *The Norton Shakespeare*. New York and London: Norton, 1997.

Grennan, Eamon. "The Women's Voices in *Othello*: Speech, Song, Silence." *Shakespeare Quarterly* 38 (1987): 275–292.

Gurr, Andrew. *Playgoing in Shakespeare's London*. Cambridge: Cambridge University Press, 1987.

Habicht, Werner. *Shakespeare and the German Imagination*. Hertford: Stephen Austin and Sons, 1994.

Hall, Kim F. *Things of Darkness: Economies of Race and Gender in Early Modern England*. Ithaca: Cornell University Press, 1995.

Haller, Mandeville, and William Haller. "The Puritan Art of Love." *Huntington Library Quarterly* 5 (1942): 235–272.

Halpern, Richard. *Shakespeare among the Moderns*. Ithaca: Cornell University Press, 1997.

Hankey, Julie. *Othello*. Plays in Performance Series. Bristol: Bristol Classical Press, 1987.

Hanson, Elizabeth. "Torture and Truth in Renaissance England." *Representations* 34 (1991): 53–84.

Harbage, Alfred. *Shakespeare and the Rival Traditions*. New York: Barnes and Noble, 1951.

———. *Shakespeare's Audience*. New York: Columbia University Press, 1941.

———, ed. *Shakespeare: Complete Works*. Baltimore: Penguin, 1969.

Hawkes, Terence. *Shakespeare's Talking Animals: Language and Drama in Society*. London: Edward Arnold, 1970.

———, ed. *Coleridge's Writings on Shakespeare*. New York: G. P. Putnam's Sons, 1959.

Hazlitt, William. *Characters of Shakespear's Plays*. In *The Complete Works of William Hazlitt*, ed. P. P. Howe, vol. 4, 165–361. London and Toronto: J. M. Dent, 1930.

Heilman, Robert B. *Magic in the Web: Action and Language in "Othello."* Lexington: University of Kentucky Press, 1956.

Henderson, Diana E. "The Theater and Domestic Culture." In *A New History of Early English Drama*, ed. John D. Cox and David Scott Kastan, 173–194. New York: Columbia University Press, 1997.

Hendricks, Margo, and Patricia Parker, eds. *Women, "Race," and Writing in the Early Modern Period*. New York and London: Routledge, 1993.

Hillman, David. "The Gastric Epic: *Troilus and Cressida*." *Shakespeare Quarterly* 48 (1997): 295–313.

Hodgdon, Barbara. "Race-ing *Othello*, Re-engendering White-out." In *Shakespeare, the Movie: Popularizing the Plays on Film, TV, and Video*, ed. Lynda E. Boose and Richard Burt, 23–44. London and New York: Routledge, 1997.

Holloway, John. "Dr. Leavis and 'Diabolic Intellect.'" In *The Story of the Night: Studies in Shakespeare's Major Tragedies*, 155–165. London: Routledge 1961.

Holmes, Stephen. "In Search of New Enemies." *London Review of Books* (24 April 1997): 3–10.

Honigmann, E. A. J. "Re-enter the Stage Direction: Shakespeare and Some Contemporaries." *Shakespeare Survey* 29, 117–125. Cambridge: Cambridge University Press, 1976.

———. *Shakespeare: Seven Tragedies: The Dramatist's Manipulation of Audience Response*. London: Macmillan, 1976.

———. *Shakespeare's Impact on His Contemporaries*. London: Macmillan, 1982.

———. *The Stability of Shakespeare's Text*. London: Edward Arnold, 1965.

———. *The Texts of "Othello" and Shakespearian Revision*. London and New York: Routledge, 1996.

———, ed. *Othello*. Arden 3 edition. Walton-on-Thames: Thomas Nelson, 1997.

Howard-Hill, Trevor. *Ralph Crane and Some Shakespeare First Folio Comedies*. Charlottesville: University Press of Virginia, 1972.

———. "Shakespeare's Earliest Editor, Ralph Crane." *Shakespeare Survey* 44, 113–129. Cambridge: Cambridge University Press, 1992.

Hughes, Alan. *Henry Irving, Shakespearean*. Cambridge: Cambridge University Press, 1981.

Hughes, Merritt Y., ed. *John Milton: Complete Poems and Major Prose*. New York: Odyssey, 1957.

Hunter, G. K. "*Othello* and Colour Prejudice." In *Dramatic Identities and Cultural Tradition: Studies in Shakespeare and His Contemporaries*, 31–59. Liverpool: Liverpool University Press, 1978.

Jameson, Anna B. *Shakespeare's Heroines: Characteristics of Women*. 1832; rpt. New York: Gordon, 1978.

Jameson, Fredric. *The Political Unconscious: Narrative as a Socially Symbolic Act*. Ithaca: Cornell University Press, 1981.

Jardine, Lisa. "Cultural Confusion and Shakespeare's Learned Heroines: 'These Are Old Paradoxes.'" *Shakespeare Quarterly* 38 (1987): 1–18.

———. "'Why Should He Call Her Whore?': Defamation and Desdemona's Case." In *Addressing Frank Kermode: Essays in Criticism and Interpretation*, ed. Margaret Tudeau-Clayton and Martin Warner, 124–153. London: Macmillan, 1991.

Johnson-Haddad, Miranda. "Patrick Stewart on Playing Othello." *Shakespeare Bulletin* 16 (1998): 11–12.

———. "The Shakespeare Theatre at the Folger, 1990–91." *Shakespeare Quarterly* 42 (1992): 472–484.

———. "The Shakespeare Theatre *Othello*." *Shakespeare Bulletin* 16 (1998): 9–11.

Jones, Ann Rosalind. "Italians and Others: Venice and the Irish in Coryat's *Crudities* and *The White Devil*." *Renaissance Drama* 18 (1987): 101–119.

Jonson, Ben. *The Alchemist*. Ed. Elizabeth Cook. London: A. C. Black, 1991.

———. *Volpone*. Ed. Philip Brockbank. London: Benn, 1968.

Kauffmann, Stanley. "Shrinking Shakespeare." *New Republic* 214 (February 12, 1996): 30–31.

Kaul, Mythili. "Background: Black or Tawny? Stage Representations of *Othello* from 1604 to the Present." In Kaul, ed., *"Othello,"* 1–22.

———. Preface to Kaul, ed., *"Othello,"* ix–xii.

———, ed. *"Othello": New Essays by Black Writers*. Washington, DC: Howard University Press, 1997.

Kernan, Alvin. *Shakespeare, the King's Playwright: Theater in the Stuart Court, 1603–1613*. New Haven: Yale University Press, 1995.

Kerrigan, William, and Gordon Braden. *The Idea of the Renaissance*. Baltimore and London: Johns Hopkins University Press, 1989.

Kirsch, Arthur. *Shakespeare and the Experience of Love*. Cambridge: Cambridge University Press, 1981.

Kittredge, George Lyman, ed. *Othello*. Boston: Ginn, 1941.

Knight, G. Wilson. "The *Othello* Music." In *The Wheel of Fire: Interpretations of Shakespearian Tragedy*, 97–119. 1930; rpt. with three new essays. London: Methuen, 1949.

Knights, L. C. "How Many Children Had Lady Macbeth? An Essay on the Theory and Practice of Shakespeare Criticism." Rpt. and revised in *Explorations: Essays in Criticism Mainly on the Literature of the Seventeenth Century*, 15–54. Harmondsworth: Penguin, 1964.

Knutson, Roslyn Lander. *The Repertory of Shakespeare's Company, 1594–1613*. Fayetteville: University of Arkansas Press, 1991.

Lamb, Charles. "On the Tragedies of Shakespeare, Considered with Reference to Their Fitness for Stage Representation." In *The Works of Charles and Mary Lamb*, ed. E. V. Lucas, vol. 1, 97–111. London: Methuen, 1903.

Laqueur, Thomas. *Making Sex: Body and Gender from the Greeks to Freud*. Cambridge: Harvard University Press, 1990.

Leavis, F. R. "Diabolic Intellect and the Noble Hero." In *The Common Pursuit*, 136–159. 1937; rpt. Harmondsworth: Penguin, 1969.

Levin, Harry. "Othello and the Motive-Hunters." *Centennial Review* 8 (1964): 1–16.

Liebler, Naomi Conn. *Shakespeare's Festive Tragedy: The Ritual Foundations of Genre*. London and New York: Routledge, 1995.

Little, Arthur, Jr. "'An essence that's not seen': The Primal Scene of Racism in *Othello*." *Shakespeare Quarterly* 44 (1993): 304–324.

Liston, William T. "*Othello*." *Shakespeare Bulletin* 16 (1998): 23–24.

Loomba, Ania. *Gender, Race, Renaissance Drama*. Manchester: Manchester University Press, 1989.

Lupton, Julia Reinhard. "*Othello* Circumcised: Shakespeare and the Pauline Discourse of Nations." *Representations* 57 (1997): 73–89.

MacDonald, Joyce Green. "Acting Black: *Othello*, *Othello* Burlesques, and the Performance of Blackness." *Theatre Journal* 46 (1994): 231–249.

Mack, Maynard. "What Happens in Shakespearean Tragedy." In *Everybody's Shakespeare: Reflections Chiefly on the Tragedies*, 231–262. Republication of "The Jacobean Shakespeare," 1960; Lincoln: University of Nebraska Press, 1993.

MacLure, Millar, ed. *Marlowe: The Critical Heritage*. London: Routledge, 1979.

Marienstras, Richard. *New Perspectives on the Shakespearean World*, trans. Janet Lloyd. Cambridge: Cambridge University Press, 1985.

Marston, John. *The Dutch Courtesan*. Ed. M. L. Wine. Regents Renaissance Drama Series. Lincoln: University of Nebraska Press, 1965.

Matteo, Gino J. *Shakespeare's "Othello": The Study and the Stage, 1604–1904*. Salzburg Studies in English Literature. Salzburg: Institut für englische Sprache und Literatur, 1974.

Matthews, G. M. "*Othello* and the Dignity of Man." In *Shakespeare in a Changing World: Essays*, ed. Arnold Kettle, 123–145. New York: International, 1964.

Maus, Katharine Eisaman. "Horns of Dilemma: Jealousy, Gender, and Spectatorship in English Renaissance Drama." *English Literary History* 54 (1987): 561–583.

———. *Inwardness and Theater in the English Renaissance*. Chicago: University of Chicago Press, 1995.

———. "Proof and Consequences: Inwardness and Its Exposure in the English Renaissance." *Representations* 34 (1991): 29–52.

McAlindon, T. *Shakespeare's Tragic Cosmos*. Cambridge: Cambridge University Press, 1991.

McDonald, Russ. *The Bedford Companion to Shakespeare: An Introduction with Documents*. Boston: Bedford, 1996.

McEachern, Claire, and Debora Shuger, eds. *Religion and Culture in Early Modern England*. Cambridge: Cambridge University Press, 1997.

McLuskie, Kathleen E. "The Shopping Complex: Materiality and the Renaissance Theatre." In *Textual and Theatrical Shakespeare: Questions of Evidence*, ed. Edward Pechter, 86–101. Iowa City: University of Iowa Press, 1996.

McPherson, David C. *Shakespeare, Jonson, and the Myth of Venice*. Newark: University of Delaware Press, 1990.

McPherson, James A. "Three Great Ones of the City and One Perfect Soul: Well Met at Cyprus." In Kaul, ed., "*Othello*," 45–76.

Michaels, Walter Benn. *Our America: Nativism, Modernism, and Pluralism*. Durham: Duke University Press, 1995.

Mikesell, Margaret Lael. Introduction to part 1. In "*Othello*": *An Annotated Bibliography*, ed. Mikesell and Virginia Mason Vaughan, xi–xxiv. New York: Garland, 1990.

Miller, Jonathan. *Subsequent Performances*. London: Faber, 1986.

Morgann, Maurice. *Morgann's Essay on the Dramatic Character of Sir John Falstaff*. Ed. William Arthur Gill. 1912; rpt. Freeport, NY: Books for Libraries, 1970.

Mowat, Barbara. "Nicholas Rowe and the Twentieth-Century Shakespeare Text." In *Shakespeare and Cultural Traditions: The Selected Proceedings of the International Shakespeare Association World Congress, Tokyo, 1991*, ed. Tetsuo Kishi, Roger Pringle, and Stanley Wells, 314–322. London and Toronto: Associated University Presses, 1994.

Muir, Kenneth, ed. *Othello.* Harmondsworth: Penguin, 1968.

Mulvey, Laura. "Afterthoughts on 'Visual Pleasure and Narrative Cinema' Inspired by *Duel in the Sun.*" *Framework* 15–17 (1981): 12–15.

———. "Changes." *Discourse* 7 (1985): 11–30.

———. *Visual and Other Pleasures.* Bloomington and Indianapolis: Indiana University Press, 1989.

———. "Visual Pleasure and Narrative Cinema." *Screen* 16 (1975): 6–18.

Munro, Alice. *The Progress of Love.* Toronto: McClelland and Stewart, 1986.

Munro, John, ed. *The Shakspere Allusion-Book: A Collection of Allusions to Shakspere from 1591 to 1700.* Vol. 1. London: Oxford University Press, 1932.

Nathan, Norman. "Othello's Marriage Is Consummated." *Cahiers elisabéthains* 34 (1988): 79–82.

Neill, Michael. "Changing Places in *Othello.*" *Shakespeare Survey* 37, 115–31. Cambridge: Cambridge University Press, 1984.

———. "'Hidden Malady': Death, Discovery, and Indistinction in *The Changeling.*" *Renaissance Drama* 22 (1991): 95–121.

———. *Issues of Death: Mortality and Identity in English Renaissance Tragedy.* Oxford: Clarendon Press, 1997.

———. "Unproper Beds: Race, Adultery, and the Hideous in *Othello.*" *Shakespeare Quarterly* 40 (1989): 383–412.

Nelson, T. G. A., and Charles Haines. "Othello's Unconsummated Marriage." *Essays in Criticism* 35 (1983): 1–18.

Newman, Karen. "'And Wash the Ethiop White': Femininity and the Monstrous in *Othello.*" In *Shakespeare Reproduced: The Text in History and Ideology*, ed. Jean E. Howard and Marion F. O'Connor, 140–162. London: Methuen, 1987.

———. *Fashioning Femininity and English Renaissance Drama.* Chicago: University of Chicago Press, 1991.

Norris, Christopher. "Post-structuralist Shakespeare: Text and Ideology." In *Alternative Shakespeares*, ed. John Drakakis, 47–66. London: Methuen, 1985.

Nuttall, A. D. "The Argument about Shakespeare's Characters." *Critical Quarterly* 7 (1965): 107–120.

———. *Openings: Narrative Beginnings from the Epic to the Novel.* Oxford: Oxford University Press, 1992.

Odell, George C. D. *Shakespeare from Betterton to Irving.* Vol. 2. New York: Scribner's, 1920.

Orgel, Stephen. "The Authentic Shakespeare." *Representations* 21 (1988): 1–25.

———. "Shakespeare and the Kinds of Drama." *Critical Inquiry* 6 (1979): 107–123.

———. "Shakespeare Imagines a Theater." In *Shakespeare, Man of the Theater: Proceedings of the Second Congress of the International Shakespeare Association, 1981*, ed. Kenneth Muir, Jay L. Halio, and D. J. Palmer, 34–46. East Brunswick, NJ, London, and Mississauga, Ont.: Associated University Presses, 1983.

Orkin, Martin. "Othello and the 'Plain Face' of Racism." *Shakespeare Quarterly* 38 (1987): 166–188.

Orwell, George. *Nineteen Eighty-Four.* London: Secker and Warburg, 1962.

Owens, W. R., and Lizabeth Goodman, eds. *Shakespeare, Aphra Behn and the Canon*. London and New York: Routledge, 1996.

Parker, Patricia. "Fantasies of 'Race' and 'Gender': Africa, *Othello*, and Bringing to Light." In Hendricks and Parker, eds., *Women, "Race," and Writing*, 84– 100.

———. "*Othello* and *Hamlet*: Dilation, Spying and the 'Secret Place' of Woman." *Representations* 44 (1993): 60–95.

———. "Prepostrous Events." *Shakespeare Quarterly* 43 (1992): 186–213.

———. "Shakespeare and Rhetoric: 'Dilation' and 'Delation.'" In *Shakespeare and the Question of Theory*, ed. Parker and Geoffrey Hartman, 57–74. London: Methuen, 1985.

Parker, R. B., ed. *Coriolanus*. Oxford: Clarendon Press, 1994.

Pechter, Edward. *Dryden's Classical Theory of Literature*. Cambridge: Cambridge University Press, 1975.

———. "'Have you not read of some such thing?': Sex and Sexual Stories in *Othello*." *Shakespeare Survey* 49, 201–216. Cambridge: Cambridge University Press, 1996.

———. "Of Ants and Grasshoppers: Two Ways (or More) to Link Texts and Power." In *What Was Shakespeare? Renaissance Plays and Changing Critical Practice*, 87–105. Ithaca: Cornell University Press, 1995.

———. "*Othello*, the Infamous Ripley and SHAKSPER." In *Shakespearean Continuities: Essays in Honour of E. A. J. Honigmann*, ed. J. B. Batchelor, T. G. S. Cain, and Claire Lamont, 138–149. London: Macmillan, 1997.

———. "*Patient Grissil* and the Trials of Marriage." *Elizabethan Theatre 14* (1996): 83- 108.

Pepys, Samuel. *The Diary of Samuel Pepys*. Vol. 1. Ed. John Warington. London: Dent, 1953.

———. *The Diary of Samuel Pepys*. Vol. 1. Ed. Robert Latham and William Matthews. London: Bell and Sons, 1970.

Phillips, Caryl. *The Nature of Blood*. New York: Knopf, 1997.

Potter, Lois. "Agonies of Lucidity." *Times Literary Supplement* (19 December 1997): 17.

Rafferty, Terence. "Fidelity and Infidelity." *New Yorker* 71 (18 December 1995): 124-127.

Raysor, Thomas Middleton, ed. *Coleridge: Shakespearean Criticism*. 2 vols. London: Dent, 1960.

Ridley, M. R., ed. *Othello*. New Arden edition. London: Methuen, 1962.

Ripley, John D. "*Coriolanus* as Tory Propaganda." In *Textual and Theatrical Shakespeare: Questions of Evidence*, ed. Edward Pechter, 102–123. Iowa City: University of Iowa Press, 1996.

Roach, Joseph. *Cities of the Dead: Circum-Atlantic Performance*. New York: Columbia University Press, 1996.

Rorty, Richard. *Contingency, Irony, and Solidarity*. Cambridge: Cambridge University Press, 1989.

Rose, Mary Beth. *The Expense of Spirit: Love and Sexuality in English Renaissance Drama*. Ithaca: Cornell University Press, 1988.

Rosenberg, Marvin. *The Masks of Othello: The Search for the Identity of Othello, Iago, and Desdemona by Three Centuries of Actors and Critics*. Berkeley, Los Angeles, and London: University of California Press, 1961.

Rosenthal, Margaret F. *The Honest Courtesan: Veronica Franco, Citizen and Writer in Sixteenth-Century Venice*. Chicago: University of Chicago Press, 1992.

Ross, Lawrence J., ed. *Othello*. Indianapolis and New York: Bobbs-Merrill, 1974.

Rudnytsky, Peter L. "The Purloined Handkerchief in *Othello*." In *The Psychoanalytic Study of Literature*, ed. Joseph Reppen and Maurice Charney, 169–190. Hillsdale, NJ: Analytic Press, 1985.

Rushdie, Salman. *The Satanic Verses*. New York: Viking, 1988.

Rymer, Thomas. *A Short View of Tragedy*. In *The Critical Works of Thomas Rymer*, ed. with an introduction and notes by Curt A. Zimansky, 227–270. New Haven: Yale University Press, 1956.

Salway, John. "Veritable Negroes and Circumcised Dogs: Racial Disturbances in Shakespeare." In *Shakespeare in a Changing Curriculum*, ed. Lesley Aers and Nigel Wheale, 108–124. New York and London: Routledge, 1991.

Sanders, Norman, ed. *Othello*. Cambridge: Cambridge University Press, 1984.

Scholes, Robert. "Pacesetter English." In *The Rise and Fall of English: Reconstructing English as a Discipline*, 128–142. New Haven: Yale University Press, 1998.

Scott, Mark W., ed. *Shakespearean Criticism: Excerpts from the Criticism of William Shakespeare's Plays and Poetry, from the First Published Appraisals to Current Evaluations*. Detroit: Gale, 1987.

Shakespeare, William. *Othello, The Moor of Venice. A Tragedy, As it hath been divers times acted at the Globe, and at the Black-Friars: And now at the Theatre Royal, By His Majesties Servants*. London, 1681; rpt. London: Cornmarket Press, 1969.

Shapiro, James. *Shakespeare and the Jews*. New York: Columbia University Press, 1996.

Shattuck, Charles H. *Shakespeare on the American Stage: From the Hallams to Edwin Booth*. Vol. 1. Washington: Folger Shakespeare Library, 1976.

Shaw, Catherine M. "'Dangerous Conceits Are in Their Natures Poisons': The Language of *Othello*." *University of Toronto Quarterly* 49 (1980): 305–319.

Shaw, John. "'What Is the Matter?' in *Othello*." *Shakespeare Quarterly* 17 (1966): 157–161.

Sheingorn, Pamela. "'Who Can Open the Doors of His Face?' The Iconography of Hell Mouth." In *The Iconography of Hell*, ed. Clifford Davidson and Thomas H. Seiler, 1–19. Early Drama, Art, and Music Monograph Series, 17. Kalamazoo, MI: Medieval Institute Publications, Western Michigan University Press, 1992.

Shuger, Debora K. *Habits of Thought in the English Renaissance: Religion, Politics, and the Dominant Culture*. Berkeley: University of California Press, 1990.

Sidney, Sir Philip. *Sir Philip Sidney's Defense of Poesy*. Ed. Lewis Soens. Lincoln: University of Nebraska Press, 1970.

Siemon, James R. "'Nay, that's not next': *Othello*, V.ii in Performance, 1760–1900." *Shakespeare Quarterly* 37 (1986): 38–51.

————. *Shakespearean Iconoclasm*. Berkeley and Los Angeles: University of California Press, 1985.

Simpson, O. J. *I Want to Tell You: My Response to Your Letters, Your Messages, Your Questions*. Boston: Little Brown, 1995.

Sinfield, Alan. *Faultlines: Cultural Materialism and the Politics of Dissident Reading*. Berkeley and Los Angeles: University of California Press, 1992.

Singh, Jyotsna. "The Interventions of History: Narratives of Sexuality." In *The Weyward Sisters: Shakespeare and Feminist Politics*, ed. Dympna Callaghan, Lorraine Helms, and Singh, 7–58. Cambridge, MA.: Blackwell, 1994.

Sisson, Charles Jasper, ed. *William Shakespeare: The Complete Works*. London: Oldhams Press, 1953.

Sloterdijk, Peter. *Critique of Cynical Reason*. Trans. Michael Eldred. Minneapolis: University of Minnesota Press, 1987.

Smith, Barbara Herrnstein. *Belief and Resistance: Dynamics of Contemporary Intellectual Controversy*. Cambridge: Harvard University Press, 1997.

Smith, Lacey Baldwin. *Treason in Tudor England: Politics and Paranoia*. Princeton: Princeton University Press, 1986.

Snow, Edward A. "Sexual Anxiety and the Male Order of Things in *Othello*." *English Literary Renaissance* 10 (1980): 384–412.

————. "Theorizing the Male Gaze: Some Problems." *Representations* 25 (1989): 30–41.

Sollors, Werner. "Ethnicity." In *Critical Terms for Literary Study*, ed. Frank Lentricchia and Thomas McLaughlin, 288–305. Chicago: University of Chicago Press, 1990.

Spencer, Hazelton. *Shakespeare Improved: The Restoration Versions in Quarto and on the Stage*. Cambridge: Harvard University Press, 1927.

Spevack, Marvin. *The Harvard Concordance to Shakespeare*. Cambridge: Harvard University Press, 1973.

Sprague, Arthur Colby. *Shakespeare and the Actors: The Stage Business in His Plays (1660–1905)*. Cambridge: Harvard University Press, 1948.

————. *Shakespearian Players and Performances*. Cambridge: Harvard University Press, 1953.

Stallybrass, Peter. "Patriarchal Territories." In *Rewriting the Renaissance: The Discourses of Sexual Difference in Early Modern Europe*, ed. Margaret Ferguson, Maureen Quilligan, and Nancy J. Vickers, 123–142. Chicago: University of Chicago Press, 1986.

Stanislavski, Constantin. *Stanislavski Produces "Othello."* Trans. Helen Nowak. New York: Theatre Arts Books, 1963.

Stewart, J. I. M. "'Steep Tragic Contrast.'" In *Character and Motive in Shakespeare: Some Recent Appraisals Examined*, 79–110. London: Longmans, 1949.

Stone, Lawrence. *The Crisis of the Aristocracy, 1558–1641*. Oxford: Clarendon Press, 1965.

————. *The Family, Sex, and Marriage in England, 1500–1800*. London: Weidenfeld and Nicholson, 1977.

Strachey, James, ed. "The Antithetical Meaning of Primary Words." In *The Standard Edition of the Complete Psychological Works of Sigmund Freud*, vol. 11, 153–162. London: Hogarth, 1957.

Swander, Homer. "Musings on the Stewart/Kelly *Othello*." *Shakespeare Bulletin* 16 (1998): 13.

Sypher, Wylie. *The Ethic of Time: Structures of Experience in Shakespeare*. New York: Seabury Press, 1976.

Tanner, Tony. *Venice Desired*. Cambridge: Harvard University Press, 1992.

Teague, Frances. "Objects in *Othello*." In *"Othello": New Perspectives*, ed. Virginia Mason Vaughan and Kent Cartwright, 177–188. London and Toronto: Associated University Presses, 1991.

Terry, Ellen. *Four Lectures on Shakespeare*. Ed., with an introduction, by Christopher St. John. London: Martin Hopkinson, 1932.

Thomson, Peter. "Rogues and Rhetoricians: Acting Styles in Early English Drama." In *A New History of English Drama*, ed. John D. Cox and David Scott Kastan, 321–336. New York: Columbia University Press, 1997.

Tillyard, E. M. W. *Shakespeare's Last Plays*. London: Chatto and Windus, 1938.

Traub, Valerie. *Desire and Anxiety: Circulations of Sexuality in Shakespearean Drama*. London and New York: Routledge, 1992.

Tuve, Rosemond. *Elizabethan and Metaphysical Imagery: Renaissance Poetic and Twentieth-Century Critics*. Chicago: University of Chicago Press, 1947.

Tynan, Kenneth, ed. *"Othello": The National Theatre Production*. New York: Stein and Day, 1967.

Updike, John. *In the Beauty of the Lilies*. New York: Fawcett Columbine, 1996.

Valéry, Paul. *The Art of Poetry*. In *The Collected Works of Paul Valéry*, trans. Denise Folliot, ed. Jackson Mathews, vol. 7. London: Routledge, 1958.

Vanita, Ruth. "'Proper' Men and 'Fallen' Women: The Unprotectedness of Wives in *Othello*." *Studies in English Literature* 34 (1994): 341–356.

Vaughan, Virginia Mason. *"Othello": A Contextual History*. Cambridge: Cambridge University Press, 1995.

Vickers, Brian, ed. *Shakespeare: The Critical Heritage. Volume 5, 1765–1774*. London: Routledge, 1979.

———. ed. *Shakespeare: The Critical Heritage. Volume 6, 1774–1801*. London: Routledge, 1981.

Wain, John, ed. *Shakespeare's "Othello": A Casebook*. Rev. ed. Basingstoke and London: Macmillan, 1994.

Walker, Alice, and John Dover Wilson, eds. *Othello*. Cambridge: Cambridge University Press, 1957.

Webster, John. *The Duchess of Malfi*. Ed. Elizabeth M. Brennan. London: A. and C. Black, 1993.

———. *The White Devil*. Ed. Christina Luckyj. London: A. and C. Black, 1996.

Weimann, Robert. *Shakespeare and the Popular Tradition in the Theater: Studies in the Social Dimension of Dramatic Form*. Baltimore and London: Johns Hopkins University Press, 1978.

Wells, Stanley. *Shakespeare: A Life in Drama*. New York: W. W. Norton, 1995.

————, and Gary Taylor, with John Jowett and William Montgomery, eds. *William Shakespeare: A Textual Companion*. Oxford: Clarendon Press, 1987.

————, and Gary Taylor, eds. *William Shakespeare: The Complete Works*. Oxford: Clarendon Press, 1986.

Wentesdorf, Karl P. "Animal Symbolism in Shakespeare's *Hamlet*: The Imagery of Sex Nausea." *Comparative Drama* 17 (1983–84): 348–382.

Whallon, William. *Inconsistencies*. Cambridge and Totowa, NJ: D. S. Brewer and Biblio, 1983.

Wickham, Glynne. *The Medieval Theatre*. Cambridge: Cambridge University Press, 1987.

Wilson, John Dover. Introduction to *Othello*, ed. Alice Walker and John Dover Wilson. Cambridge: Cambridge University Press, 1957.

Wine, Martin L. *"Othello": Text and Performance*. London: Macmillan, 1984.

Winter, William. *Life and Art of Edwin Booth*. New York: Macmillan, 1893.

————. *Shakespeare on the Stage*. First series. 1911; rpt. New York: Benjamin Blom, 1969.

Worthen, W. B. *Shakespeare and the Authority of Performance*. Cambridge: Cambridge University Press, 1997.

Yachnin, Paul. *Stage-Wrights: Shakespeare, Jonson, Middleton, and the Making of Theatrical Value*. Philadelphia: University of Pennsylvania Press, 1997.

Young, Robert J. C. *Colonial Desire: Hybridity in Theory, Culture and Race*. London and New York: Routledge, 1995.

Ziegler, Georgiana. "'My Lady's Chamber': Female Space, Female Chastity in Shakespeare." *Textual Practice* 4 (1990): 73–90.

INDEX

divided between Othello and Iago; racial interests/anxieties; re-evaluated after Bradley; re-evaluated with Romanticism; sexual interests/ anxieties

Inchbald, Elizabeth, 121

Irving, Sir Henry, 15, 26, 27, 39, 55–57, 81, 82, 83, 123, 148, 195 n.18

Jackson, Henry, 11, 21, 125, 126, 130– 131, 147, 180, 225 n.1

Jacobus, Mary, 207 n.4

James I, 36

James, Emrys, 196 n.20

James, Henry, 155

Jameson, Anna, 120, 131,

Jameson, Fredric, 195 n.11

Jardine, Lisa, 74–75, 222 n.26

Jew of Malta, The (Marlowe), 56

Johnson, Samuel, 14, 53, 118, 154–156, 157, 158, 167, 169–171, 216 n.3

Johnson-Haddad, Miranda, 19, 133, 143, 222 n.2

Jones, Ann Rosalind, 198 n.10, 221 n.23, 226 n.4

Jones, James Earl, 196 n.20

Jonson, Ben, 21, 39, 56, 177, 180, 199 n.12

Kauffmann, Stanley, 196 n.21

Kaul, Mythili, 3, 179, 227 n.11

Kean, Charles, 12

Kean, Edmund, 7, 12, 15, 26–27, 38, 54, 97, 98, 150, 156, 165, 195 n.17

Keats, John, 38

Kee, Robert, 215 n.39

Kelly, Jude, 70, 132, 143

Kemble, Fanny, 122, 125, 219 n.13

Kemble, John Philip, 97, 150

Kendal, Madge, 123

Kenrick, William, 226 n.8

Kernan, Alvin, 226 n.1

Kerrigan, William, 199 n.12

Kirsch, Arthur, 48–50, 52, 84, 86, 105, 196 n.24, 201 n.26, 205 n.14, 213 n.31

Kittredge, George Lyman, 89

Knight, Wilson G., 24, 184, 196 n.23, 228 n.4

Knight of the Burning Pestle, The (Beaumont), 204 n.5

Knights, L. C., 228 n.4

Knutson, Roslyn Lander, 218 n.9, 226 n.1

Kreutzer Sonata, The (Tolstoy), 193 n.2

Lacan, Jacques, 106, 214 n.36

Lamb, Charles, 15, 55

Laqueur, Thomas, 193 n.10

Leavis, F. R., 16–17, 18, 20, 21, 28, 29, 105, 194 n.8, 201 n.26, 216 n.41, 228 n.2

Lepanto, Battle of, 36

Levin, Harry, 194 n.4

Lewes, George Henry, 26, 82

Lewis, Wyndham, 111

Liebler, Naomi Conn, 224 n.10

Lipking, Joanna, 195 n.13

Liston, William T., 210 n.15

Little, Arthur, Jr., 208 n.8

Lodovico, 6, 69–70, 92, 103, 115, 139, 150, 214 n.35

London Prodigal, The, 218 n.9

Loomba, Ania, 106, 124, 130, 163, 174, 186, 205 n.14

Luckyj, Christina, 196 n.1

Lupton, Julia Reinhard, 197 n.4

Lyly, John, 205 n.18

MacDonald, Joyce Green, 7

Mack, Maynard, 131, 133, 134

Macklin, Charles, 7

MacLure, Millar, 204 n.7

Macready, William, 7, 13, 14, 15, 26, 97, 98, 150, 156, 195 n.17, 196 n.19, 218 n.13

Malcontent, The (Marston), 33

Marienstras, Richard, 206 n.21

Marlowe, Christopher, 204 n.7

Marston, John, 162, 197 n.3, 220 n.19, 221 n.23, 225 n.17

Martin, Sir Theodore, 122, 148

Mason, Brewster, 196 n.20

Matteo, Gino J., 158, 211 n.20
Matthews, G. M., 151, 165, 185–186, 189, 205 n.14, 207 n.3, 228 n.4
Maus, Katharine Eisaman, 198 n.8, 208 n.8
McAlindon, T., 217 n.5
McCullough, John, 211 n.21
McDonald, Russ, 195 n.14
McEachern, Claire, 204 n.8
McKellen, Sir Ian, 97, 210 n.17
McLuskie, Kathleen E., 23, 32
McPherson, David, 198 n.10
McPherson, James, 2
Mendes, Sam, 100, 210 n.15
Michaels, Walter Benn, 198 n.5
Mikesell, Margaret, 219 nn.16–17
Miller, Jonathan, 15–16, 59–60, 110, 196 n.20
Miller, Mary, 133
Milton, John, 69
Montaigne, Michel de, 38
Montano, 105, 126, 140, 163, 250
Morgann, Maurice, 86, 87
Morris, Clara, 210 n.18
Morris, Mowbray, 57
Mowat, Barbara, 221 n.21
Muir, Kenneth, 107, 133, 134, 221 n.24
Mulvey, Laura, 208 n.9
Munro, Alice, 69
Munro, John, 26

Nathan, Norman, 194 n.8
National Theatre, The, 19, 100, 210 n.15, 216 n.41
Nature of Blood, The (Phillips), 207 n.4
Neill, Michael, 19, 50, 74, 87, 88, 94, 96, 105, 126, 134, 165, 179, 180, 187, 196 n.1, 198 n.11, 202 n.31, 208 n.8, 222 n.27
Nelson, T. G. A., 194 n.8
Newman, Karen, 25, 50, 56, 163, 164, 172–175, 178–179, 181, 197 n.4, 199 n.13, 205 n.14, 226 nn.3–4, 227 n.11
Norris, Christopher, 16–17, 28

Nunn, Trevor, 60, 133, 210 n.17, 216 n.41
Nuttall, A. D., 187, 199 n.15

Odell, George C. D., 27, 54, 114, 211 n.20, 216 n.2
Olivier, Laurence, 7, 19, 28, 60, 99–100, 123, 143, 165, 196 n.21, 210 n.19, 215 n.39, 216 n.41, 223 n.2, 224 n.8
Orgel, Stephen, 10, 114, 216 n.3
Orkin, Martin, 227 n.11
Oroonoko (Behn), 24, 195 n.13
Orwell, George (Eric Blair), 206 n.22
Othello (key references only): contradictory first impressions, 33–42; heroic or normative protagonist, 16, 105–112; ineffectual scapegoat, 153; in eighteenth-century and earlier criticism, 14, 80, 81–82, 142, 145, 154, 156; in nineteenth-century criticism, 15 80–81, 105, 108–109, 141–142, 144–147, 150–153; in twentieth-century criticism, 16–20, 49, 86–87, 94–95, 106–108, 109–112, 143–144, 145, 159–161; on eighteenth-century and earlier stages, 15, 80, 81–82, 98, 142, 145; on nineteenth-century stages, 12–13, 15, 26–28, 38–39, 82–84, 95–99, 101, 147–150, 153–154, 155, 156, 165; on twentieth-century stages, 13, 15–16, 19, 99–100, 103, 143, 159, 165–166; self-deluding at the end, 141–143; transformation of, 4, 82–104: determined by alien status, 84–85, 104–105; gradual process on nineteenth-century stages, 82–84; sexual anxiety and identity enacted in performance, 95–104; sexual anxiety and the disintegration of identity, 86–94. *See also Othello* and interpretive interests: divided between Othello and Iago; racial interests/anxieties; re-evaluated after Bradley; re-evaluated with

STUDIES IN THEATRE HISTORY AND CULTURE